Steelers' 1974 season: 2

Steelers' 1975 season: 112

Steelers' 1978 season: 203

Steelers' 1979 season: 303

Edited by John Schaefer
Copyright 2012, John Schaefer

1974

Season Review

The Steelers' strong 6-0 preseason showing was less surprising than Joe Gilliam's winning the starting quarterback job away from Terry Bradshaw.

Gilliam faltered in midseason and was benched in favor of Bradshaw, but the Steelers had so much talent that they easily captured first place in the Central Division.

The Steelers had a solid offensive line, a copious supply of wide receivers, a superb fullback in Franco Harris and a brutally effective defense featuring Mean Joe Greene, L.C. Greenwood, Andy Russell and Jack Ham.

The biggest bonus of the year was the play of halfback Rocky Bleier, who had recovered well enough from leg injuries suffered in the Vietnam War to claim a starting job in the offensive backfield.

Week 1

		Sept. 15 Three Rivers Stadium Pittsburgh, PA			

Baltimore Colts					Pittsburgh Steelers
	1Q	2Q	3Q	4Q	Total
Colts	0	0	0	0	0
Steelers	3	13	7	7	30

Joe Gilliam, whose right arm can now be officially declared a natural resource, black gold, calmly shrugged off a slow start Sunday before pitching the Pittsburgh Steelers to a 30-0 victory over the Baltimore Colts.

Gilliam, booed by some of the 48,000 opening day football fans after failing to effectively move the Steelers in the first quarter, turned those taunts to cheers after firing a pair of touchdown passes in the closing minutes of the second quarter.

Most Pittsburgh fans, on the strength of Gilliam's 17 completions in 31 attempts for a total of 257 yards, left Three Rivers Stadium believing that Jefferson Street is the road to victory, possibly all the way to the Super Bowl.

"Joe was off-target early," said Steeler coach Chuck Noll, "but he didn't get upset. That's one of his qualities. He hangs in there and eventually gets on top."

The smattering of boos in the first quarter apparently had little or no effect on the wispy black man whose brilliant play in the Steelers' undefeated exhibition season earned him Sunday's start of Terry Bradshaw, the No. 1 draft pick by the pros in 1970.

"The fans want performance, man. I can dig it. That's where it's at," Gilliam said.

They call the third-year pro from Tennessee State "Jefferson Street Joe," Nashville's equivalent to New York City, which boasts of a quarterback they call "Broadway Joe."

The two Joes, despite their obvious differences, are similarly talented. Both are exciters. But while Namath is declining, Pittsburgh's Joe Gilliam is a star on the ascent.

The Steelers' offensive line treated Gilliam as if he were royalty. Gilliam could have played Sunday in his street clothes. Not once in his 31 passing attempts did the Baltimore Colts' defenders so much as lay a hand on him.

The Steelers had taken an early 3-0 lead on Roy Gerela's 31-yard field goal in the first quarter after Baltimore's Bruce Laird fumbled away a Bobby Walden punt at the Colts' 46-yard line.

A fumble by rookie wide receiver Lynn Swann, the Steelers' No. 1 draft pick this spring, put the Colts in a threatening position as they drove down to the Pittsburgh one-yard line.

However, the massive Steelers defense, headed by Joe Greene, L.C. Greenwood, Ernie Holmes and Dwight White, shut out the Colts on a goal-line stand that seemed to shake awake the offense.

Gilliam marched the Steelers 99 yards to their first touchdown, 54 of them on a brilliant pass to Swann for the score. On the next series, Gilliam took the Steelers on a 64-yard march for a touchdown that convinced everyone in the stadium, Colts alike, that Gilliam was for real.

In that second drive, Gilliam hit Swann for another bomb, this one for 40 yards to the four. Frank Lewis caught a four-yard pass for the TD on the very next play.

In the third quarter, a Bert Jones pass was intercepted by Mel Blount after the Colts drove to the Steelers' 18. The Steelers then marched 66 yards to another score, including a 41-yard screen pass to Steve Davis and a four-yard touchdown blast by Franco Harris.

With only 53 seconds gone from the fourth quarter, Frenchy Fuqua crashed over for the final Steelers score and the defense preserved the shutout, the first for Pittsburgh since the 12th game of the 1972 season.

Bradshaw charted Gilliam's every play throughout the game and in the fourth quarter Noll used Terry Hanratty, the third-string quarterback.

The Steelers' next game is 4 p.m. Sunday, Sept. 22 at mile-high Denver. That's about where Gilliam is following the opening victory, a mile high.

		SCORING	BAL	PIT
1st	Steelers	Roy Gerela 31 yard field goal	0	3
2nd	Steelers	Lynn Swann 54 yard pass from Joe Gilliam (kick failed)	0	9
	Steelers	Frank Lewis 4 yard pass from Joe Gilliam (Roy Gerela kick)	0	16
3rd	Steelers	Franco Harris 4 yard rush (Roy Gerela kick)	0	23
4th	Steelers	John Fuqua 4 yard rush (Roy Gerela kick)	0	30

	TEAM STATS	
	BAL	PIT
First downs	11	18
Rush-Yards-TD	34-118-0	29-103-2
Comp-Att-Yards-TD-INT	9-20-102-0-2	18-37-289-2-1
Sacked-Yards	6-54	0-0
Net pass yards	48	289
Total yards	166	392
Fumbles-Lost	3-2	3-1
Turnovers	4	2
Penalties-Yards	3-20	4-32

PASSING, RUSHING and RECEIVING

Colts

Passing

Bert Jones: 8-of-17, 100 yards, 0 TD, 2 INT
Marty Domres: 1-of-3, 2 yards

Rushing

Bert Jones: 2 carries for 5 yards
Lydell Mitchell: 9 carries for 44 yards
Don McCauley: 8 carries for 38 yards
Bill Olds: 14 carries for 33 yards
John Andrews: 1 carry for -2 yards

Receiving

Glenn Doughty: 3 catches for 58 yards
Lydell Mitchell: 1 catch for 5 yards
Don McCauley: 1 catch for 3 yards
Bill Olds: 1 catch for 2 yards
Raymond Chester: 3 catches for 34 yards

Steelers

Passing

Joe Gilliam: 17-of-31, 257 yards, 2 TD, 1 INT
Terry Hanratty: 1-of-6, 32 yards

Rushing

Franco Harris: 13 carries for 49 yards, 1 TD
Steve Davis: 3 carries for 9 yards
Preston Pearson: 9 carries for 36 yards
John Fuqua: 4 carries for 9 yards, 1 TD

Receiving

Lynn Swann: 2 catches for 94 yards, 1 TD
Franco Harris: 3 catches for 19 yards
Steve Davis: 2 catches for 44 yards
Randy Grossman: 3 catches for 52 yards
Preston Pearson: 1 catch for 4 yards
John Fuqua: 1 catch for 18 yards
Frank Lewis: 3 catches for 26 yards, 1 TD
John Stallworth: 2 catches for 25 yards
Larry Brown: 1 catch for 7 yards

DEFENSE

Colts

Interceptions

Rick Volk: 1 for 0 yards

Steelers

Interceptions

Mel Blount: 1 for 22 yards
Glen Edwards: 1 for 4 yards

KICK RETURNS

Colts

Kickoffs

Freddie Scott: 1 for 26 yards, 26.0 avg.
Cotton Speyrer: 3 for 70 yards, 23.3 avg.

Punts

Bruce Laird: 3 for 2 yards, 0.7 avg.

Steelers

Punts

Glen Edwards: 2 for 14 yards, 7.0 avg.
Lynn Swann: 4 for 33 yards, 8.3 avg.

KICKING and PUNTING

Colts

Punting

David Lee: 8 for 266 yards, 33.3 avg.

Steelers

Kicking

Roy Gerela: 3-for-4 PAT, 1-for-1 FG

Punting

Bobby Walden: 4 for 182 yards, 45.5 avg.

Week 2

Sept. 22
Mile High Stadium
Denver, CO

Pittsburgh Steelers   Denver Broncos

	1Q	2Q	3Q	4Q	OT	Total
Steelers	7	7	14	7	0	35
Broncos	21	0	7	7	0	35

It had to be the "Gone With the Wind" of regular-season pro football games.

After three hours and 49 minutes, five quarters and 160 plays, the Steelers and the Denver Broncos were still tied yesterday at 35-35. And that's the way it ended.

Nobody was asking for money back. There was no nonsense about a tie being like kissing your sister. There was only mild criticism of Chuck Noll's decision to run the ball on the final two plays from inside the Steeler 25 to kill the clock and accept the exhausted deadlock.

This was the first time since George Halas and his pals gathered in that auto showroom in Canton a half century ago to create the league that a regular-season game in the National Football League has gone into overtime.

Neither team was able to break the tie – Jim Turner's 41-yard field goal attempt with 3:13 left in sudden death was wide to the right – but that didn't make the spectacle any less exciting.

Of course, the Steelers were bitterly disappointed in the tie. They were favored, they expected to win. They came back from a 21-7 deficit and led 35-28 midway in the final period. They even had a chance to win it on the final play of the fourth period when Roy Gerela's 25-yard field goal attempt was low and blocked.

Once Gerela's attempt was blocked, the new rules in the NFL call for a 15-minute sudden-death period to break the tie.

Noll thought 60 minutes was enough. "I don't like the idea of overtime," he said. "I have a tired football team that has to get ready for a football game next week. If we'd have one of these every week, it'd kill our team."

Naturally, Denver coach John Ralston disagreed. He likes the idea of overtime. He's a rah-rah type who runs out onto the field before the kickoffs and is always patting his guys on the back.

Ralston set the tempo of the game when he had Jim Turner try a successful onside kick to start the game. That didn't lead to a score but the Broncos seemed to be higher than Mile High Stadium.

Before the game was 10 minutes old, the Broncos were leading 21-7 – scoring 3 touchdowns on just eight plays – and the Denver fans were wondering about the Steeler defense.

So was Noll. "I don't know what it was. We'll have to look at it," he said. "They weren't doing anything different."

What the Broncos were doing was breaking tackles, especially Otis Armstrong, who rushed 19 times for 131 yards and caught five passes for 86 yards. Noll said, "When the other guys are running through your arms, that's the first indication you're not ready to do something."

The exciting play, though, had just started. Joe Gilliam was to put on what Ralston called "possibly the finest performance I've ever seen by a quarterback."

Steve Davis ran 61 yards on a spectacular run with a screen pass for the Steelers' first touchdown, and before it was over Gilliam would pass 50 times for 31 completions – both Steeler records. He's now completed 48 of 81 in two games, and if he keeps that pace up he's going to break every single-season NFL record in the book.

Ralston devised what Noll called a "four deep zone" to take away Gilliam's long game, but Gilliam patiently ran an 87-yard drive in 18 plays in the second period to cut the deficit to 21-14 at halftime.

Franco Harris was especially valuable, running 20 times for 70 yards and catching nine passes – a Steeler record for a back – for 84 yards as Gilliam used the short game.

The Steeler defense seemed to come alive in the second half for a while.

Joe Greene knocked Charley Johnson out of the game with a sprained shoulder on a play that led to an interception by Mike Wagner on the third play of the second half and set up a TD.

Andy Russell rammed into Steve Ramsey, Johnson's replacement, to set up Marv Kellum's interception that led to another touchdown, and Fats Holmes sacked Ramsey again to set up an L.C. Greenwood recovery.

These big plays gave the Steelers a 35-28 lead in the fourth quarter and possession on the Denver 32. The Steelers marched to the Denver 14 and seemed to be ready to take control of the game, but Gilliam got sacked and then Calvin Jones tipped a pass and Tom Jackson intercepted it and that seemed to change the game.

"That missed being a touchdown by just an inch," Gilliam said.

Five plays later, Ramsey threw a 23-yard touchdown pass to Armstrong and the game was tied 35-35 with 7:06 left.

It was to remain that way for 22 more minutes – although no one knew it at the time.

Gerela's missed field goal – after the officials somehow let 50 seconds tick away on the clock just before Denver punted – blew a chance to win the game in regulation time for Pittsburgh.

In the overtime, John Rowser – a former Steeler – intercepted a pass on a third-and-22 play when third-string receiver Reggie Garrett – playing because of injuries to end Ron Shanklin and Lynn Swann – ran a poor route.

That set up Turner's missed 41-yarder and neither team threatened again.

So it was a tie. But it couldn't have been more exciting. Did somebody once say something about dull, ball-control NFL games? Maybe it's the thin air here.

		SCORING	PIT	DEN
1st	Broncos	Otis Armstrong 45 yard pass from Charley Johnson (Jim Turner kick)	0	7
	Steelers	Steve Davis 61 yard pass from Joe Gilliam (Roy Gerela kick)	7	7
	Broncos	Haven Moses 7 yard pass from Charley Johnson (Jim Turner kick)	7	14
	Broncos	Jon Keyworth 1 yard rush (Jim Turner kick)	7	21
2nd	Steelers	Joe Gilliam 1 yard rush (Roy Gerela kick)	14	21
3rd	Steelers	Steve Davis 1 yard rush (Roy Gerela kick)	21	21
	Broncos	Riley Odoms 3 yard pass from Steve Ramsey (Jim Turner kick)	21	28
	Steelers	Steve Davis 1 yard rush (Roy Gerela kick)	28	28
4th	Steelers	John Fuqua 1 yard rush (Roy Gerela kick)	35	28
	Broncos	Otis Armstrong 23 yard pass from Steve Ramsey (Jim Turner kick)	35	35

	TEAM STATS	
	PIT	DEN
First downs	33	20
Rush-Yards-TD	40-160-4	37-156-1
Comp-Att-Yards-TD-INT	31-50-348-1-2	12-27-191-4-2
Sacked-Yards	3-24	3-15
Net pass yards	324	176
Total yards	484	332

Fumbles-Lost	3-2	1-1
Turnovers	4	3
Penalties-Yards	12-91	7-61

PASSING, RUSHING and RECEIVING

Steelers

Passing

Joe Gilliam: 31-of-50, 348 yards, 1 TD, 2 INT

Rushing

Joe Gilliam: 4 carries for 21 yards, 1 TD
Franco Harris: 20 carries for 70 yards
Steve Davis: 6 carries for 16 yards, 2 TD
Preston Pearson: 8 carries for 47 yards
John Fuqua: 2 carries for 6 yards, 1 TD

Receiving

Franco Harris: 9 catches for 84 yards
Steve Davis: 5 catches for 58 yards, 1 TD
John Stallworth: 3 catches for 67 yards
Frank Lewis: 5 catches for 65 yards
Preston Pearson: 1 catch for 6 yards
Randy Grossman: 5 catches for 43 yards
Lynn Swann: 2 catches for 15 yards
Larry Brown: 1 catch for 10 yards

Broncos

Passing

Charley Johnson: 6-of-15, 129 yards, 2 TD, 1 INT
Steve Ramsey: 6-of-12, 62 yards, 2 TD, 1 INT

Rushing

Otis Armstrong: 19 carries for 131 yards
Floyd Little: 14 carries for 21 yards
Jon Keyworth: 4 carries for 4 yards, 1 TD

Receiving

Otis Armstrong: 5 catches for 86 yards, 2 TD
Haven Moses: 3 catches for 61 yards, 1 TD
Floyd Little: 1 catch for 18 yards
Riley Odoms: 3 catches for 26 yards, 1 TD

DEFENSE

Steelers

Interceptions

Marv Kellum: 1 for 0 yards
Mike Wagner: 1 for 4 yards

Broncos

Interceptions

Tom Jackson: 1 for 39 yards
John Rowser: 1 for 7 yards

KICK RETURNS

Steelers

Kickoffs

Steve Davis: 1 for 23 yards, 23.0 avg.
Preston Pearson: 2 for 43 yards, 21.5 avg.

Punts

Dick Conn: 2 for 26 yards, 13.0 avg.
Glen Edwards: 2 for 25 yards, 12.5 avg.

Broncos

Kickoffs

Otis Armstrong: 3 for 72 yards, 24.0 avg.

Punts

Charlie Greer: 3 for 23 yards, 7.7 avg.
Bill Thompson: 1 for 4 yards, 4.0 avg.

KICKING and PUNTING

Steelers

Kicking

Roy Gerela: 5-for-5 PAT, 0-for-1 FG

Punting

Bobby Walden: 6 for 250 yards, 41.7 avg.

Broncos

Kicking

Jim Turner: 5-for-5 PAT, 0-for-1 FG

Punting

Billy Van Heusen: 7 for 311 yards, 44.4 avg.

Week 3

Sept. 29
Three Rivers Stadium
Pittsburgh, PA

Oakland Raiders   Pittsburgh Steelers

	1Q	2Q	3Q	4Q	Total
Raiders	7	10	0	0	17
Steelers	0	0	0	0	0

By SAM BECHTEL
TIMES Sports Editor

PITTSBURGH — The post-mortum was brief and to the point.

"Every time I looked out over the field, I saw the guys in the white jerseys up and running and pursuing. I also saw all the guys in the black jerseys knocked down," Steeler coach Chuck Noll remembered.

Just in case you don't know by now, the Oakland Raiders' white uniforms were still white after it was all over yesterday afternoon at Three Rivers Stadium.

Proving once again that they are truly one of the soundest teams in football week in and week out, John Madden's "Pride and Poise" bunch did a cute little number on the Steelers yesterday to the tune of 17-0.

Not only was it the first time Pittsburgh had been shutout in 132 games, but the first time since 1951 (when Cleveland did it 28-0) that the Steelers failed to score in front of a home crowd.

There were no trite excuses on the part of the Steelers, who fell one-half game behind the Cincinnati Bengals in the Central Division race.

"We got our fannies (cleaned up quote) beat," said a rather calm, cool and collected Noll. "Oakland is a team that can embarrass your fanny, and they did today.

"We couldn't block or tackle anybody, and you can't win football games that way. They beat us physically in every department."

Not really.

As a matter of fact, the Steeler defense is to be excused for the 17 points here, since Oakland's two TDs were set up on a 47-yard punt return to the Steeler 28 by Ron Smith and an Al Atkinson interception of a Joe Gilliam pass, which wound up on the Steeler 19.

Smith, who went into the season with more kick return yardage than any man to ever play the game (7,804 yards in nine seasons), later returned another punt 37 yards to the Steeler 24, which led to a 25-yard field goal by George Blanda to conclude the game's scoring with four minutes and 52 seconds still left in the second period.

Other than the three short scoring drives, the Raiders legitimately drove into Steeler territory only two times all day, once to the 37 and again to the 45.

But where the Raiders did excell was on defense, a Chinese fire drill-like concoction that did what eight other teams before it could not.

Reduce the up-to-yesterday sensational Steeler offensive line to silly putty, and ground the Jefferson Street Airplane as a result.

Jefferson Street Joe Gilliam's Aerial Circus couldn't get out of the hangar against a constantly shifting and stunting Raider defense that had more different looks to it than Lon Chaney.

The grim facts are that Gilliam completed only eight of 31 passes for 106 yards, and even more a credit to Oakland,only two to wide receivers, one each to rookies Lynn Swann and John Stallworth.

Although Gilliam was the first to admit that he didn't have a very good day throwing the ball, much of it was not his fault.

Because, as Noll put it "you can't throw the ball on your back."

Gilliam did end up on his back three times, eating the football, but it was only his quick release that prevented that number from being in double figures.

He was constantly under pressure. Heaps of it. Both of his interceptions were thrown as he was hit, and just about everything else he put up came in self defense.

And as Noll pointed out, "their coverage was fantastic, which makes the pass rush even more of a factor."

"We knew what we had to do," Madden related. "They have passed the ball so very well against everybody. We started out playing against two basically running teams (Buffalo and Kansas City) and then we had to come in here and play somebody that has been passing the bleep out of the ball."

So what the Raiders did was never let Gilliam know what they were doing. On one play they used three down linemen, four linebackers, and four defensive backs.

The next play they used three linemen, three linebackers, and five defensive backs. The next time the conventional 4-3-4, etc.

"We didn't do all that because he's a young quarterback, Madden insisted. "We don't like any quarterback to know what we're doing.

"We'd planned it all week. To give him different substitutions on every play. To move people in and out and around. The idea wasn't so much to throw him off as it was to give us solid coverage."

"It threw our blocking off a little," Steeler center Ray Mansfield said, alluding to some confusion on the offensive line. "And as a result we didn't give him (Gilliam) very much protection."

"Their defense just swallowed our offense," Noll lamented. They were effective," he said of the Oakland switching around. "We didn't do much did we?"

Gilliam refused to admit that the different Oakland looks gave him any problems, suffice it to say that the Raiders "went to a prevent defense earlier than I expected." Which shows just how effective the Raider camouflage was.

He also failed to agree with any criticism of his offensive line.

"What we do we do as a football team," he fired at a guy who pointed out he had about as much protection as Custer did at Little Big Horn.

"Our strength lies in our ability to play as a team. They are only human," he said of the Steeler offensive linemen. "They can't keep everybody out all the time. Things like this happen."

Most of the 48,304 who showed up in yesterday's rain however, chose to castigate Gilliam personally for failing to put points on the board.

He was unmercifully booed as early as the second quarter, and at the start of the fourth period the chants of "we want Bradshaw, we want Bradshaw" echoed through Pittsburgh's North Side from the same people who cheered when he lay on the ground with his shoulder separated against Cincinnati last year.

"The fans are gonna' be fans," Gilliam said, kissing off the apparent end of a love affair.

Noll, even though he put in Terry Bradshaw with 1:52 left in the game, put it more directly.

"No, I had no thoughts about replacing Joe," he said. "I would have liked to replace the offensive line, the receivers, everything else. A quarterback is only as good as his supporting cast. Today that cast wasn't any good. It wasn't Joe's fault. It was a total team loss."

Or, as John Madden put it, "I think we beat them with a an all-around performance".

The guys in the white jerseys did their thing. . Very well.

		SCORING	OAK	PIT
1st	Raiders	Ken Stabler 1 yard rush (George Blanda kick)	7	0
2nd	Raiders	Cliff Branch 19 yard pass from Ken Stabler (George Blanda kick)	14	0
	Raiders	George Blanda 35 yard field goal	17	0

	TEAM STATS	
	OAK	PIT
First downs	17	16
Rush-Yards-TD	47-177-1	27-117-0
Comp-Att-Yards-TD-INT	5-12-70-1-0	9-33-117-0-3
Sacked-Yards	0-0	2-31
Net pass yards	70	86
Total yards	247	203
Fumbles-Lost	3-0	2-1

| Turnovers | 0 | 4 |
| Penalties-Yards | 11-92 | 7-66 |

PASSING, RUSHING and RECEIVING

Raiders

Passing

Ken Stabler: 5-of-12, 70 yards, 1 TD, 0 INT

Rushing

Marv Hubbard: 19 carries for 96 yards
Clarence Davis: 16 carries for 63 yards
Ken Stabler: 2 carries for -4 yards, 1 TD
Pete Banaszak: 7 carries for 21 yards
Mark van Eeghen: 2 carries for 11 yards
Frank Pitts: 1 carry for -10 yards

Receiving

Marv Hubbard: 1 catch for 7 yards
Bob Moore: 2 catches for 31 yards
Cliff Branch: 1 catch for 19 yards, 1 TD
Fred Biletnikoff: 1 catch for 13 yards

Steelers

Passing

Joe Gilliam: 8-of-31, 106 yards, 0 TD, 2 INT
Terry Bradshaw: 1-of-2, 11 yards, 0 TD, 1 INT

Rushing

Steve Davis: 10 carries for 49 yards
Joe Gilliam: 3 carries for 13 yards
John Fuqua: 8 carries for 25 yards
Terry Bradshaw: 2 carries for 18 yards
Preston Pearson: 2 carries for 4 yards
Franco Harris: 1 carry for 6 yards
Rocky Bleier: 1 carry for 2 yards

Receiving

Steve Davis: 2 catches for 43 yards
John Fuqua: 1 catch for 2 yards
Preston Pearson: 2 catches for 18 yards
Larry Brown: 2 catches for 21 yards
John Stallworth: 1 catch for 19 yards
Lynn Swann: 1 catch for 14 yards

DEFENSE

Raiders

Interceptions

George Atkinson: 1 for 26 yards
Jack Tatum: 1 for 0 yards
Skip Thomas: 1 for -13 yards

KICK RETURNS

Raiders

Kickoffs

Ron Smith: 1 for 41 yards, 41.0 avg.

Punts

Ron Smith: 6 for 81 yards, 13.5 avg.

Steelers

Kickoffs

Steve Davis: 2 for 53 yards, 26.5 avg.
Preston Pearson: 2 for 32 yards, 16.0 avg.

Punts

Glen Edwards: 1 for 8 yards, 8.0 avg.
Lynn Swann: 3 for 25 yards, 8.3 avg.

KICKING and PUNTING

Raiders

Kicking

George Blanda: 2-for-2 PAT, 1-for-1 FG

Punting

Ray Guy: 8 for 323 yards, 40.4 avg.

Steelers

Kicking

Roy Gerela: 0-for-1 FG

Punting

Bobby Walden: 6 for 254 yards, 42.3 avg.

Week 4

Pittsburgh Steelers

Oct. 6
Astrodome
Houston, TX

Houston Oilers

	1Q	2Q	3Q	4Q	Total
Steelers	0	3	3	7	13
Oilers	0	7	0	0	7

HOUSTON—For a half, the vital signs were there. A listless running game, an inconsistent passing attack and infrequent but crippling defensive mistakes. In short, the Pittsburgh Steelers acted as if they were an accident waiting to happen.

But stretchers, ambulances and blood donors weren't needed. With Preston Pearson injecting much-needed adrenalin into a sluggish offense and L. C. Greenwood, Jack Lambert and Jack Ham making the big plays defensively, the Steelers transformed a 7-3 deficit into a 13-7 victory over the Houston Oilers before an Astrodome crowd of 30,049 yesterday.

It was the Steelers' second win against one loss and one tie. It was the Oilers' third loss in four starts. For both it was a familiar script.

The Steelers, painfully deficient in establishing their running game in recent weeks, finally made it work, satisfying themselves with gouging out three yards and a cloud of AstroTurf until Pearson's 53-yard run on the game's final snap.

The Oilers, meanwhile, continued to transform a silk purse of opportunity into a sow's ear of success. Twice in the first half, Pittsburgh turnovers permitted the Oilers to penetrate the Steelers' 20.

In combination with Billy Johnson's scintilating 37-yard touchdown run, two more scores would have broken the game open. Instead, Skip Butler missed his sixth straight field goal and Mike Wagner stole Lynn Dickey's tardy pass toward George Amundson in the end zone.

Given a boost by Roy Gerela's 37-yard field goal with 49 seconds left in the half, the Steelers trailed only 7-3 at intermission.

After sticking with Steve Davis and Frenchy Fuqua for the first half, Steeler Head Coach Chuck Noll inserted Pearson and Rocky Bleier into the lineup at the running back spots as the second half began.

"I had intended to use my four healthy backs as much as possible," said Noll. "There was no pre-determined pattern. I just wanted to use them all and see what would happen. Pearson and Bleier were definitely the difference."

Pearson rung up his first 100-yard total as a pro, milking 15 carries for 117 yards. He also grabbed three passes for 42 yards. Bleier added 37 yards on eight rushes and, like Pearson, his blocking bordered on the extraordinary.

"The blocking of the backs in the second half was a big thing," Noll enthused. "Bleier made a sensational block to spring Pearson for that last big run and Pearson made some real good blocks for Rocky.

In the first half, the Steelers gained only 31 yards on 14 running plays for a paltry 2.2 average. In the second half, the figures read 24 attempts, 153 yards. The 6.4 average thrilled Noll.

"That is what happens when you use your running game properly," he explained. "You will go along for awhile with little to show for it and then you break loose and the average goes way up. We got a lot more balance in our offense today and maybe we ran the ball a little too often at times.

"But we had been doing with that for the last four years, so it really was not that new to us. We don't go back that far in our offensive thinking but the balance was nice to see."

Joe Gilliam provided the necessary passing, completing 16 of 32 for 202 yards. Two interceptions stifled his production but not his enthusiasm.

"I wasn't bothered by the interceptions. I thought I threw both of those passes well," he explained. "I'll have to look at the film to see what went wrong or whether or not they were just great defensive plays.

"There wasn't much change of thinking because we went to the running game more. Most people think it is, I don't. I'm not going to shake because of interceptions and I'm not bothered when I throw less. What matters is execution, no matter what type of offense you run.

"If you don't execute well, you lose, and, if you execute well, you win."

The Steelers executed with clinical precision for most of the second half, rolling up 241 yards to Houston's 83, scoring 10 points while the Oilers scored none.

"I'm very satisfied with the win," said Noll. "Houston is a lot finer team than most people give them credit for being. They have excellent people at the skilled positions on offense and their defense is aggressive and strong. They will beat a lot of people before the year is over."

For the record, Gerela's 27-yard field goal, Pearson's nine-yard run and Gerela's PAT provided the Steelers' second-half points, all of which might have gone to waste had it not been for timely fumble recoveries by Lambert and Ham and Greenwood's ferocious pass rushing.

Lambert's recovery came when Dan Pastorini, playing for the first time during the regular season after a hamstring injury, fumbled on the first play after Tommy Maxwell's interception and 15-yard return gave the Oilers life at the Steeler 18 with 4:50 left.

Ham's came when Ken Burrough fumbled after gaining only 29 of the needed 30 yards on a pass from Pastorini on the game's next-to-last play.

"Our defensive play was excellent," said Noll. "They came up with some big plays when we really needed them."

Oiler Head Coach Sid Gillman's analysis went thusly: "I know you people are tired of hearing this, but we have a helluva football team. Untimely turnovers continue to be our problem. It would be nice to win one of these big games and see what might happen."

To be sure, both coaches were sounding an S.O.S. — same old story.

		SCORING	PIT	HOU
2nd	Oilers	Billy Johnson 47 yard rush (Skip Butler kick)	0	7
	Steelers	Roy Gerela 37 yard field goal	3	7
3rd	Steelers	Roy Gerela 27 yard field goal	6	7
4th	Steelers	Preston Pearson 9 yard rush (Roy Gerela kick)	13	7

	TEAM STATS	
	PIT	HOU
First downs	18	10
Rush-Yards-TD	38-184-1	24-119-1
Comp-Att-Yards-TD-INT	16-32-202-0-2	12-23-148-0-1
Sacked-Yards	0-0	3-27

Net pass yards	202	121
Total yards	386	240
Fumbles-Lost	1-1	3-2
Turnovers	3	3
Penalties-Yards	7-53	7-50

PASSING, RUSHING and RECEIVING

Steelers

Passing

Joe Gilliam: 16-of-32, 202 yards, 0 TD, 2 INT

Rushing

Preston Pearson: 15 carries for 117 yards, 1 TD
John Fuqua: 7 carries for 16 yards
Rocky Bleier: 8 carries for 37 yards
Steve Davis: 8 carries for 14 yards

Receiving

Preston Pearson: 3 catches for 42 yards
Ron Shanklin: 4 catches for 49 yards
John Fuqua: 3 catches for 32 yards
Larry Brown: 3 catches for 46 yards
Frank Lewis: 3 catches for 33 yards

Oilers

Passing

Lynn Dickey: 9-of-17, 79 yards, 0 TD, 1 INT
Dan Pastorini: 3-of-6, 69 yards

Rushing

Willie Rodgers: 12 carries for 48 yards
Fred Willis: 2 carries for 9 yards
Lynn Dickey: 1 carry for 0 yards
Billy Johnson: 2 carries for 38 yards, 1 TD

Dan Pastorini: 1 carry for 0 yards
Vic Washington: 6 carries for 24 yards

Receiving

Willie Rodgers: 1 catch for 4 yards
Fred Willis: 3 catches for 34 yards
Jerry Broadnax: 1 catch for 42 yards
Ken Burrough: 3 catches for 30 yards
Vic Washington: 1 catch for 2 yards
George Amundson: 2 catches for 22 yards
Billy Parks: 1 catch for 14 yards

DEFENSE

Steelers

Interceptions

Mike Wagner: 1 for 9 yards

Oilers

Interceptions

Tommy Maxwell: 2 for 30 yards

KICK RETURNS

Steelers

Kickoffs

Preston Pearson: 2 for 43 yards, 21.5 avg.

Punts

Lynn Swann: 3 for 22 yards, 7.3 avg.

Oilers

Kickoffs

Bob Gresham: 1 for 12 yards, 12.0 avg.
Billy Johnson: 2 for 47 yards, 23.5 avg.
Jeff Severson: 1 for 21 yards, 21.0 avg.

Punts

Billy Johnson: 1 for 37 yards, 37.0 avg.

KICKING and PUNTING

Steelers

Kicking

Roy Gerela: 1-for-1 PAT, 2-for-2 FG

Punting

Bobby Walden: 5 for 193 yards, 38.6 avg.

Oilers

Kicking

Skip Butler: 1-for-1 PAT, 0-for-1 FG

Punting

David Beverly: 6 for 230 yards, 38.3 avg.

Week 5

Oct. 13
Arrowhead Stadium
Kansas City, MO

Pittsburgh Steelers **Kansas City Chiefs**

	1Q	2Q	3Q	4Q	Total
Steelers	7	17	10	0	34
Chiefs	3	7	7	7	24

The '74 Steelers still remain a puzzle.

Five games into the season, the questions remain. Is this a team on the threshold of greatness or is it one that has the muscle to overpower the weaker teams but lacks the class and finesse to be a real Super Bowl contender?

There weren't too many answers yesterday when the Steelers turned back the slipping Chiefs 34-24 in a sloppy game before 65,517 diehards who braved the early rain to watch a game that had moments of high drama and some of low comedy.

There were some brilliant moments for the Steelers. Like Glen Edwards' 49-yard touchdown run with an intercepted pass that helped Pittsburgh take a 24-10 halftime lead.

It was one of seven Steeler interceptions.

"When I saw the whole thing develop, it was as pretty as a picture," Edwards said. "I got a quick read on the quarterback and knew it was an interception when it left (Mike) Livingston's hand."

And Joe Gilliam's 31-yard touchdown pass on a third-down play to Frank Lewis in the third period that wrapped the game up was another thing of beauty.

Gilliam picked up the blitz, called an audible at the line of scrimmage and hit Lewis perfectly for his first TD pass in 15 quarters.

But in between there were a lot of frustrating moments for the Steelers. They fumbled the ball away the first two times they had it and even though Kansas City had nine turnovers, the Steelers let them stay alive until late in the third period.

"We made too many mistakes on offense," coach Chuck Noll said in an understatement. "Fumbles and penalties hurt what could have been a great offensive performance."

It was the fourth consecutive game in which the Steelers, now 3-1-1, have made more than their share of mistakes. Not since the opener, when they bombed Baltimore 30-0, have they shown the promise of the exhibition season. With a record-tying seven interceptions, it should have been an easier win.

As expected, Gilliam started for the Steelers at the QB spot. He went all the way, completing 14 of 36 for 214 yards and a TD, but the defense made things easy for him in the first half with the turnovers.

The front four was blowing in so hard that Livingston barely had time to take the snap from center before Joe Greene and his friends were hounding him.

The Steelers also blitzed more than normal and that was effective, too. Andy Russell set up the first TD when he blitzed Livingston, knocking the ball out of his hands and recovered it on the Chiefs' 34. Six plays later, Rocky Bleier swept the right end with a pitch for the TD.

K.C. came back to take a 10-7 lead on the first play of the second period on a 13-yard pass from Livingston to former Steeler Barry Pearson. It came the play after a Mike Wagner interception was nullified when Dwight White was nailed for roughing the passer on a controversial call.

Livingston's next pass – after Roy Gerela missed a 37-yard field goal – was picked off by Jack Lambert. Five plays later, Preston Pearson swept the right end for a TD and the Steelers were back ahead 14-10.

Five plays later, Edwards stepped in front of Pearson, intercepted the pass and all he had in front of him was 49 yards of soggy artificial turf.

That made it 21-10 and Chiefs coach Hank Stram, who's under fire here, tried Len Dawson. That didn't work as Dawson's first pass was intercepted by Ham and that led to a Gerela 32-yard field goal. Gerela hit on two of four for the afternoon.

With a 24-10 halftime lead, the Steelers seemed ready to make it a rout. But it didn't materialize. The Steelers took the second-half kickoff but got only one first down from five running plays and punted.

Stram went back to Livingston and he directed an 83-yard touchdown drive in 11 plays. It was the type of drive that characterized the game. Lambert intercepted a pass and fumbled it back to Otis Taylor to keep the drive going. A 48-yard Livingston-Pearson pass was another key play and Livingston hit Otis Taylor on a 10-yarder to strike paydirt on third down with 6:28 left in the quarter.

Suddenly it was 24-17 and the Steelers knew it wasn't going to be easy.

In fact, the Chiefs forced the Steelers to punt and were in a good position to tie. But the Chiefs were called for holding and that handed the ball back to Pittsburgh and Gerela eventually kicked a 45-yard field goal with 2:41 left for a 27-17 margin and some breathing room.

After the next four plays it was all over. Loren Toews recovered a fumble by Larry Brunson on the ensuing kickoff. Three plays later, on a third-and-eight, Gilliam caught the Chiefs in a blitz, called the audible and fired the touchdown strike to Lewis that made it 34-17.

"That was a super play," Noll said. "Gilliam missed on some third-down plays but he made some great plays on third down, too."

Stram also gave Gilliam a vote of confidence. "He's a tremendous quarterback," Stram said. "He has poise and confidence and a lot of daring. He threw some balls that were unbelievable and he completed them. He's a brilliant young quarterback. We tried to create as many different looks as possible but he read them extremely well."

Livingston brought the Chiefs back to within 10 with a 13-yard touchdown pass to Elmo Wright on the first play of the final period but the Chiefs never really threatened again.

The Chiefs wound up trying 49 passes – the most ever in one game in the history of the club – in a vain effort to come from behind.

With the Chiefs trying to come from behind and Gilliam doing his usual throwing for the Steelers, the game lasted three hours and 17 minutes and took 155 plays. The Denver overtime game lasted 160 plays.

Lambert, Edwards and Ham wound up with two interceptions each while J.T. Thomas chipped in with one and Russell and Toews recovered fumbles.

"You can't give the ball up nine times and expect to win," Stram said.

But the Steelers can't expect too many teams to give it up that many times, either. Against a tougher foe, the mistakes they made could have been costly.

		SCORING	PIT	KAN
1st	Chiefs	Jan Stenerud 31 yard field goal	0	3
	Steelers	Rocky Bleier 2 yard rush (Roy Gerela kick)	7	3
2nd	Chiefs	Barry Pearson 13 yard pass from Mike Livingston (Jan Stenerud kick)	7	10
	Steelers	Preston Pearson 3 yard rush (Roy Gerela kick)	14	10
	Steelers	Glen Edwards 49 yard interception return (Roy Gerela kick)	21	10
	Steelers	Roy Gerela 32 yard field goal	24	10
3rd	Chiefs	Otis Taylor 10 yard pass from Mike Livingston (Jan Stenerud kick)	24	17
	Steelers	Roy Gerela 45 yard field goal	27	17
	Steelers	Frank Lewis 31 yard pass from Joe Gilliam (Roy Gerela kick)	34	17
4th	Chiefs	Elmo Wright 13 yard pass from Mike Livingston (Jan Stenerud kick)	34	24

	TEAM STATS	
	PIT	KAN
First downs	19	19
Rush-Yards-TD	41-119-2	25-58-0
Comp-Att-Yards-TD-INT	14-36-214-1-1	16-49-235-3-7
Sacked-Yards	1-12	3-36
Net pass yards	202	199
Total yards	321	257
Fumbles-Lost	3-3	6-2
Turnovers	4	9
Penalties-Yards	11-132	7-35

PASSING, RUSHING and RECEIVING

Steelers

Passing

Joe Gilliam: 14-of-36, 214 yards, 1 TD, 1 INT

Rushing

Joe Gilliam: 3 carries for 7 yards
Rocky Bleier: 12 carries for 45 yards, 1 TD
Preston Pearson: 12 carries for 27 yards, 1 TD
Frank Lewis: 1 carry for 3 yards
John Fuqua: 9 carries for 29 yards
Steve Davis: 4 carries for 8 yards

Receiving

Rocky Bleier: 3 catches for 41 yards
Preston Pearson: 3 catches for 45 yards
Frank Lewis: 3 catches for 55 yards, 1 TD
Lynn Swann: 2 catches for 28 yards
John Stallworth: 2 catches for 25 yards
Ron Shanklin: 1 catch for 20 yards

Chiefs

Passing

Mike Livingston: 15-of-43, 243 yards, 3 TD, 5 INT
David Jaynes: 0-of-2, 0 yards, 0 TD, 1 INT
Len Dawson: 1-of-4, -8 yards, 0 TD, 1 INT

Rushing

Mike Livingston: 1 carry for 5 yards
Willie Ellison: 7 carries for 26 yards
Ed Podolak: 5 carries for 16 yards
Woody Green: 4 carries for 12 yards
Wendell Hayes: 5 carries for 1 yard
David Jaynes: 1 carry for 0 yards
Jeff Kinney: 2 carries for -2 yards

Receiving

Barry Pearson: 4 catches for 92 yards, 1 TD
Willie Ellison: 3 catches for 47 yards
Ed Podolak: 2 catches for 21 yards
Otis Taylor: 3 catches for 37 yards, 1 TD
Andy Hamilton: 1 catch for 19 yards
Morris Stroud: 1 catch for 14 yards
Elmo Wright: 1 catch for 13 yards, 1 TD
Jeff Kinney: 1 catch for -8 yards

DEFENSE

Steelers

Interceptions

Glen Edwards: 2 for 64 yards, 1 TD
Jack Ham: 2 for 8 yards
Jack Lambert: 2 for 19 yards
J.T. Thomas: 1 for 14 yards

Chiefs

Interceptions

Kerry Reardon: 1 for 0 yards

KICK RETURNS

Steelers

Kickoffs

Steve Davis: 4 for 73 yards, 18.3 avg.
Preston Pearson: 1 for 23 yards, 23.0 avg.

Punts

Lynn Swann: 3 for 62 yards, 20.7 avg.

Chiefs

Kickoffs

Larry Brunson: 6 for 128 yards, 21.3 avg.
Cleo Miller: 1 for 28 yards, 28.0 avg.

Punts

Larry Brunson: 2 for 29 yards, 14.5 avg.

KICKING and PUNTING

Steelers

Kicking

Roy Gerela: 4-for-4 PAT, 2-for-4 FG

Punting

Bobby Walden: 6 for 263 yards, 43.8 avg.

Chiefs

Kicking

Jan Stenerud: 3-for-3 PAT, 1-for-1 FG

Punting

Jerrel Wilson: 4 for 184 yards, 46.0 avg.

Week 6

Oct. 20
Three Rivers Stadium
Pittsburgh, PA

Cleveland Browns — **Pittsburgh Steelers**

	1Q	2Q	3Q	4Q	Total
Browns	0	13	0	3	16
Steelers	7	7	3	3	20

PITTSBURGH — In the old days of the famed Turnpike Series between the Cleveland Browns and the Pittsburgh Steelers, football fans imbibed freely and frequently.

Anything from canned heat to Chevas Regal was fair game for Steelers or Browns fans. They toasted every play, every time out, everything. Sunday night in Pittsburgh was a ritual headache.

Yesterday, for most of the 48,100 fans at Three Rivers Stadium, the Steelers 20-16 win over the Browns was a sobering experience. Cleveland was not as bad as its 1-5 record and certainly the Steelers aren't as good as their 4-1-1 record.

Oh, sure, the Steelers are in first place in the Central Division of the American Football Conference, but only because Cincinnati lost later in the day to the Oakland Raiders, 30-27.

"If thass a team thass gonna go to the Super Bowl, I'm O. J. Simpson," said one very heavy, very drunk, very white fellow to another.

"I'll drink to that," said his companion. And he did.

Mostly, I assume, they were drinking to forget the performance on the field by the Pittsburgh offense. Either that, or they were trying to find warmth in the amber liquid.

In truth, there were more boos from the fans than there was booze in them. And once gain, only sooner Sunday, the chant "We want Bradshaw" wafted over quarterback Joe Gilliam.

Gilliam completed five of 18 passes for 96 yards and directed the offense to 15 first downs and 165 yards rushing.

He drew his loudest Bradshaw number at his appearance on the series following the one-yard touchdown plunge by Franco Harris in the second quarter. Three gives to Frenchy Fuqua on a first and goal from the four had moved the ball only to the one before Gilliam called on Harris for the TD.

Pittsburgh fans, spoiled in two seasons by contending clubs after 40 years of illegitimacy, vocally murdered Gilliam and head coach Chuck Noll.

Preston Pearson had scored Pittsburgh's first touchdown in the early minutes of the game after the Steelers recovered a fumbled at the Cleveland 29.

Harris's fourth-down touchdown capped a 28-yard drive that was set up by Lynn Swann's 17-yard return of a low punt by Don Cockroft who was punting from his own endzone.

Trailing 14-0 with just 2:38 left in the second quarter, Mike Phipps marched the Browns to within one point of the Steelers before the intermission.

Phipps scrambled 18 yards for the first Cleveland score with 1:57 left in the half, capping a 50-yard drive set up when Billy Lefleur returned the Steeler's kickoff 41-yards.

Unable to move the ball and preserve the 14-7 lead, Pittsburgh punted it away, and with eight seconds showing on the clock, Phipps had the Browns only one point away from the lead.

Gloster Richardson caught a 46-yard pass from Phipps, beating the coverage by defender J. T. Thomas, then aging tight end Milt Morin threaded his way past the secondary and took a 14-yard scoring toss from Phipps.

Halftime celebrators toasted L. C. Greenwood who got a hand up in time to deflect Cockroft's conversion kick for the 14-13 halftime lead.

Roy Gerela, who could not kick off due to a pulled thigh muscle, booted a pair of field goals in the second half, while Cockroft converted a 21-yard field goal on the opening series of the fourth quarter to end Cleveland's scoring.

However, the Browns were not through and it took an interception by safety Glen Edwards late in the game to preserve the win.

Phipps had marched the Browns 54 yards to the Steelers 17 before the Pittsburgh defense, led by Joe Greene, stiffened. The desperation fourth-down pass by Phipps was picked off by Edwards and returned 59 yards to preserve the win and send the frozen fans streaming for the exits and their favorite clubs.

		SCORING	CLE	PIT
1st	Steelers	Preston Pearson 6 yard rush (Roy Gerela kick)	0	7
2nd	Steelers	Franco Harris 1 yard rush (Roy Gerela kick)	0	14
	Browns	Mike Phipps 18 yard rush (Don Cockroft kick)	7	14

	Browns	Milt Morin 9 yard pass from Mike Phipps (kick failed)	13	14
3rd	Steelers	Roy Gerela 31 yard field goal	13	17
4th	Browns	Don Cockroft 21 yard field goal	16	17
	Steelers	Roy Gerela 26 yard field goal	16	20

	TEAM STATS	
	CLE	PIT
First downs	16	15
Rush-Yards-TD	35-135-1	45-165-2
Comp-Att-Yards-TD-INT	10-23-160-1-1	5-18-78-0-0
Sacked-Yards	6-33	1-12
Net pass yards	127	66
Total yards	262	231
Fumbles-Lost	3-2	5-1
Turnovers	3	1
Penalties-Yards	5-32	8-65

PASSING, RUSHING and RECEIVING

Browns

Passing

Mike Phipps: 10-of-23, 160 yards, 1 TD, 1 INT

Rushing

Mike Phipps: 4 carries for 38 yards, 1 TD
Hugh McKinnis: 13 carries for 46 yards
Greg Pruitt: 8 carries for 37 yards
Ken Brown: 10 carries for 14 yards

Receiving

Hugh McKinnis: 4 catches for 38 yards
Gloster Richardson: 2 catches for 62 yards
Greg Pruitt: 1 catch for 14 yards
Milt Morin: 3 catches for 46 yards, 1 TD

Steelers

Passing

Joe Gilliam: 5-of-18, 78 yards

Rushing

Franco Harris: 14 carries for 81 yards, 1 TD
Rocky Bleier: 9 carries for 48 yards
Joe Gilliam: 3 carries for 4 yards
Preston Pearson: 10 carries for 21 yards, 1 TD
John Fuqua: 5 carries for 11 yards
Steve Davis: 3 carries for 9 yards
John Stallworth: 1 carry for -9 yards

Receiving

Ron Shanklin: 2 catches for 42 yards
Randy Grossman: 1 catch for 12 yards
Frank Lewis: 1 catch for 10 yards
John Stallworth: 1 catch for 14 yards

DEFENSE

Steelers

Interceptions

Glen Edwards: 1 for 59 yards

KICK RETURNS

Browns

Kickoffs

Billy Lefear: 4 for 101 yards, 25.3 avg.
Jim Romaniszyn: 1 for 17 yards, 17.0 avg.

Punts

Thom Darden: 2 for 14 yards, 7.0 avg.
Greg Pruitt: 3 for 20 yards, 6.7 avg.

Steelers

Kickoffs

Steve Davis: 4 for 100 yards, 25.0 avg.

Punts

Glen Edwards: 1 for 13 yards, 13.0 avg.
Lynn Swann: 4 for 32 yards, 8.0 avg.

KICKING and PUNTING

Browns

Kicking

Don Cockroft: 1-for-2 PAT, 1-for-1 FG

Punting

Don Cockroft: 6 for 258 yards, 43.0 avg.

Steelers

Kicking

Roy Gerela: 2-for-2 PAT, 2-for-2 FG

Punting

Bobby Walden: 7 for 275 yards, 39.3 avg.

Week 7

		Oct. 28 Three Rivers Stadium Pittsburgh, PA			
Atlanta Falcons					**Pittsburgh Steelers**
	1Q	2Q	3Q	4Q	Total
Falcons	0	14	0	3	17

| Steelers | 14 | 0 | 3 | 7 | 24 |

PITTSBURGH (AP) — Terry Bradshaw predicted it. He's back, so is Franco Harris and so is the Pittsburgh Steelers' running game.

"And it feels good, real good," Bradshaw said after he made his first quarterback start this year and Harris rushed for a career high of 141 yards in a 24-17 victory over the Atlanta Falcons in Monday night's nationally televised National Football League game.

On opening day, Bradshaw was on the bench behind Joe Gilliam, who led the NFL preseason passers by throwing almost twice as often as Bradshaw had in Pittsburgh's two previous playoff seasons.

"Joe's had the hot hand," Bradshaw said in September, "but the time will come when we have to establish a running threat. My style is ball control and I'll wait until this thing run its course."

After Gilliam's 5-for-18 passing day in a narrow win last week over Cleveland, Coach Chuck Noll opted for Bradshaw, even though the Steelers were atop the AFC Central Division.

"It was pretty much a return to the bread and butter," Noll said after the Pittsburgh climbed to 5-1-1 and Atlanta fell to 2-5 under beleaguered Coach Norm Van Brocklin.

"We battled them. We fought as hard as we could," said Van Brocklin, target of a "Dump the Dutchman" campaign in Atlanta.

"They blocked tough and that Spaghetti Strangler or whatever he is (a reference to Harris' Afro-Italian lineage) can run pretty good."

The Steelers pounded out a season high of 235 yards rushing against the Falcons, and stumpy Rocky Bleier added 78 yards to Harris' career high total.

"I get a kick out of making the running game go," said Bradshaw, who completed nine of 20 passes for 130 yards with two interceptions.

"I don't care about getting a lot of yards passing as long as we control the ball and score some points. That's the way I've been schooled here."

It was the first 100-yard game of the season for Harris, who had a career high of 28 carries, and he gained all but 29 of his ground yards in the second half.

"I feel I'm the kind of back who has to carry the ball 20-25 times a game to be effective," said Harris, who also ran 29 yards with a swing pass from Bradshaw to set up the winning touchdown.

"So many things can go wrong with the pass, but the basic thing you have to do in running game is to beat the other team physically. It's that simple," he added.

Harris, who had rushed for 206 yards previously this season, powered seven yards for what proved to be the winning touchdown in the final quarter.

"The offensive line really did a super job out there, and Franco was the best I've seen

See STEELERS, 3B

Continued From 1B
him in quite a while," said Bradshaw. "He was really cutting that corner, and he wasn't chopping. He was running with straight power."

Pittsburgh jumped to a 14-0 lead in the first quarter. Bleier plunged one yard for the first touchdown, set up by Lynn Swann's 52-yard punt return, and Bradshaw dove in from the one for the second score to cap a 57-yard march.

Atlanta quarterback Bob Lee, sacked seven times by the hard-charging Steeler front, fired a pair of touchdown passes in the second quarter to knot the score at 14-14 by halftime.

		SCORING	ATL	PIT
1st	Steelers	Rocky Bleier 10 yard rush (Roy Gerela kick)	0	7
	Steelers	Terry Bradshaw 1 yard rush (Roy Gerela kick)	0	14
2nd	Falcons	Al Dodd 9 yard pass from Bob Lee (Nick Mike-Mayer kick)	7	14
	Falcons	Ken Burrow 24 yard pass from Bob Lee (Nick Mike-Mayer kick)	14	14
3rd	Steelers	Roy Gerela 33 yard field goal	14	17
4th	Steelers	Franco Harris 7 yard rush (Roy Gerela kick)	14	24
	Falcons	Nick Mike-Mayer 32 yard field goal	17	24

	TEAM STATS	
	ATL	PIT
First downs	13	21
Rush-Yards-TD	33-108-0	52-235-3
Comp-Att-Yards-TD-INT	8-20-122-2-2	9-21-130-0-2
Sacked-Yards	7-63	1-10
Net pass yards	59	120
Total yards	167	355
Fumbles-Lost	3-1	4-2
Turnovers	3	4
Penalties-Yards	5-25	5-35

PASSING, RUSHING and RECEIVING

Falcons

Passing

Bob Lee: 8-of-20, 122 yards, 2 TD, 2 INT

Rushing

Jim R. Mitchell: 1 carry for 5 yards
Bob Lee: 2 carries for 5 yards
Dave Hampton: 17 carries for 55 yards
Art Malone: 13 carries for 43 yards

Receiving

Jim R. Mitchell: 2 catches for 62 yards
Dave Hampton: 1 catch for 7 yards
Ken Burrow: 2 catches for 42 yards, 1 TD
Art Malone: 1 catch for -1 yard
Al Dodd: 1 catch for 9 yards, 1 TD
Haskel Stanback: 1 catch for 3 yards

Steelers

Passing

Terry Bradshaw: 9-of-21, 130 yards, 0 TD, 2 INT

Rushing

Franco Harris: 28 carries for 141 yards, 1 TD
Rocky Bleier: 15 carries for 78 yards, 1 TD
Terry Bradshaw: 9 carries for 16 yards, 1 TD

Receiving

Franco Harris: 2 catches for 37 yards
Rocky Bleier: 1 catch for 24 yards
Frank Lewis: 3 catches for 26 yards
Ron Shanklin: 1 catch for 22 yards
John Stallworth: 1 catch for 14 yards
Larry Brown: 1 catch for 7 yards

DEFENSE

Falcons

Interceptions

Clarence Ellis: 1 for 0 yards
John Zook: 1 for 14 yards

Steelers

Interceptions

Jack Ham: 1 for 5 yards
J.T. Thomas: 1 for 0 yards

KICK RETURNS

Falcons

Kickoffs

Rick Byas: 3 for 81 yards, 27.0 avg.
Ray Easterling: 1 for 13 yards, 13.0 avg.
Paul Ryczek: 1 for 0 yards, 0.0 avg.

Punts

Ray Brown: 1 for 9 yards, 9.0 avg.
Al Dodd: 1 for 6 yards, 6.0 avg.

Steelers

Kickoffs

Rocky Bleier: 2 for 57 yards, 28.5 avg.
Preston Pearson: 1 for 25 yards, 25.0 avg.

Punts

Lynn Swann: 7 for 102 yards, 14.6 avg.

KICKING and PUNTING

Falcons

Kicking

Nick Mike-Mayer: 2-for-2 PAT, 1-for-1 FG

Punting

John James: 7 for 313 yards, 44.7 avg.

Steelers

Kicking

Roy Gerela: 3-for-3 PAT, 1-for-2 FG

Punting

Bobby Walden: 4 for 137 yards, 34.3 avg.

Week 8

	1Q	2Q	3Q	4Q	Total
Eagles	0	0	0	0	0
Steelers	7	10	10	0	27

Nov. 3
Three Rivers Stadium
Pittsburgh, PA

Philadelphia Eagles vs. Pittsburgh Steelers

By VITO STELLINO
Post-Gazette Sports Writer

Who are the real Steelers?

Are they the team that has been meandering around aimlessly for several weeks, beating clubs but not looking very impressive in the process? Or are they the efficient, well-polished unit that practically bulldozed the big, bad Eagles all the way back to Philadelphia with a 27-0 victory that wasn't as close as the score sounded?

The definitive answer may not come until next Sunday when the Steelers travel to Cincinnati but if the effort against the Eagles is any indication, the Steelers have finally found themselves.

It was so one-sided that Roman Gabriel was able to lead the Eagles into Steeler territory just once before he left in the third period — and that was with the help of three penalties.

And the Steelers gave his replacement, John Reaves, a royal welcome when Mel Blount picked off his third pass and ran 52 yards for his first NFL touchdown that wrapped it up.

It was so satisfying that Joe Greene, whose fumble recovery led to a touchdown, almost liked it. "We're getting better every week and when the time comes for the playoffs, the Steelers will be standing there," he insisted. The Steelers are still 1½ games ahead of Cincinnati in the AFC Central Division.

The defense was mainly responsible for 17 of the points on Greene's recovery and interceptions by Blount and Glen Edwards, whose theft made Eagle coach Mike McCormack decide to yank Gabriel.

The offense gets credit for the other 10 on an eight-yard pass from Terry Bradshaw to Frank Lewis and a 35-yard field goal by Roy Gerela. Franco Harris scored on a five-yard run after Greene's recovery and Gerela kicked a 28-yarder after Edwards' interception.

Defense has been the heart of the Steeler team since the team has been rebuilt in recent years and Blount said the unit, "is definitely playing better than it has in previous years."

The offense is showing a lot of zing, too. Ray Mansfield, the offensive center, said, "I'm much, much happier the way the team has looked the last two weeks. I hate to stumble around out there, even when you're winning. It's hard to stop you when you get your running game going and you're beating the other team physically."

Even coach Chuck Noll beamed, "It felt good to get our first shutout."

First shutout? The Steelers blitzed Baltimore 30-0 in their opener but it seems so long ago that even Noll had forgotten. It was the first time the Steelers have had two shutouts in the modern era. The first time was in 1942.

For those people who like omens, the only NFL team to get two shutouts last year was Miami. You know where the Dolphins played last January.

When he was asked about the Steeler improvement, Noll first tried to be coy. "I thought we've played pretty well several times," he smiled as he looked at the writers, "but nobody agreed with me."

But he then added, "We've eliminated a lot of mistakes we were making earlier that hurt us."

As usual, the Steelers got a quick lead. It was the third straight game in which the Steelers jumped to a 14-0 margin. But in previous games, the defense has been guilty of lapses and let the opposing team get close. This time, the defense controlled the whole game.

"It was a matter of concentration," Noll said "In other games they've lost their concentration by stuff like arguing with the refs (a reference in particular to the Kansas City game) but this time they avoided that."

The only people who had a worse day than the Steelers were the refs. But it evened out; they handed the Steelers one TD they didn't deserve and took one back that they did.

Lewis seemed to be out of the end zone when he came down with Bradshaw's pass and defensive back Joe Lavendar said, "I know he was out because I was and he was in front of me. It doesn't look like much because of the score but that was a critical play."

However, the officials took away a third period TD from the Steelers with a holding penalty on Mansfield when Bradshaw went over from the one. The Steelers had to settle for a field goal.

It would be difficult for

Mansfield, who centered the ball, to hold before Bradshaw went over. "I just flopped down on my man and when I heard the call holding, I was ready to get up and chew out whoever it was called on. I couldn't believe it was on me."

The improved Steeler running game, which grinded out 238 yards, played a big role in the triumph.

Noll said Bradshaw, who replaced Joe Gilliam last Monday night, was "much sharper" yesterday although he showed signs of the layoff a couple of times. Franco Harris, who had 70 yards, and Rocky Bleier again ran well and the offensive line of Mansfield, Sam Davis, Jim Clack, Jon Kolb and Gordon Gravelle, who played for injured Gerry Mullins, opened up the holes repeatedly.

The Steelers moved 85 yards in eight plays, six runs, and passes of 35 yards to tight end Larry Brown and eight yards to Lewis for the TD the first time they had the ball.

The Eagles then made their only real drive of the first three periods, moving to the Steeler 27 before Tom Dempsey missed a 44-yard field goal. But they did it only with the help of two off-side penalties on Greene and a pass interference call against J. T. Thomas.

That was the Eagle offense for the day. "They couldn't do anything," Greene said, and

(Continued on Page 23)

that summed it up.

A holding penalty on Sam Davis foiled the next Steeler drive but Greene recovered Tom Bailey's fumble on the 26 and returned it 11 yards to the 15 before he was hit by several Eagles.

Four plays later, Harris scored from the five and it was 14-0 with 12:47 left in the second period. The familiar pattern of Steeler games was set but this time they never let Philadelphia get back in the contest.

The next time they had the ball, Gercia kicked a 35-yarder to make it 17-0 although he missed a 40-yard attempt on the next-to-the-last play of the second period.

The Steelers got just one first down the first three times they had the ball in the third period as the Eagles stifled their running game with several blitzes, forcing Bradshaw to throw a bit.

But the defense took over and knocked the Eagles out of it. First, Edwards intercepted a Gabriel pass intended for Harold Carmichael and returned it 26 yards to the Eagle nine. The penalty on Mansfield nullified the TD and the Steelers settled for the 28-yarder by Gereal with 4:21 left in the third period for a 20-0 lead.

Gabriel simply threw the pass over the head of the 6-foot-8 Carmichael right into the hands of Edwards, who was standing on the 35. "I saw he overthrew the receiver so I just stayed there and didn't break for the receiver and it came right to me," Edwards said.

Reaves then tried his luck on his third play, a spot pass to Charley Young was picked off by Blount, who was escorted in by half the team as he tightroped down the sidelines. Dwight White pushed the last defender, Reaves, out of the way.

"He threw it into the zone and the receiver didn't get there, so I made a break on the ball," Blount explained.

That made it 27-0 with 2:33 left in the third period and that was it. The only other interesting point came in the fourth period when John Stallworth and the Eagles' John Bunting were ejected after a brief skirmish. That got Stallworth a lecture from Noll.

A little fracas during a game with the Eagles seems to be normal procedure and Greene called them a "bunch of hot dogs."

But Bill Bergey, who's noted for getting into controversies, had a rather mild day. "That wasn't the Bill Bergey I know out there," Mansfield smiled. "Maybe he thought I was serious in the off-season when I said we had a man assigned just to get him."

So, all-in-all, it was a day for the Steelers to savor. It was the kind of game title teams play.

One of the few words of caution was provided by Edwards. "We gave them a little and on a championship defense, you don't want to give them anything. You don't want to make even little mistakes. That's the way Miami played the last two years when it was in its stride," Edwards said.

If the Steelers can play the way Miami has, their season won't be over until January.

Steeler Notes

		SCORING	PHI	PIT
1st	Steelers	Frank Lewis 8 yard pass from Terry Bradshaw (Roy Gerela kick)	0	7

2nd	Steelers	Franco Harris 5 yard rush (Roy Gerela kick)	0	14
	Steelers	Roy Gerela 35 yard field goal	0	17
3rd	Steelers	Roy Gerela 28 yard field goal	0	20
	Steelers	Mel Blount 52 yard interception return (Roy Gerela kick)	0	27

	TEAM STATS	
	PHI	PIT
First downs	10	20
Rush-Yards-TD	22-66-0	48-238-1
Comp-Att-Yards-TD-INT	9-31-104-0-2	12-22-146-1-0
Sacked-Yards	4-27	1-9
Net pass yards	77	137
Total yards	143	375
Fumbles-Lost	2-1	0-0
Turnovers	3	0
Penalties-Yards	6-68	10-99

PASSING, RUSHING and RECEIVING

Eagles

Passing

John Reaves: 4-of-14, 75 yards, 0 TD, 1 INT
Roman Gabriel: 5-of-17, 29 yards, 0 TD, 1 INT

Rushing

Tom Sullivan: 16 carries for 35 yards
John Reaves: 1 carry for 8 yards
Tom Bailey: 5 carries for 23 yards

Receiving

Tom Sullivan: 3 catches for 38 yards
Charle Young: 3 catches for 30 yards
Harold Carmichael: 1 catch for 29 yards
Tom Bailey: 1 catch for -1 yard
Randy Jackson: 1 catch for 8 yards

Steelers

Passing

Terry Bradshaw: 12-of-22, 146 yards, 1 TD, 0 INT

Rushing

Terry Bradshaw: 4 carries for 48 yards
Franco Harris: 20 carries for 70 yards, 1 TD
Preston Pearson: 7 carries for 47 yards
Rocky Bleier: 9 carries for 37 yards
John Fuqua: 6 carries for 23 yards
Steve Davis: 2 carries for 13 yards

Receiving

Franco Harris: 1 catch for 8 yards
Larry Brown: 4 catches for 70 yards
Ron Shanklin: 4 catches for 40 yards
Frank Lewis: 3 catches for 28 yards, 1 TD

DEFENSE

Steelers

Interceptions

Mel Blount: 1 for 52 yards, 1 TD
Glen Edwards: 1 for 26 yards

KICK RETURNS

Eagles

Kickoffs

Randy Jackson: 1 for 27 yards, 27.0 avg.
Larry Marshall: 5 for 113 yards, 22.6 avg.

Punts

Bill Bradley: 1 for 7 yards, 7.0 avg.
Larry Marshall: 1 for 21 yards, 21.0 avg.

Steelers

Kickoffs

Rocky Bleier: 1 for 10 yards, 10.0 avg.

Punts

Dick Conn: 4 for 21 yards, 5.3 avg.
Glen Edwards: 3 for 30 yards, 10.0 avg.

KICKING and PUNTING

Eagles

Kicking

Tom Dempsey: 0-for-1 FG

Punting

Merritt Kersey: 7 for 351 yards, 50.1 avg.

Steelers

Kicking

Roy Gerela: 3-for-3 PAT, 2-for-3 FG

Punting

Bobby Walden: 6 for 252 yards, 42.0 avg.

Week 9

Nov. 10
Riverfront Stadium
Cincinnati, OH

Pittsburgh Steelers **Cincinnati Bengals**

	1Q	2Q	3Q	4Q	Total
Steelers	0	3	0	7	10

| Bengals | 0 | 10 | 7 | 0 | 17 |

If he were an escape artist, you could compare him to Houdini. If he were a hypnotist, you could compare him to Svengali. If he were a detective, you could compare him to Sherlock Holmes.

But all Ken Anderson is, was or ever hopes to be is a quarterback, and comparisons in that league are at best risky and even more subjective than grading a college English theme. Let it be said, however, that yesterday in the dank and dark that pervaded Riverfront Stadium, he was closer to perfection than any quarterback you, me or Amos Alonzo Stagg ever laid eyes upon.

Completing 20 of 22 passes for 227 yards, Anderson directed the Cincinnati Bengals to a 17-10 decision over the Pittsburgh Steelers before 57,532 fans.

The victory was the Bengals' sixth in nine starts; the loss was the Steelers' second as opposed to six wins and a tie. So instead of Pittsburgh taking an almost insurmountable 2 ½-game lead in the American Conference Central Division, Cincinnati now trails by only a half game.

Anderson completed his first eight passes to stretch a record-breaking string of 16 over a two-game period.

He has now completed 37 of his last 43 passes and Glen Edwards, the Steelers' free safety, thinks he knows why.

"He dumps the ball off to his backs an awful lot," said Edwards, who was ejected for clotheslining Anderson on a violent sideline tackle late in the third quarter. "He is a very patient man. He is not bomb-happy like some quarterbacks.

"We were willing to give him three or four yards on every pass to a back if it meant stopping the big play. We stopped the big play but we might have given their backs a little too much room to operate."

As a result, Doug Dressler, replacing the injured Boobie Clark at fullback, was Cincinnati's leading receiver with nine catches for 84 yards. Rookie Charlie Davis, making his first pro start, was next in line with four receptions for 45 yards.

"They showed us a lot of deep zones in order to cut off (Isaac) Curtis," said Anderson. "But they gave us the backs coming out. You have to take what you can get and be happy with it."

Technically speaking, the Steelers' strategy against Curtis and his disarming 9.3 speed was a huge success. He caught only one pass for a meager five-yard gain and was, statistically at least, a non-factor.

"Our plan was to take away the big play and that of course meant stopping Curtis," admitted Steelers head coach Chuck Noll. "We saw nothing we hadn't expected from them and we had coverages designed to handle their backs, but we just didn't execute them well at all.

"As for Anderson, his statistics speak for themselves. He was great."

Anderson's accuracy only served to magnify the ineffective performance of his Steeler counterpart, Terry Bradshaw. Hitting only 13 of 35 passes for 140 yards, Bradshaw frequently threw into double and triple coverages and above or beyond open receivers.

"That was what got me," said Bradshaw. "We'd have a receiver open and I'd miss him bad. That frustrates me. It has to. But we knew we'd have to throw into that kind of coverage and we had passes designed to handle them.

"We wanted to throw into the seam between coverages but I just didn't get it done enough."

The Steelers fell behind 10-0 in the second quarter. Actually, the Bengals' first scoring drive began on the final play of the first quarter when Lemar Parrish returned Bobby Walden's 44-yard punt three yard to the Cincy 30.

They covered the 70 yards in only six plays, with Davis' 22-yard run and Anderson's 32-yard pass to Davis the most significant plays. On second-and-goal from the two, Ed Williams – the Bengals' 250-pound rookie fullback – scored the game's first touchdown. Horst Muhlmann converted, making it 7-0 with 11:23 left in the first half.

Tommy Casanova returned Walden's next punt 74 yards, breaking at least five tackles along the way.

"The coverage wasn't bad, but apparently he was strong enough to break a lot of tackles," said Noll.

Despite a first-and-10 from the Pittsburgh 12, the Bengals could net only three points, those coming on Muhlmann's 30-yard field goal with 7:47 left in the quarter.

Meanwhile, Bradshaw, after completing his first pass, had thrown eight successive incompletions. He snapped out of it with a 20-yard pitch to rookie tight end Randy Grossman, triggering a clock-beating drive that ended with Roy Gerela's 24-yard field goal on the final play of the half.

Cincinnati increased the margin to 17-3 on Williams' one-yard run with 2:09 left in the third quarter and Muhlmann's ensuing PAT. Those points followed a 47-yard drive highlighted by two Steeler penalties, Edwards' ejection, Anderson's temporary departure and Wayne Clark's temporary appearance at quarterback.

The Steelers countered with a six-minute, six-second scoring march of their own. It was culminated when Preston Pearson, subbing for the injured Rocky Bleier (sprained ankle), took a pitchout and swept right end to score from the one. Gerela converted, slicing the Bengals' lead to 17-10 with 10:54 left in the game.

Pittsburgh's next possession lasted only one play as Bradshaw's bomb down the left sideline for Frank Lewis was picked off by Ken Riley at the Bengals' 26. Cincy's possession ended abruptly at the Steelers' 10 when Davis fumbled and Mike Wagner recovered.

After chasing Wags most of the 69 yards, Anderson (who else?) dropped him at the Cincinnati 16.

"After Wagner's fumble recovery and run," said Bradshaw ruefully, "we should have scored. Something, anything. But we didn't cash in. It really hurt us bad."

The Steelers got one last chance after Dave Green's 46-yard punt downed on the Pittsburgh 16 with 1:33 left. Three quick passes to Franco Harris, Frenchy Fuqua and Grossman – in that order – gained 30 yards. After an incompletion, Fuqua swept right end for six and Ron Pritchard's last hit added 15 more yards to the gain.

Bradshaw scrambled for 11, giving Pittsburgh the ball on the Cincy 22 with 22 seconds left. An incompletion, a loss of 12 attempting to pass and a one-yard loss followed on the final three plays, an imperfect ending to be sure.

		SCORING	PIT	CIN
2nd	Bengals	Ed Williams 2 yard rush (Horst Muhlmann kick)	0	7
	Bengals	Horst Muhlmann 30 yard field goal	0	10
	Steelers	Roy Gerela 24 yard field goal	3	10
3rd	Bengals	Ed Williams 1 yard rush (Horst Muhlmann kick)	3	17
4th	Steelers	Preston Pearson 1 yard rush (Roy Gerela kick)	10	17

	TEAM STATS	
	PIT	CIN
First downs	20	22
Rush-Yards-TD	39-161-1	35-136-2
Comp-Att-Yards-TD-INT	13-35-140-0-1	20-22-227-0-0
Sacked-Yards	1-12	4-34
Net pass yards	128	193
Total yards	289	329
Fumbles-Lost	0-0	3-3
Turnovers	1	3

| Penalties-Yards | 7-42 | 5-43 |

PASSING, RUSHING and RECEIVING

Steelers

Passing

Terry Bradshaw: 13-of-35, 140 yards, 0 TD, 1 INT

Rushing

Terry Bradshaw: 6 carries for 31 yards
Franco Harris: 17 carries for 75 yards
Rocky Bleier: 8 carries for 31 yards
John Fuqua: 1 carry for 6 yards
Preston Pearson: 7 carries for 18 yards, 1 TD

Receiving

Franco Harris: 2 catches for 10 yards
Rocky Bleier: 2 catches for 14 yards
Ron Shanklin: 2 catches for 39 yards
Frank Lewis: 3 catches for 29 yards
Randy Grossman: 2 catches for 29 yards
John Fuqua: 1 catch for 16 yards
Preston Pearson: 1 catch for 3 yards

Bengals

Passing

Ken Anderson: 20-of-22, 227 yards

Rushing

Doug Dressler: 14 carries for 45 yards
Ken Anderson: 3 carries for 15 yards
Charlie Davis: 13 carries for 63 yards
Charlie Joiner: 1 carry for 3 yards
Isaac Curtis: 1 carry for 5 yards
Ed Williams: 3 carries for 5 yards, 2 TD

Receiving

Doug Dressler: 9 catches for 84 yards
Charlie Davis: 4 catches for 45 yards
Charlie Joiner: 2 catches for 43 yards
Chip Myers: 3 catches for 39 yards
Bob Trumpy: 1 catch for 11 yards
Isaac Curtis: 1 catch for 5 yards

DEFENSE

Bengals

Interceptions

Ken Riley: 1 for 0 yards

KICK RETURNS

Steelers

Kickoffs

Preston Pearson: 4 for 92 yards, 23.0 avg.

Punts

Dick Conn: 1 for 0 yards, 0.0 avg.
Glen Edwards: 2 for 12 yards, 6.0 avg.
Lynn Swann: 1 for -3 yards, -3.0 avg.

Bengals

Kickoffs

Bernard Jackson: 1 for 15 yards, 15.0 avg.
Lemar Parrish: 1 for 21 yards, 21.0 avg.

Punts

Lyle Blackwood: 1 for 2 yards, 2.0 avg.
Tommy Casanova: 2 for 81 yards, 40.5 avg.
Lemar Parrish: 2 for 6 yards, 3.0 avg.

KICKING and PUNTING

Steelers

Kicking

Roy Gerela: 1-for-1 PAT, 1-for-1 FG

Punting

Bobby Walden: 7 for 255 yards, 36.4 avg.

Bengals

Kicking

Horst Muhlmann: 2-for-2 PAT, 1-for-1 FG

Punting

Dave Green: 5 for 229 yards, 45.8 avg.

Week 10

Nov. 17
Municipal Stadium
Cleveland, OH

Pittsburgh Steelers   Cleveland Browns

	1Q	2Q	3Q	4Q	Total
Steelers	7	6	0	13	26
Browns	3	3	10	0	16

CLEVELAND — At halftime, Pete Rozelle called the stadium and asked to have his name erased from the ball. Amos Alonzo Stagg sat on some heavenly vista with his head in his hands, fighting nausea. Vince Lombardi's gravestone heaved and trembled.

It was a game only a mother could've loved. Knute Rockne's mother.

But for the Steelers, now 7-2-1 and owners of a magic number of three, it had its virtues. History had been had. For the first time since 1964, the Pittsburgh Steelers, those children of despair among the buckeyes, had survived the Cleveland Browns. By a score of 26-16 and solely because of a defense that reminds you of Ali Baba and the 40 Thieves.

But it will probably be Thursday before they quite believe they own a game and a half edge over Cincinnati with four left. Even when a club official jumped on the team bus to announce "Houston beat Cincinnati, 20-3," the Steelers could muster only the sort of hollow cheer given by the teacher's pet on the last day of school.

As Joe Greene had put it, more than once, "any damn thing can happen in Cleveland." And in a game that would've been embarrassing if Baldwin-Wallace and John Carroll had been out there stumbling around, anything that could've happened did.

There were 11 turnovers, some caused as Andy Russell insisted, by "a lot of hard hitting;" others refuting that old theory about the hand being quicker than the eye and smacking of something produced for The Three Stooges.

Of the Steelers' 26 points, 16 were the direct result of Cleveland misplays, which included three fumbles and three interceptions. All 16 of the Browns' points came as the result of Steeler mistakes, or in one memorable instance, their own. One Cleveland field goal occurred after a Brown fumble that gained six yards.

All told, there were eight fumbles and six interceptions and it was wholly appropriate, even poetic, that the game was decided on a play in which Cleveland quarterback Brian Sipe and back Billy LeFear collided on a handoff.

Greene, whose earlier interception had accounted for a field goal, scooped up the ensuing fumble, deftly lateraled to J.T. Thomas and he ran 14 yards to dissolve a 16-all tie with 12:51 remaining in the game. It was that sort of an afternoon.

There were 77,739 fans on hand at Municipal Stadium and when perhaps a hundred of them staged a furious fight in one end zone, it was generally agreed they had produced the day's most coordinated physical activity.

When Chuck Noll said later, "Joe Greene got the offensive game ball for his broken-field running," not one eyebrow was raised.

This was Cleveland, where yearly fate had slipped a horse's head into the Steeler bed. And when the Browns (3-7) had erased deficits of 10-3 and 13-6 to go ahead, 16-13, midway in the third quarter, and when Joe Gilliam started warming up because in 15 attempts Terry Hanratty had completed more passes to the Browns (3) than he had to the Steelers (2), Joe Greene knew the gods were thinking of making the Steelers an offer they couldn't refuse.

"Here we go again," thought Greene. "And I came close to saying it," he smiled after his interception and fumble recovery led to 10 points. "I thought, 'this is the same old stuff in Cleveland.' I shouldn't have been thinking that, but I was. They've been a nemesis for us. There's no such thing as a jinx, but it builds when you keep losing. Anybody who calls himself a man or part of a football team has to be bothered when you keep hearing you can't win in a certain place."

Along the sidelines, "as excited as I ever saw him," according to Mike Wagner, Andy Russell was telling Steeler defenders to keep the faith.

Russell, who is what they're talking about when they use the term an old pro, was sure the defense would suck one more turnover from the Browns, who seemed willing.

"Every so often there's a game the defense has to win," Russell said. "This was one of them. We talked to each other on the sidelines. We were sure we'd make the play that would win the game."

And so the Steeler defenders did. Russell hit Sipe from behind on a blitz and knocked the ball loose. L.C. Greenwood recovered. In a few minutes, the third of Roy Gerela's four field goals tied it, 16-16, with three minutes gone in the final quarter.

Exactly 16 seconds later, Greene and Thomas untied it. Greene's lateral — (I like laterals when they go for touchdowns," Noll grinned — hit Thomas in stride and he went in untouched, the touchdown and two earlier interceptions bringing the first game ball of his career.

"It was meant for us to win." Greene said. "This game was a classic example of being in the right place at the right time."

More often than the Browns, the Steelers were. "Weird is probably a good way to describe the game," Noll agreed. "But nice weird."

It wouldn't have been nice weird if a Steeler defense that seems capable of overcoming its most serious problem, the Steeler offense, hadn't been as reliable as a Mafia hit man.

By virtue of a process that seems to be part Pin-the-tail-on-the-donkey and part the divine right of coaches, Noll

(Continued from Page 27.)

elected Hanratty to start his first game in a year. And as might have reasonably been expected of a guy who had thrown only six passes this season and hadn't even played in nine games, Hanratty completed two of 15 passes, fumbled once, botched a few handoffs and in general conducted himself as though in an alien environment.

Or, as he put it, "I felt strange out there without my baseball hat on."

It was good that Franco Harris was quite comfortable because he composed much of the Steeler offense, running for a career high 156 yards that included a 54-yard burst which set up Gerela's second field goal.

Beyond Harris and Steve Davis, who returned with a vengeance and gained 52 yards in nine pops, all was darkness. Until Greene and the defense removed a rather large bag from Noll's hand.

As Terry Bradshaw, apparently now the No. 3 quarterback said, "We helped the coach out."

The coach appreciated it. "Our offensive play was filled with errors," Noll understated, "but we survived our mistakes. Usually, when we come over here, we don't."

The Steelers almost didn't again yesterday, but Noll had a thought for any purists wondering how long the Steelers might survive in the playoffs should they reach them.

"We've got to keep our defense playing good offense," he smiled.

And that is the rock-bottom line on the Steelers, who are, regardless of who is playing quarterback, still winning them on dee-fense.

		SCORING	PIT	CLE
1st	Browns	Don Cockroft 44 yard field goal	0	3
	Steelers	Ron Shanklin 28 yard pass from Terry Hanratty (Roy Gerela kick)	7	3
2nd	Steelers	Roy Gerela 32 yard field goal	10	3
	Browns	Don Cockroft 35 yard field goal	10	6
	Steelers	Roy Gerela 32 yard field goal	13	6
3rd	Browns	Van Green 36 yard interception return (Don Cockroft kick)	13	13
	Browns	Don Cockroft 18 yard field goal	13	16
4th	Steelers	Roy Gerela 23 yard field goal	16	16
	Steelers	J.T. Thomas 14 yard fumble return (Roy Gerela kick)	23	16
	Steelers	Roy Gerela 22 yard field goal	26	16

	TEAM STATS	
	PIT	CLE
First downs	10	13
Rush-Yards-TD	41-233-0	31-80-0
Comp-Att-Yards-TD-INT	3-19-81-1-3	15-35-162-0-3
Sacked-Yards	0-0	4-24
Net pass yards	81	138
Total yards	314	218
Fumbles-Lost	4-3	6-4
Turnovers	6	7
Penalties-Yards	9-111	2-20

PASSING, RUSHING and RECEIVING

Steelers

Passing

Terry Hanratty: 2-of-15, 63 yards, 1 TD, 3 INT
Joe Gilliam: 1-of-4, 18 yards

Rushing

Franco Harris: 23 carries for 156 yards
Steve Davis: 9 carries for 52 yards
John Fuqua: 8 carries for 31 yards
Terry Hanratty: 1 carry for -6 yards

Receiving

Ron Shanklin: 3 catches for 81 yards, 1 TD

Browns

Passing

Brian Sipe: 15-of-30, 162 yards, 0 TD, 3 INT
Mike Phipps: 0-of-5, 0 yards

Rushing

Brian Sipe: 2 carries for 17 yards
Hugh McKinnis: 14 carries for 49 yards
Ken Brown: 5 carries for 16 yards
Greg Pruitt: 6 carries for -2 yards
Billy Lefear: 4 carries for 0 yards

Receiving

Milt Morin: 6 catches for 59 yards
Hugh McKinnis: 1 catch for 3 yards
Dave Sullivan: 2 catches for 49 yards
Ken Brown: 1 catch for 12 yards
Steve Holden: 2 catches for 27 yards
Greg Pruitt: 3 catches for 12 yards

DEFENSE

Steelers

Interceptions

Joe Greene: 1 for 26 yards
J.T. Thomas: 2 for 0 yards

Browns

Interceptions

Bob Babich: 1 for 4 yards
Van Green: 1 for 36 yards, 1 TD
Clarence R. Scott: 1 for 25 yards

KICK RETURNS

Steelers

Kickoffs

Jimmy Allen: 1 for 7 yards, 7.0 avg.
Mel Blount: 3 for 103 yards, 34.3 avg.
Steve Davis: 1 for 20 yards, 20.0 avg.

Punts

Dick Conn: 2 for 11 yards, 5.5 avg.
Glen Edwards: 1 for 0 yards, 0.0 avg.

Browns

Kickoffs

Eddie Brown: 1 for 17 yards, 17.0 avg.
Billy Lefear: 4 for 94 yards, 23.5 avg.
Greg Pruitt: 1 for 26 yards, 26.0 avg.

Punts

Thom Darden: 1 for 3 yards, 3.0 avg.
Billy Lefear: 2 for 1 yard, 0.5 avg.
Greg Pruitt: 1 for 0 yards, 0.0 avg.

KICKING and PUNTING

Steelers

Kicking

Roy Gerela: 2-for-2 PAT, 4-for-5 FG

Punting

Bobby Walden: 4 for 152 yards, 38.0 avg.

Browns

Kicking

Don Cockroft: 1-for-1 PAT, 3-for-3 FG

Punting

Don Cockroft: 6 for 259 yards, 43.2 avg.

Week 11

Nov. 25
Tulane Stadium
New Orleans, LA

Pittsburgh Steelers   New Orleans Saints

	1Q	2Q	3Q	4Q	Total
Steelers	7	7	14	0	28
Saints	0	0	7	0	7

NEW ORLEANS (AP) — "If I'd been O.J. Simpson, I'd have scored a couple more," said Pitsburgh quarterback Terry Bradshaw after he led the Steelers to a 28-7 runaway victory over the New Orleans Saints in Monday night's National Football League game.

Simpson, star running back of the Buffalo Bills, has had better nights than the blond quarterback had against the Saints Monday. But Bradshaw's performance was more than sufficient, netting 99 yards rushing—including a touchdown—and 80 yards and two more touchdowns through the air.

The fourth Steeler touchdown came on a 64-yard punt return by Lynn Swann.

"The Saints' coverage was really excellent, but they opened some huge lanes," he said in the noisy, steamy dressing room. "You saw it. You could have run for a hundred yards yourself.

"I would have liked to have thrown the ball a little better, but our running game was going, and I wasn't about to disturb a good thing."

Bradshaw hit eight of 19 with two interceptions.

Pittsburgh Coach Chuck Noll wouldn't commit himself to ending the game of musical quarterbacks he's been playing all season, but he did praise Bradshaw's performance.

"Bradshaw played a heck of a fine game," Noll said.

Noll has rotated quarterback chores among Bradshaw, Joe Gilliam and Terry Hanratty, saying he was waiting for a leader to emerge and "take the bull by the horns."

Saints' Coach John North was more vehement in his comments about Bradshaw's performance: "We made Terry Bradshaw into an all-pro tonight."

Bradshaw threw 31 yards to Frank Lewis for a first-quarter score, ran 18 yards for a touchdown in the second quarter and tossed one yard to Larry Brown for a third-period marker.

Swann's 64-yard scamper also came in the third period.

Between Brown's touchdown and the one by Swann, the Saints notched their single score of the night—a 10-yard pass from reserve quarterback Bobby Scott to rookie tight end Paul Seal.

Scott stepped in late in the first half, after starting quarterback Archie Manning had gone 2-10-3 in passing. Scott hit eight of 22 without being picked off.

Joe Greene and Steve Furness sacked Manning twice. They got to Scott for two more sacks, and Dwight White nailed Scott to add a fifth sack to the Steeler defensive statistics. They came into the game with 40 sacks in 10 games and the NFL's third-ranked defense. The Saints were ranked fourth.

The Steeler defense held the Saints to a total of 178 yards from scrimmage, while the Pittsburgh offense was garnering 334—272 of it ground yardage.

Franco Harris again went over 100 yards for the night, picking up 114 on 19 carries.

		SCORING	PIT	NOR
1st	Steelers	Frank Lewis 31 yard pass from Terry Bradshaw (Roy Gerela kick)	7	0
2nd	Steelers	Terry Bradshaw 18 yard rush (Roy Gerela kick)	14	0
3rd	Steelers	Lynn Swann 64 yard punt return (Roy Gerela kick)	21	0
	Saints	Paul Seal 10 yard pass from Bobby Scott (Bill McClard kick)	21	7
	Steelers	Larry Brown 1 yard pass from Terry Bradshaw (Roy Gerela kick)	28	7

	TEAM STATS	
	PIT	NOR
First downs	18	15
Rush-Yards-TD	43-272-1	33-109-0
Comp-Att-Yards-TD-INT	8-19-80-2-2	10-32-117-1-3
Sacked-Yards	2-18	6-48
Net pass yards	62	69
Total yards	334	178
Fumbles-Lost	3-2	1-1
Turnovers	4	4
Penalties-Yards	10-115	1-11

PASSING, RUSHING and RECEIVING

Steelers

Passing

Terry Bradshaw: 8-of-19, 80 yards, 2 TD, 2 INT

Rushing

Terry Bradshaw: 9 carries for 99 yards, 1 TD
Franco Harris: 19 carries for 114 yards
Steve Davis: 14 carries for 53 yards
Reggie Harrison: 1 carry for 6 yards

Receiving

Franco Harris: 2 catches for -1 yard
Frank Lewis: 2 catches for 42 yards, 1 TD
Ron Shanklin: 1 catch for 22 yards
Randy Grossman: 1 catch for 10 yards
Lynn Swann: 1 catch for 6 yards
Larry Brown: 1 catch for 1 yard, 1 TD

Saints

Passing

Bobby Scott: 8-of-22, 108 yards, 1 TD, 0 INT
Archie Manning: 2-of-10, 9 yards, 0 TD, 3 INT

Rushing

Alvin Maxson: 15 carries for 70 yards
Howard Stevens: 5 carries for 19 yards
Jess Phillips: 10 carries for 13 yards
Archie Manning: 1 carry for 6 yards
Rod McNeill: 2 carries for 1 yard

Receiving

Alvin Maxson: 1 catch for 1 yard
Paul Seal: 3 catches for 47 yards, 1 TD
Bob Newland: 2 catches for 34 yards
Joel Parker: 3 catches for 30 yards
Howard Stevens: 1 catch for 5 yards

DEFENSE

Steelers

Interceptions

Jack Ham: 1 for 0 yards
Andy Russell: 1 for 0 yards
J.T. Thomas: 1 for 8 yards

Saints

Interceptions

Ernie Jackson: 1 for 13 yards
Tom Myers: 1 for 5 yards

KICK RETURNS

Steelers

Kickoffs

Mel Blount: 2 for 49 yards, 24.5 avg.

Punts

Glen Edwards: 1 for 14 yards, 14.0 avg.
Lynn Swann: 6 for 106 yards, 17.7 avg., 1 TD

Saints

Kickoffs

Howard Stevens: 2 for 40 yards, 20.0 avg.

Punts

Howard Stevens: 4 for 16 yards, 4.0 avg.

KICKING and PUNTING

Steelers

Kicking

Roy Gerela: 4-for-4 PAT, 0-for-1 FG

Punting

Bobby Walden: 5 for 207 yards, 41.4 avg.

Saints

Kicking

Bill McClard: 1-for-1 PAT

Punting

Tom Blanchard: 7 for 291 yards, 41.6 avg.

Week 12

	Dec. 1 Three Rivers Stadium Pittsburgh, PA				
Houston Oilers					Pittsburgh Steelers
	1Q	2Q	3Q	4Q	Total
Oilers	0	7	3	3	13

| Steelers | 3 | 7 | 0 | 0 | 10 |

It was the kind of day when you had to think more about getting the last seat on the ark than about winning a football game.

A nasty, sleeting rain dropped on the Steelers' parade yesterday and helped turn what was supposed to be a cakewalk to the division crown into a dogfight.

A one-time meek bunch of players named the Houston Oilers, who seem bent on eventually inheriting the National Football League, rose up and dealt the Steelers a soggy, gritty 13-10 setback.

"You're going to have to print some retractions," said a chagrined Joe Greene, who confidently predicted last week that the Steelers were going to win the Super Bowl despite their previous failure to beat a winning team this year.

"I was overflowing with confidence before but I'm scared now. I've got to admit it," Greene said. "We let it get away."

The Steelers are now only a game ahead of Cincinnati and the Bengals could close to within a half-game tonight with an upset victory at Miami that could set the stage for a title showdown on national TV against the Steelers on Dec. 14.

It might have been poetic justice that Houston ruined the Steelers' dream of clinching it this weekend because the Steelers had the lead in the first place because the Oilers had upset Cincinnati twice.

But it's gotten to the point where Oiler victories no longer rate as upsets. In fact, the Steelers' 13-7 victory in the first meeting now is the team's only win against a .500 team because the Oilers are now 6-6. The Steelers are 8-3-1 and Cincinnati is 7-4.

"I kept thinking, 'when are they going to come up and be Houston again and make a mistake?' but they didn't," Greene said.

Instead, the Steelers' offense, which had its lowest net yardage total of the season (84) besides the lowest rushing (75) and passing (9) totals of the year, made the mistakes.

While the Steelers' didn't get a single turnover for only the second time of the year, the Oilers swiped three Steeler passes, sacked Terry Bradshaw and Terry Hanratty four times and drove Bradshaw out of the game with bruised ribs. X-rays proved negative and he says he can play next week.

The Steeler defense was almost as tough, holding Houston to 158 yards, and the Oilers needed the help of a controversial officials' call to set the stage for Skip Butler's 34-yard field goal with.

for Skip Butler's 34-yard field goal with 2:32 left in the game that snapped a 10-10 tie. The Oilers picked off two Hanratty passes in the last two minutes to wrap it up.

The Steelers scored in the first period on Roy Gerela's 44-yard field goal and the teams traded touchdowns in the second period. Dan Pastorini tossed a six-yard pass to Fred Willis and Bradshaw hit Franco Harris with a 32-yard strike with 32 seconds left in the first half after he scrambled all over the field.

That made it 10-7 at the half but Butler's 42-yarder midway in the third period — set up when Greg Bingham stole a pass that bounced off Ron Shanklin's hands — tied it up. It was a strange period in which Houston scored but failed to get a first down and the Steelers got just two.

As the rain continued to pelt down on the diehards in the crowd of 41,195 at Three Rivers who refused to be driven away by the miserable weather, it looked as if neither team would score again — even if it went to overtime.

But Houston got two breaks on a pair of third down plays involving Willis. First, Pastorini threw a pass to Willis on 3rd-and-4 from the Houston 41 and Jack Ham reached over his shoulder and knocked it away but was called for interference.

Since the Oilers were holding, the play was nullified by offsetting penalties and then Pastorini passed seven yards to Willis for a first down that kept the drive alive.

Three plays later on 3rd-and-7 from the Steeler 31 came the real controversial call that cost the Steelers again. This time it was on Glen Edwards — and was it mere coincidence that Al DeRogatis was broadcasting the game?

Willis went in the left flat and the Pastorini pass went over his head with no Steeler seemingly close enough to touch him. When the flag went down and Edwards was called for defensive holding, both Andy Russell and Edwards jumped in the air in protest.

Russell was complaining that Billy Johnson had illegally "picked" — or screened him — for a second consecutive play. Edwards simply said he was innocent.

"I was in the middle of the field," Edwards said. "It couldn't possibly be me. I jumped for the sky when he pointed to me. I didn't do anything."

But the Oilers had an automatic first down on the Steelers 26 and four plays later, the Oilers had their winning field goal.

Oiler coach Sid Gillman smiled and said with his tongue-in-cheek, "I'm sure the official was right." Steeler coach Chuck Noll said he didn't see the play.

Willis said he wasn't aware a penalty had been called until he turned around and saw the flag because, "I was just concentrating on getting free." But then he said maybe somebody hooked him around the waist.

The Steelers can't blame the officials, though. As Greene said, "The handwriting was already on the wall."

Bradshaw said, "We looked terrible. It was the worst day offensively I can remember since I've been here. No excuses or pointing fingers. We just looked bad."

Then, sounding like George Allen, he said, "There were too many distractions." And he added some excuses. "It was a short week after a Monday night game and Thanksgiving was in there. We weren't ready, maybe it was too much turkey."

Noll said, "The defense and special teams played well enough to win but you don't win many wars playing defense alone. We didn't throw the ball well at times and we didn't make the blocks and the running game won't go if you don't sustain the blocks."

He added, "What we have to do now is not dwell on this. This is history. We've got two games left and if we win them both, we'll win the division. If we dwell on what could and should have happened, it'll kill us."

Greene had one final thing to dwell on. "You feel bad when you get whipped on your own field on a day when you don't even want to be out. But if we had to lose, I don't feel too bad about them winning, especially Pastorini. He's spent a lot of days flat on his back. I was happy for him.".

But there wasn't much else for the Steelers to be happy about on a drizzly, dismal day.

		SCORING	HOU	PIT
1st	Steelers	Roy Gerela 44 yard field goal	0	3
2nd	Oilers	Fred Willis 6 yard pass from Dan Pastorini (Skip Butler kick)	7	3
	Steelers	Franco Harris 31 yard pass from Terry Bradshaw (Roy Gerela kick)	7	10
3rd	Oilers	Skip Butler 42 yard field goal	10	10
4th	Oilers	Skip Butler 34 yard field goal	13	10

	TEAM STATS	
	HOU	PIT
First downs	11	6
Rush-Yards-TD	43-97-0	20-75-0
Comp-Att-Yards-TD-INT	10-19-84-1-0	6-25-60-1-3

Sacked-Yards	3-23	4-51
Net pass yards	61	9
Total yards	158	84
Fumbles-Lost	1-0	1-0
Turnovers	0	3
Penalties-Yards	8-64	4-30

PASSING, RUSHING and RECEIVING

Oilers

Passing

Dan Pastorini: 10-of-19, 84 yards, 1 TD, 0 INT

Rushing

Willie Rodgers: 15 carries for 63 yards
Fred Willis: 23 carries for 34 yards
Dan Pastorini: 5 carries for 0 yards

Receiving

Willie Rodgers: 2 catches for 37 yards
Fred Willis: 6 catches for 36 yards, 1 TD
Mack Alston: 1 catch for 10 yards
Billy Johnson: 1 catch for 1 yard

Steelers

Passing

Terry Bradshaw: 6-of-20, 60 yards, 1 TD, 1 INT
Terry Hanratty: 0-of-5, 0 yards, 0 TD, 2 INT

Rushing

Franco Harris: 7 carries for 29 yards
Frank Lewis: 1 carry for 22 yards
Terry Bradshaw: 2 carries for 2 yards

Rocky Bleier: 6 carries for 15 yards
Steve Davis: 4 carries for 7 yards

Receiving

Franco Harris: 3 catches for 39 yards, 1 TD
Frank Lewis: 1 catch for 12 yards
Ron Shanklin: 1 catch for 9 yards
Steve Davis: 1 catch for 0 yards

DEFENSE

Oilers

Interceptions

Bob Atkins: 1 for 5 yards
Gregg Bingham: 2 for 31 yards

KICK RETURNS

Oilers

Kickoffs

Billy Johnson: 3 for 77 yards, 25.7 avg.

Punts

Billy Johnson: 4 for 36 yards, 9.0 avg.
Jeff Severson: 3 for 6 yards, 2.0 avg.

Steelers

Kickoffs

Glen Edwards: 2 for 31 yards, 15.5 avg.
Reggie Harrison: 2 for 43 yards, 21.5 avg.

Punts

Glen Edwards: 3 for 12 yards, 4.0 avg.
Lynn Swann: 5 for 54 yards, 10.8 avg.

KICKING and PUNTING

Oilers

Kicking

Skip Butler: 1-for-1 PAT, 2-for-2 FG

Punting

David Beverly: 10 for 344 yards, 34.4 avg.

Steelers

Kicking

Roy Gerela: 1-for-1 PAT, 1-for-1 FG

Punting

Bobby Walden: 9 for 330 yards, 36.7 avg.

Week 13

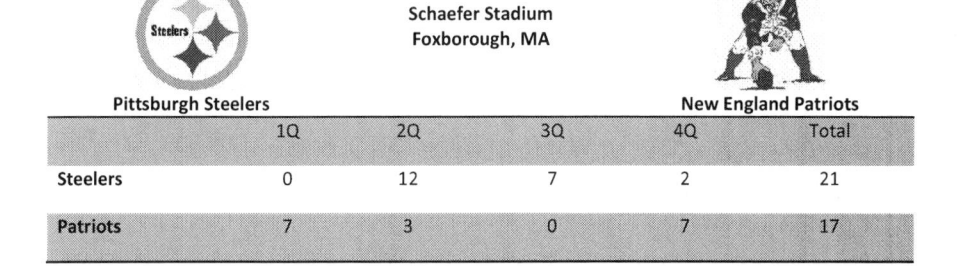

	Dec. 8 Schaefer Stadium Foxborough, MA				
Pittsburgh Steelers				**New England Patriots**	
	1Q	2Q	3Q	4Q	Total
Steelers	0	12	7	2	21
Patriots	7	3	0	7	17

Franco Harris said that all he could think of going into Sunday's game between the Pittsburgh Steelers and the New England Patriots was that a victory for his Steelers would clinch the Central Division title of the American Conference in the National Football League.

Harris rushed for 136 yards and a touchdown to help the Steelers win 21-17.

"This makes it three years in a row in the playoffs," said veteran Steeler linebacker Andy Russell. "Now we've got to do something – get into the big game."

The Steelers are 2 ½ games ahead of the second-place team in their division, Cincinnati, with one game remaining for each team – a game next Sunday against each other at Pittsburgh.

"If we play this type of ball, we'll be very strong going into the playoffs," said Harris, a 230-pound fullback from Penn State.

The Steelers, who now have a 9-3-1 record, will be host to the conference wild-card team, the Buffalo Bills, on Dec. 22.

Harris' touchdown put the Steelers ahead 9-7 after 4 minutes, 25 seconds of play in the second quarter, five plays after defensive back Mel Blount had recovered a fumble by Mack Herron at the New England 19.

Mistakes by the Patriots gave the Steelers two fumbles, an intercepted pass, a 16-yard punt and a safety.

The Patriots scored their first touchdown early after a weak punt by Pittsburgh into a strong wind. They moved 38 yards in six plays and scored on a 17-yard pass from Jim Plunkett to Herron. Except for a 20-yard field goal by John Smith, the Patriots were held until only 71 seconds remained in the game. Then Plunkett passed 48 yards to Herron to set up Herron's five-yard touchdown run.

Roy Gerela kicked two field goals for the Steelers, of 40 yards and 27 yards. Lynn Swann caught a seven-yard touchdown pass and L.C. Greenwood tackled Plunkett for the safety.

The Patriots are the only team with a record of better than .500 that the Steelers have beaten. The Steelers have lost to Oakland, Cincinnati and Houston and tied Denver. They have not played Buffalo.

		SCORING	PIT	NWE
1st	Patriots	Mack Herron 17 yard pass from Jim Plunkett (John Smith kick)	0	7
2nd	Steelers	Roy Gerela 40 yard field goal	3	7
	Steelers	Franco Harris 2 yard rush (kick failed)	9	7
	Steelers	Roy Gerela 27 yard field goal	12	7
	Patriots	John Smith 20 yard field goal	12	10
3rd	Steelers	Lynn Swann 7 yard pass from Terry Bradshaw (Roy Gerela kick)	19	10
4th	Steelers	Safety, Greenwood tackled Plunkett in end zone	21	10
	Patriots	Mack Herron 5 yard rush (John Smith kick)	21	17

	TEAM STATS	
	PIT	NWE
First downs	16	12
Rush-Yards-TD	46-184-1	32-79-1
Comp-Att-Yards-TD-INT	10-18-86-1-1	8-18-127-1-1

Sacked-Yards	2-17	3-22
Net pass yards	69	105
Total yards	253	184
Fumbles-Lost	1-1	2-2
Turnovers	2	3
Penalties-Yards	7-44	5-25

PASSING, RUSHING and RECEIVING

Steelers

Passing

Terry Bradshaw: 10-of-16, 86 yards, 1 TD, 1 INT
Joe Gilliam: 0-of-2, 0 yards

Rushing

Franco Harris: 29 carries for 136 yards, 1 TD
Rocky Bleier: 12 carries for 42 yards
Terry Bradshaw: 1 carry for 6 yards
Steve Davis: 3 carries for 4 yards
Joe Gilliam: 1 carry for -4 yards

Receiving

Franco Harris: 1 catch for 4 yards
Rocky Bleier: 1 catch for 8 yards
Frank Lewis: 3 catches for 39 yards
Larry Brown: 4 catches for 28 yards
Lynn Swann: 1 catch for 7 yards, 1 TD

Patriots

Passing

Jim Plunkett: 8-of-18, 127 yards, 1 TD, 1 INT

Rushing

Mack Herron: 19 carries for 55 yards, 1 TD
Jim Plunkett: 1 carry for 4 yards
John Tarver: 11 carries for 18 yards
Joe Wilson: 1 carry for 2 yards

Receiving

Mack Herron: 3 catches for 69 yards, 1 TD
Randy Vataha: 2 catches for 35 yards
Bob Adams: 2 catches for 23 yards
John Tarver: 1 catch for 0 yards

DEFENSE

Steelers

Interceptions

Jack Ham: 1 for 0 yards

Patriots

Interceptions

Prentice McCray: 1 for 0 yards

KICK RETURNS

Steelers

Kickoffs

Reggie Harrison: 1 for 2 yards, 2.0 avg.
Lynn Swann: 2 for 11 yards, 5.5 avg.

Punts

Lynn Swann: 2 for 32 yards, 16.0 avg.

Patriots

Kickoffs

Mack Herron: 1 for 21 yards, 21.0 avg.
Andy Johnson: 1 for 17 yards, 17.0 avg.

Punts

Eddie Hinton: 1 for 0 yards, 0.0 avg.

KICKING and PUNTING

Steelers

Kicking

Roy Gerela: 1-for-2 PAT, 2-for-3 FG

Punting

Bobby Walden: 6 for 207 yards, 34.5 avg.

Patriots

Kicking

John Smith: 2-for-2 PAT, 1-for-2 FG

Punting

Dave Chapple: 5 for 179 yards, 35.8 avg.

Week 14

Dec. 14
Three Rivers Stadium
Pittsburgh, PA

Cincinnati Bengals — Pittsburgh Steelers

	1Q	2Q	3Q	4Q	Total
Bengals	0	0	3	0	3
Steelers	7	10	7	3	27

The pro-Joe Gilliam faction can occupy itself with sugar-coated thoughts of what might have been or what glories lie ahead. The pro-Terry Hanratty faction can cheer itself with a rousing chorus or two of the Notre Dame Fight Song.

For, if nothing else of substance emerged from the Steelers' 27-3 thrashing of Cincinnati at Three Rivers Stadium Saturday, the fact that, in the short second season that is the National Football league playoffs, Pittsburgh will breathe or suffocate with Terry Bradshaw at quarterback, became obvious.

"Well, I wouldn't say the team was mine at last," said Bradshaw in the wake of the Steelers 10th win against three losses and a tie. "But The Man (Coach Chuck Noll) has stuck with me the last few weeks, and I think both the team and I have responded with confidence."

On Saturday Bradshaw's response came in the form of an eight-for-13 passing performance that netted 132 yards and two first-half touchdowns.

yards and two first-half touchdowns.

"The big thing is my confidence is finally coming back," said Bradshaw. "Any quarterback who sits on the bench for six weeks like I did has to have a lot of his confidence destroyed. Nothing destroys your confidence more than idleness, and I think the timing and instincts a quarterback needs come back a lot faster than the confidence.

"I'm making progress now, I'm not having to rely solely on instincts any more. I'm into every game and I'm picking up the things in the defense I have to pick up. Playing as much as I did today really helped me. Some quarterbacks might not need as much work as I do to stay sharp, but I need every minute I can get.

"Until now, the running game has made things easy for me while I shook off the rust. But now I feel that, at last, I'm contributing a lot to our offense. I hope I can contribute even more next week."

And next week means against Buffalo in the first round of the American Conference playoffs.

"Getting to watch them on TV (yesterday against Los Angeles) is going to help me get a head start. I find I can pick up a lot of little things from watching a team on television. I'll make a lot of mental notes on who does what and who lines up where.

"But working on the things we worked on against Cincinnati was a lot more help. There were a lot of little things we needed to iron out and the best place to do it is in a game, not in practice.

"A big thing, too, was not getting my ribs hurt any further. I didn't take a single lick on them. Right now I'd say I'm about 90 percent healthy as far as the ribs go and I think I've got a good shot at being 100 percent for Buffalo."

While the Steeler offense profited from Saturday's otherwise meaningless encounter, the defense derived no benefits, particularly since the Bengals refined non-aggression tactics to an art in the last 30 minutes.

"About the only thing we gained from that was exercise," said end L. C. Greenwood, who blocked a field goal and recovered a fumble. "We needed that of course, but in terms of getting ready for Buffalo we got nothing out of it.

"Will I watch Buffalo on TV? Probably not. If I involve myself with too much football I get bored and this would be the wrong time to get bored with football. Anyways, the films will give us as much help as TV and I'll see all the films I could want to see starting Tuesday."

Noll, though obviously displeased with Cincinnati's no-show offense, was cheered by the Steelers' know-how and will-to. Particularly the will-to.

"The enthusiasm we showed toward a game that meant nothing was very

Steeler Notes

Mel Blount, the right cor- even though he registered 30

gratifying," he explained. "We could have just gone through the motions, but instead we accepted the challenge and carried the battle. That shows me a lot. "Right now, I'n very optimistic about the playoffs. I'll take things in the state they are right now. I'm convinced we have a good football team and a team that will do whatever it takes to win."

Against Buffalo the thrust must be threefold: Stop O. J. Simpson's running, control Joe Ferguson's short-passing game and perhaps most significantly, give Bradshaw the freedom to be as steady and efficient as he was against Cincinnati.

		SCORING	CIN	PIT
1st	Steelers	John Stallworth 5 yard pass from Terry Bradshaw (Roy Gerela kick)	0	7
2nd	Steelers	Gerry Mullins 7 yard pass from Terry Bradshaw (Roy Gerela kick)	0	14
	Steelers	Roy Gerela 26 yard field goal	0	17
3rd	Bengals	Horst Muhlmann 32 yard field goal	3	17
	Steelers	Reggie Harrison 1 yard rush (Roy Gerela kick)	3	24
4th	Steelers	Roy Gerela 42 yard field goal	3	27

	TEAM STATS	
	CIN	PIT
First downs	11	21
Rush-Yards-TD	41-170-0	37-171-1

Comp-Att-Yards-TD-INT	3-8-23-0-1	12-21-183-2-0
Sacked-Yards	0-0	0-0
Net pass yards	23	183
Total yards	193	354
Fumbles-Lost	1-1	3-2
Turnovers	2	2
Penalties-Yards	4-29	3-63

PASSING, RUSHING and RECEIVING

Bengals

Passing

Wayne Clark: 3-of-8, 23 yards, 0 TD, 1 INT

Rushing

Charlie Davis: 13 carries for 73 yards
Ed Williams: 18 carries for 67 yards
Doug Dressler: 8 carries for 16 yards
Charlie Joiner: 1 carry for 8 yards
Isaac Curtis: 1 carry for 6 yards

Receiving

Ed Williams: 1 catch for -1 yard
Bruce Coslet: 2 catches for 24 yards

Steelers

Passing

Terry Bradshaw: 8-of-13, 132 yards, 2 TD, 0 INT
Joe Gilliam: 4-of-8, 51 yards

Rushing

Franco Harris: 17 carries for 79 yards
Terry Bradshaw: 1 carry for 4 yards

Lynn Swann: 1 carry for 14 yards
Rocky Bleier: 8 carries for 38 yards
Reggie Harrison: 5 carries for 24 yards, 1 TD
Steve Davis: 5 carries for 12 yards

Receiving

John Stallworth: 6 catches for 105 yards, 1 TD
Lynn Swann: 2 catches for 44 yards
Reggie Harrison: 1 catch for 2 yards
Steve Davis: 1 catch for 7 yards
Randy Grossman: 1 catch for 18 yards
Gerry Mullins: 1 catch for 7 yards, 1 TD

DEFENSE

Steelers

Interceptions

Donnie Shell: 1 for 0 yards

KICK RETURNS

Bengals

Kickoffs

Bernard Jackson: 4 for 110 yards, 27.5 avg.
John McDaniel: 2 for 40 yards, 20.0 avg.

Punts

Tommy Casanova: 1 for 9 yards, 9.0 avg.

Steelers

Kickoffs

Dick Conn: 1 for 34 yards, 34.0 avg.
Reggie Harrison: 1 for 27 yards, 27.0 avg.

Punts

Dick Conn: 1 for 11 yards, 11.0 avg.
Lynn Swann: 3 for 112 yards, 37.3 avg.

KICKING and PUNTING

Bengals

Kicking

Horst Muhlmann: 1-for-2 FG

Punting

Dave Green: 5 for 211 yards, 42.2 avg.

Steelers

Kicking

Roy Gerela: 3-for-3 PAT, 2-for-2 FG

Punting

Bobby Walden: 3 for 83 yards, 27.7 avg.

AFC Divisional Playoffs

		Dec. 22 Three Rivers Stadium Pittsburgh, PA			
Buffalo Bills					**Pittsburgh Steelers**
	1Q	2Q	3Q	4Q	Total
Bills	7	0	7	0	14
Steelers	3	26	0	3	32

PITTSBURGH (AP) — It was Terry Bradshaw's 86th game as a pro football quarterback. Or was it his first?

"I've never felt in full control like that before," he said with a subdued smile after helping the Pittsburgh Steelers defeat the Buffalo Bills 32-14 Sqnday in an American Football Conference playoff.

Booed and benched early this season, Bradshaw hit seven of nine passes in the second quarter to key a 26-point spurt that included three short touchdown runs by Franco Harris.

"It was the best game I've ever had in the pros," Bradshaw said after Pittsburgh advanced to next week's title game against the Oakland Raiders.

"I've never seen Terry so calm and confident, calling plays cooly and quickly," said Steeler tackle Jon Kolb.

Fans who had booed himhfor past incompletions cheered lustily as Bradshaw left the game after hitting 12 of 19 pass attempts for 203 yards. He also rushed five times for 48 more key yards.

"I enjoyed the cheers, but ovations don't last long if you don't produce," said Bradshaw, who charted plays the first six games of this season while Joe Gilliam was at quarterback.

The game also marked a redemption for the Steeler offense, maligned by some as a weak sister to Pittsburgh's dominant defense.

On a day when the Steeler defense forced only one turnover, Jack Ham's recovery of a Jim Braxton fumble, the Steeler offense outgained Buffalo 438 yards to 264.

"They did a great job offensively," said Bills' Coach Lou Swban, whose club ranks second only to Pittsburgh in AFC defensive statistics.

"I'm not sure how they did what they did again us, but they blew us out," Saban added.

"I was surprised by their offense. Looking at the films, I didn't think they'd score that much against us," said Buffalo linebacker Jim Cheyunski.

"They had a real good game plan," he added, "and every time there was a key down they made the big play."

One guy who said he wasn't surprised was Steeler Coach Chuck Noll.

"Not too many people believed me, but I never lost confidence in our offense," said Noll.

"Early in the season with Gilliam we passed well, then we ran very well with Bradshaw, and today we put both together for the first time."

Pittsburgh's 26-point second quarter came two points shy of the AFC playoff record for one period, set by Oakland against Houston in 1969.

The Steelers also set a new AFC playoff record with 29 first downs, and Harris' three touchdowns tied the AFC single game playoff mark of Oakland's Fred Biletnikoff against Kansas City in 1968.

"They were hot today," conceded Buffalo's O.J. Simpson, held to 49 yards rushing on 15 carries.

"We thought we would be able to do well on offense," he added. "But when they got that huge lead we had to throw."

Pittsburgh took a 3-0 lead on the game's opening series on a 21-yard field goal by Roy Gerela. Buffalo countered in the same period with a 22-yard touchdown pass from Joe Ferguson to tight end Paul Seymour.

Then Bradshaw's 27-yard touchdown pass to running back Rocky Bleier started the second-quarter assault.

The next three Steelers drives, all better than 50 yards, ended with touchdown runs of one, four and one yards by Harris, who led all rushers with 79 yards.

"Our offense went crazy," said Steeler linebacker Jack Ham. "I'd have hated to have been Buffalo's defense. They were out there all day."

"We were rolling today," echoed rookie reciever Lynn Swann, who caught three passes for 60 yards in the second quarter and added 25 yards on an end-around.

In the third quarter, Buffalo closed to within 29-14 on a three-yard touchdown pass from Ferguson to Simpson, but Gerela's 23-yard field goal in the final quarter was the only score the rest of the way.

"We're out of it and I'm going home," said Saban.

"This was a game where we had to let it all hang out," said Noll. "We've got two more like that."

At Pittsburgh—40,321
Bills 7 0 7 0—14 Steelers 3 26 0 3—32
Pitt—FG Gerela 21
Buff—Seymour 22 pass from Ferguson (Leypoldt kick)
Pitt—Bleier 27 pass from Bradshaw (kick failed)
Pitt—Harris 1 run (Gerela kick)
Pitt—Harris 4 run (kick failed)
Pitt—Harris 1 run (Gerela kick)
Buff—Simpson 3 pass from Ferguson (Leypoldt kick)
Pitt—FG Gerela 22
INDIVIDUAL LEADERS
RUSHING—Buffalo, Simpson 15 49, Braxton 5 48, Ferguson 1-3. Pittsburgh, Harris 24-74, Bradshaw 5-48. Bleier 14 45, Davis 5-32, Swann 2-24, Gilliam 1 12
RECEIVING—Buffalo, Hill 4 59, Simpson 3 37, Seymour 2-35 Pittsburgh, Swann 3-60, Bleier 3 54, Lewis 2 18
PASSING—Buffalo, Ferguson 11 26-0, 164. Pittsburgh, Bradshaw 12 19-0, 203; Gilliam 0-2-0, 0.

		SCORING	BUF	PIT
1st	Steelers	Roy Gerela 21 yard field goal	0	3
	Bills	Paul Seymour 22 yard pass from Joe Ferguson (John Leypoldt kick)	7	3
2nd	Steelers	Rocky Bleier 27 yard pass from Terry Bradshaw (kick failed)	7	9
	Steelers	Franco Harris 1 yard rush (Roy Gerela kick)	7	16
	Steelers	Franco Harris 4 yard rush (kick failed)	7	22
	Steelers	Franco Harris 1 yard rush (Roy Gerela kick)	7	29

| 3rd | Bills | O.J. Simpson 3 yard pass from Joe Ferguson (John Leypoldt kick) | 14 | 29 |
| 4th | Steelers | Roy Gerela 22 yard field goal | 14 | 32 |

	TEAM STATS	
	BUF	PIT
First downs	15	29
Rush-Yards-TD	21-100-0	51-235-3
Comp-Att-Yards-TD-INT	11-26-164-2-0	12-21-203-1-0
Sacked-Yards	0-0	0-0
Net pass yards	164	203
Total yards	264	438
Fumbles-Lost	2-1	2-0
Turnovers	1	0
Penalties-Yards	3-15	2-10

PASSING, RUSHING and RECEIVING

Bills

Passing

Joe Ferguson: 11-of-26, 164 yards, 2 TD, 0 INT

Rushing

O.J. Simpson: 15 carries for 49 yards
Joe Ferguson: 1 carry for 3 yards
Jim Braxton: 5 carries for 48 yards

Receiving

O.J. Simpson: 3 catches for 37 yards, 1 TD
J.D. Hill: 4 catches for 59 yards
Jim Braxton: 1 catch for 8 yards

Paul Seymour: 2 catches for 35 yards, 1 TD
Ahmad Rashad: 1 catch for 25 yards

Steelers

Passing

Terry Bradshaw: 12-of-19, 203 yards, 1 TD, 0 INT
Joe Gilliam: 0-of-2, 0 yards

Rushing

Terry Bradshaw: 5 carries for 48 yards
Rocky Bleier: 14 carries for 45 yards
Lynn Swann: 2 carries for 24 yards
Franco Harris: 24 carries for 74 yards, 3 TD
Steve Davis: 5 carries for 32 yards
Joe Gilliam: 1 carry for 12 yards

Receiving

Rocky Bleier: 3 catches for 54 yards, 1 TD
Lynn Swann: 3 catches for 60 yards
Franco Harris: 1 catch for 5 yards
Larry Brown: 1 catch for 29 yards
John McMakin: 1 catch for 22 yards
Frank Lewis: 2 catches for 18 yards
Ron Shanklin: 1 catch for 15 yards

KICK RETURNS

Bills

Kickoffs

Donnie Walker: 6 for 118 yards, 19.7 avg.

Punts

Donnie Walker: 2 for 11 yards, 5.5 avg.

Steelers

Kickoffs

Mel Blount: 2 for 56 yards, 28.0 avg.
Steve Davis: 1 for 30 yards, 30.0 avg.

Punts

Glen Edwards: 2 for 13 yards, 6.5 avg.
Lynn Swann: 2 for 12 yards, 6.0 avg.

KICKING and PUNTING

Bills

Kicking

John Leypoldt: 2-for-2 PAT

Punting

Marv Bateman: 5 for 197 yards, 39.4 avg.

Steelers

Kicking

Roy Gerela: 2-for-4 PAT, 2-for-2 FG

Punting

Bobby Walden: 3 for 116 yards, 38.7 avg.

AFC Championship Game

	1Q	2Q	3Q	4Q	Total
Steelers	0	3	0	21	24
Raiders	3	0	7	3	13

Dec. 29
Oakland-Alameda County Coliseum
Oakland, CA

Pittsburgh Steelers — Oakland Raiders

If winning is everything, how do you account for the fact that the Oakland Raiders have the best won-loss record for the past 12 years and only one Super Bowl appearance to show for it?

In that span, they've win 116 games, lost 43 and tied one – by far the best in the National Football League. Loss No. 43 brought the 1974 season to an abrupt end Sunday.

"Winning 13 out of 16 this year wasn't enough," said one Raider after a 24-13 defeat at the hands of the Pittsburgh Steelers in the American Football Conference championship game.

So it means no Super Bowl – except on television – and another long, long winter.

"It's tough to come this far and lose," said John Madden, the dejected Raider coach after the defeat. "We had the feeling everything was going our way. We had the best record in the NFL. We beat Miami. And we had the opportunity to play the title conference game at home. But look at what happened."

"We got tired of hearing that last week's Oakland-Miami game was the real Super Bowl," Pittsburgh center Ray Mansfield said. "When you get stung like that, you become just a little more dedicated to winning."

With frightening efficiency, the Steelers' defense choked off the Raiders' running game and that ended Oakland's hopes of Super Bowl glory in New Orleans two weeks from now.

"The Steelers beat us because they gave us nothing on the ground," said Madden. "Our passing was sufficient but we couldn't get the run going. I can't remember when our ground game was shut down that effectively."

But what Madden didn't mention was that the Steelers showed why they were the best defensive team in the AFC this year.

The Raiders gained only 29 yards on 21 rushes and relied primarily on the passing of quarterback Ken Stabler, who connected on 19 of 38 for 271 yards. However, with the unbalanced yardage ratio, Pittsburgh's linebackers and secondary laid low and intercepted two passes which eventually were converted into touchdowns.

"We said before the game that turnovers would decide it," Madden said. "And that's what happened. They played well on defense and gave us nothing on the ground.

"You can't play a team like Pittsburgh and just do one thing. You have to mix the run with the pass and you have to have confidence when you do run."

To whip the Raiders, who were six-point favorites, the Steelers totally manhandled Oakland's defensive line while toying with their offensive line.

"We wanted to gear our attack to working against their tackles (Otis Sistrunk and Art Thomas," said exuberant Steelers quarterback Terry Bradshaw, who was a benchwarmer for the first half of the regular season.

"Not because they are weak, but because that's where our strength lies. We wanted to be the aggressor. So we forgot about their weaknesses and depended upon our strengths.

"We worked outside tackle all day, using a lot of double- and triple-teaming on them."

As a result, Franco Harris and Rocky Bleier muscled up for 111 and 98 yards, respectively.

"We're a completely different team now," discerned Bleier. "In the past we looked for weaknesses and attacked from there. Now we depend on our strengths, not other people's weaknesses. That's what a little confidence and maturity will do for you."

Bradshaw threw sparingly, completing eight of 17 for 95 yards and one touchdown. He had a second touchdown pass called back incorrectly.

"I was so far inside the end zone it was ridiculous," said rookie wide receiver John Stallworth, whose one-handed catch of Bradshaw's eight-yard pass was rubbed out by head linesman Ray Dodez's ruling.

Lynn Swann had less misfortune. After fumbling Ray Guy's first punt and setting up George Blanda's 40-yard first-quarter field goal, Swann thirsted for retribution.

He got it early in the fourth quarter when he beat Alonza Thomas and Jack Tatum to catch Bradshaw's go-ahead touchdown pass.

"I called the play myself," said Swann. "A couple of plays earlier, I discovered it was open. So I told Bradshaw and he was ready to call it."

Pittsburgh coach Chuck Noll said that the key was a 61-yard drive that immediately followed a Stabler-to-Cliff Branch touchdown pass.

The drive included only one pass, a third-and-10 Bradshaw-to-Stallworth toss that gained 13 yards. Bleier gained 35 and Harris 13, the last eight producing the touchdown.

"From that moment on, I knew we were in," said Bradshaw. "You could feel it. I've never felt anything like it, either."

Oakland's only bright spot was a record nine receptions for 186 yards and one touchdown by the speedy Branch.

Stabler, the AFC's Player of the Year, was in no mood to answer questions in the gloom-like atmosphere of the Oakland dressing room.

"Let me off the hook," he said. "I have nothing to say. I've cooperated all year so give me a break this one time."

Marv Hubbard, who rushed for 865 yards during the regular season but was held to only six by the Steelers, gave credit where credit was due.

"Their defense played a whale of a game," he said. "And (rookie middle linebacker Jack) Lambert played a lot better than we expected."

Sistrunk summed it up as he took off his black-and-silver uniform for the last time this year.

"They've got a good ball club, but I'm not saying they are better than us. Mistakes just killed us."

The Steelers' Dwight White countered by saying, "The best team won. That shouldn't surprise anybody."

		SCORING	PIT	OAK
1st	Raiders	George Blanda 40 yard field goal	0	3
2nd	Steelers	Roy Gerela 23 yard field goal	3	3
3rd	Raiders	Cliff Branch 38 yard pass from Ken Stabler (George Blanda kick)	3	10
4th	Steelers	Franco Harris 8 yard rush (Roy Gerela kick)	10	10
	Steelers	Lynn Swann 6 yard pass from Terry Bradshaw (Roy Gerela kick)	17	10
	Raiders	George Blanda 24 yard field goal	17	13
	Steelers	Franco Harris 21 yard rush (Roy Gerela kick)	24	13

	TEAM STATS	
	PIT	OAK
First downs	20	15
Rush-Yards-TD	50-224-2	21-29-0
Comp-Att-Yards-TD-INT	8-17-95-1-1	19-36-271-1-3
Sacked-Yards	0-0	2-22
Net pass yards	95	249
Total yards	319	278
Fumbles-Lost	3-2	0-0
Turnovers	3	3
Penalties-Yards	4-30	5-60

PASSING, RUSHING and RECEIVING

Steelers

Passing

Terry Bradshaw: 8-of-17, 95 yards, 1 TD, 1 INT

Rushing

Rocky Bleier: 18 carries for 98 yards
Franco Harris: 29 carries for 111 yards, 2 TD
Terry Bradshaw: 4 carries for 1 yard

Receiving

Rocky Bleier: 2 catches for 25 yards
Larry Brown: 2 catches for 37 yards
Lynn Swann: 2 catches for 17 yards, 1 TD
John Stallworth: 2 catches for 16 yards

Raiders

Passing

Ken Stabler: 19-of-36, 271 yards, 1 TD, 3 INT

Rushing

Ken Stabler: 1 carry for 0 yards
Clarence Davis: 10 carries for 16 yards
Pete Banaszak: 3 carries for 7 yards
Marv Hubbard: 7 carries for 6 yards

Receiving

Cliff Branch: 9 catches for 186 yards, 1 TD
Fred Biletnikoff: 3 catches for 45 yards
Bob Moore: 4 catches for 32 yards
Clarence Davis: 2 catches for 8 yards
Pete Banaszak: 1 catch for 0 yards

DEFENSE

Steelers

Sacks

Joe Greene (1) and L.C. Greenwood (1)

Interceptions

Jack Ham: 2 for 19 yards
J.T. Thomas: 1 for 37 yards

Raiders

Interceptions

Nemiah Wilson: 1 for 37 yards

KICK RETURNS

Steelers

Kickoffs

Steve Davis: 3 for 76 yards, 25.3 avg.
Preston Pearson: 1 for 28 yards, 28.0 avg.

Punts

Glen Edwards: 1 for 15 yards, 15.0 avg.
Lynn Swann: 3 for 30 yards, 10.0 avg.

Raiders

Kickoffs

Harold Hart: 3 for 63 yards, 21.0 avg.
Ron Smith: 2 for 42 yards, 21.0 avg.

KICKING and PUNTING

Steelers

Kicking

Roy Gerela: 3-for-3 PAT, 1-for-2 FG

Punting

Bobby Walden: 4 for 164 yards, 41.0 avg.

Raiders

Kicking

George Blanda: 1-for-1 PAT, 2-for-3 FG

Punting

Ray Guy: 5 for 217 yards, 43.4 avg.

Super Bowl IX

Jan. 12
Tulane Stadium
New Orleans, LA

Pittsburgh Steelers — **Minnesota Vikings**

	1Q	2Q	3Q	4Q	Total
Steelers	0	2	7	7	16
Vikings	0	0	0	6	6

NEW ORLEANS (AP) — Pittsburgh Coach Chuck Noll preaches basic football blocking and tackling and pounding out the yardage along the ground.

And that's just the way his Steelers destroyed the Minnesota Vikings Sunday to win the ninth Super Bowl game 16-6.

They said they would run the football and that's exactly what they did, with Franco Harris churning out a Super Bowl record 158 yards. They said they would stop Minnesota's running game and that's just what they did, permitting the Vikings a mere 21 yards on the ground.

And when Commissioner Pete Rozelle presented the gleaming silver trophy that goes with victory in this National Football League championship game, Mean Joe Greene, leader of the stubborn Steeler defense, positively glowed.

"It's fantastic," said Greene. "Never in my wildest dreams did I think I would get this big a charge out of winning it."

A major part of the credit for that victory must go to Greene and the ferocious Steeler front line that harassed Minnesota quarterback Fran Tarkenton all day long.

The Steeler defenders put the game's first points on the scoreboard with the first safety in Super Bowl history and kept Tarkenton in a tizzy.

"The best thing we did all day was keeping Fran from throwing when he wanted to," said Greene, who intercepted a pass and recovered a fumble.

Greene, L.C. Greenwood, Ernie Holmes and Dwight White, the rush-line Pittsburgh fans have nicknamed the "Steel Curtain," never did sack Tarkenton, but it hardly mattered. They forced him into mistakes, batting down his passes and never allowing the Minnesota offense to get started.

"We came in with the idea of getting the job done," said Noll. "The defense let nothing stand in its way. They shut out the champions of the National Football Conference. I can't think of anything more fitting." Minnesota's only points were scored by the defense on a blocked punt.

Minnesota Coach Bud Grant suggested that those fierce Steeler defenders might have had help in beating his team.

"It wasn't a very good game," said Grant. "Both teams had enough chances to score and to win, but the penalties, the interceptions and the official bumbles...it was just a game of errors by all three teams."

Grant was particularly annoyed by a third-quarter play that left much of the crowd in Tulane Stadium confused.

Greene and his defensive buddies picked up a first-half safety when Tarkenton's pitchout to Dave Osborn missed connecting and the football rolled into the end zone. Fran fell on the football and the Steelers grabbed him for the two points, the only ones of the first half.

Late in the second quarter, Tarkenton seemed to have something going and moved the Vikes downfield smartly. But the drive ended dismally when Glen Edwards batted an apparently completed pass out of John Gilliam's hands and into the waiting arms of Mel Blount. That sent Pittsburgh into the lockerroom with a 2-0 halftime edge.

Then Noll, the football fundamentalist, threw a gimmick at Minnesota, with Roy Gerela delivering a squibbler for the second half kickoff.

When Bill Brown fumbled it, Marv Kellum recovered for the Steelers. Harris ripped off a 24yard run and a couple of plays later Franco barrelled into the end zone for a touchdown.

Now the score was 9-0 and clearly Tarkenton had to get something going for Minnesota—and soon. Three plays picked up nine yards and with fourth-and-one at their own 37, it seems a certain punting situation.

But Minnesota—criticized so often for being conservative kept punter Mike Eischeid on the sidelines. The Vikings were going for the first down. Or were they?

Tarkenton ducked under the center and both teams set at the line of scrimmage. But nothing happened. It was a long count, a play designed to draw the Steeler offside.

Suddenly there was a whistle, and confusion. The officials ruled both teams had gone offside—offsetting penalties.

"In effect, they made no call," said Grant. "Nobody saw anything. It seems to me that if we ran the play, it was their ball with first and 10. If we didn't, they were offside."

Instead, it amounted to a doover and Grant wasn't gambling again. This time, the Vikes punted the ball away.

On their next series of downs, Minnesota started at its own 20. On second down, Tarkenton rolled right and passed again. Again, the Steeler defense was there. Greenwood batted the ball and it flew crazily back into Fran's arms. Flustered, Fran threw again for what would have been a good gain to Gilliam—except for the NFL rule that permits only one forward pass per play. That episode cost Tarkenton a penalty and a valuable down.

Once again, Tarkenton had to throw over. At last he seemed to have the Vikes moving and he got them as far as midfield. But another deflected pass settled into the arms of Greene and the Steelers had stalled Minnesota again.

It was still 9-0 in the early stages of the fourth quarter. And by now, Fran was becoming frantic to get the Vikes on the scoreboard. He uncorked a long pass that fell incomplete at the Steeler five, but Mike Wagner was tagged with an interference call and suddenly the Vikes were in business.

Just as quickly, they were out of it. Foreman fumbled and there was Greene for the recovery.

"That was the biggest and best defensive play," said Noll. "They tried to run a counter play, but we got the ball loose and Joe Greene got it. That was the best."

A few moments later, Minnesota got its first and only— break of the day Matt Blair blocked Bobby Walden's punt and Terry Brown recovered it in the end zone for a touchdown. But Fred Cox missed the extra points when his kick hit the goalpost and the Vikes were still down by three points

If the Steelers were going to fold, this would be the time. But they weren't bending. Terry Bradshaw moved them smartly up the field.

With a third-and-two at his own 32, Bradshaw hit Larry Brown for a 30-yard gain. But the ball squirted loose and when a purple-shirted Viking fell on it, Minnesota seemed to have another break. But the officials ruled that the play was over, a decision Grant hardly agreed with.

"From our vantage point, Brown had not reached the

ground when the ball came loose," said the grim coach. "Our bench reacted immediately. There wasn't any question in their minds it was a fumble. But the officials ruled the ball dead.

"The official who called it was across the field and behind him. When they didn't give it to us, it became a very big play bigger than any we could make."

Shortly after that, the Vikings were dead. Bradshaw took Pittsburgh to the end zone, scoring on a four-yard pass to Larry Brown that provided the game's final points.

For Bradshaw, it was vindication a crowning ending to a season he started on the bench as a third-stringer.

"I've looked at all sides," the quarterback said, "being a hero and being a jerk. I've faced adversity and withstood the trials, and they enabled me to do this."

Then he kissed Art Rooney, the owner of the Steelers, who had waited 42 years for an NFL championship.

For the Vikings, the trial and waiting continued. Sunday they became the first team ever to lose three Super Bowls.

"We're not frustrated or dejected," said Tarkenton. "We did not capitalize on our opportunities and Pittsburgh did. We came to win and we couldn't do it."

INDIVIDUAL LEADERS
RUSHING Pittsburgh, Harris 34-158, Bleier 17-65, Bradshaw 5-33. Minnesota, Foreman 12-22, Osborn 8-minus 1
RECEIVING Pittsburgh, L. Brown 3-21 Stallworth 3-24, Bleier 2-11, Lewis 1-12. Minnesota, Foreman 5-50, Voigt 2-31, Osborn 2-7, Gilliam 1-16
PASSING Pittsburgh, Bradshaw 9-14-0, 96 yards. Minnesota, Tarkenton 11-27-3, 102

		SCORING	PIT	MIN
2nd	Steelers	Safety, White downed Tarkenton in end zone	2	0
3rd	Steelers	Franco Harris 9 yard rush (Roy Gerela kick)	9	0
4th	Vikings	Terry Brown blocked punt return for touchdown (kick failed)	9	6
	Steelers	Larry Brown 4 yard pass from Terry Bradshaw (Roy Gerela kick)	16	6

	TEAM STATS	
	PIT	MIN
First downs	17	9
Rush-Yards-TD	57-249-1	21-17-0
Comp-Att-Yards-TD-INT	9-14-96-1-0	11-26-102-0-3
Sacked-Yards	2-12	0-0

Net pass yards	84	102
Total yards	333	119
Fumbles-Lost	4-2	3-2
Turnovers	2	5
Penalties-Yards	8-122	4-18

PASSING, RUSHING and RECEIVING

Steelers

Passing

Terry Bradshaw: 9-of-14, 96 yards, 1 TD, 0 INT

Rushing

Franco Harris: 34 carries for 158 yards, 1 TD
Terry Bradshaw: 5 carries for 33 yards
Rocky Bleier: 17 carries for 65 yards
Lynn Swann: 1 carry for -7 yards

Receiving

Rocky Bleier: 2 catches for 11 yards
Larry Brown: 3 catches for 49 yards, 1 TD
John Stallworth: 3 catches for 24 yards
Frank Lewis: 1 catch for 12 yards

Vikings

Passing

Fran Tarkenton: 11-of-26, 102 yards, 0 TD, 3 INT

Rushing

Chuck Foreman: 12 carries for 18 yards
Fran Tarkenton: 1 carry for 0 yards
Dave Osborn: 8 carries for -1 yard

Receiving

Chuck Foreman: 5 catches for 50 yards
Stu Voigt: 2 catches for 31 yards
John Gilliam: 1 catch for 16 yards
Dave Osborn: 2 catches for 7 yards
Oscar Reed: 1 catch for -2 yards

DEFENSE

Steelers

Interceptions

Mel Blount: 1 for 10 yards
Joe Greene: 1 for 10 yards
Mike Wagner: 1 for 26 yards

Vikings

Sacks

Bob Lurtsema (1) and Alan Page (1)

KICK RETURNS

Steelers

Kickoffs

Reggie Harrison: 2 for 17 yards, 8.5 avg.
Preston Pearson: 1 for 15 yards, 15.0 avg.

Punts

Glen Edwards: 2 for 2 yards, 1.0 avg.
Lynn Swann: 3 for 34 yards, 11.3 avg.

Vikings

Kickoffs

Bill Brown: 1 for 2 yards, 2.0 avg.
Brent McClanahan: 1 for 22 yards, 22.0 avg.
Sam McCullum: 1 for 26 yards, 26.0 avg.

Punts

Sam McCullum: 3 for 11 yards, 3.7 avg.
Nate Wright: 1 for 1 yard, 1.0 avg.

KICKING and PUNTING

Steelers

Kicking

Roy Gerela: 2-for-2 PAT, 0-for-1 FG

Punting

Bobby Walden: 6 for 243 yards, 40.5 avg.

Vikings

Kicking

Fred Cox: 0-for-1 PAT, 0-for-1 FG

Punting

Mike Eischeid: 6 for 223 yards, 37.2 avg.

1974 NFL Standings

AFC					
East	W	L	T	PF	PA
Miami Dolphins	11	3	0	327	216
Buffalo Bills	9	5	0	264	244
New York Jets	7	7	0	279	300
New England Patriots	7	7	0	348	289
Baltimore Colts	2	12	0	190	329
Central	W	L	T	PF	PA
Pittsburgh Steelers	10	3	1	305	189
Houston Oilers	7	7	0	236	282
Cincinnati Bengals	7	7	0	283	259
Cleveland Browns	4	10	0	251	344
West	W	L	T	PF	PA
Oakland Raiders	12	2	0	355	228
Denver Broncos	7	6	1	302	294
San Diego Chargers	5	9	0	212	285
Kansas City Chiefs	5	9	0	233	293

NFC					
East	W	L	T	PF	PA
Washington Redskins	10	4	0	320	196
St. Louis Cardinals	10	4	0	285	218
Dallas Cowboys	8	6	0	297	235
Philadelphia Eagles	7	7	0	242	217
New York Giants	2	12	0	195	299

Central	W	L	T	PF	PA
Minnesota Vikings	10	4	0	320	196
Detroit Lions	7	7	0	256	270
Green Bay Packers	6	8	0	210	206
Chicago Bears	4	10	0	152	279
West	W	L	T	PF	PA
Los Angeles Rams	10	4	0	263	181
San Francisco 49ers	6	8	0	226	236
New Orleans Saints	5	9	0	166	263
Atlanta Falcons	3	11	0	111	271

Steelers 1974 Draft Picks

Round 1 (21): Lynn Swann, WR, USC
Round 2 (46): Jack Lambert, LB, Kent State
Round 4 (82): John Stallworth, WR, Alabama A&M
Round 4 (100): Jimmy Allen, DB, UCLA
Round 5 (125): Mike Webster, C, Wisconsin
Round 6 (149): Jim Wolf, DT, Prairie View
Round 6 (150): Rich Druschel, T, North Carolina State
Round 7 (165): Allen Sitterle, T, North Carolina State
Round 7 (179): Scott Garske, TE, Eastern Michigan
Round 8 (204): Mark Gefert, LB, Purdue
Round 9 (223): Tommy Reamon, RB, Missouri
Round 9 (229): Charles Davis, DT, TCU
Round 10 (243): Jim Kregel, G, Ohio State
Round 10 (254): Dave Atkinson, DB, BYU
Round 11 (283): Dickie Morton, RB, Arkansas
Round 12 (308): Hugh Lickiss, LB, Simpson
Round 13 (333): Frank Kolch, QB, Eastern Michigan
Round 14 (358): Bruce Henley, DB, Rice
Round 15 (387): Larry Hunt, DT, Iowa State
Round 16 (412): Octavus Morgan, LB, Illinois
Round 17 (437): Larry Moore, DE

1975

Season Review

Despite a 37-0 triumph over San Diego to start the season, the Steelers looked better and better as the campaign wore on.

After losing to Buffalo in their second game, the Steelers then tore through the league with 11 straight victories.

The Pittsburgh defense smothered enemy attacks week after week, even while losing Joe Greene for a time with neck and groin injuries.

Franco Harris led the offense with 1,246 yards on the ground, but the performances of Terry Bradshaw, Lynn Swann and the yeoman line ranked as high in excellence.

The Steelers beat back challenges from the Oilers and Bengals to brand themselves the team to beat in the playoffs.

Week 1

Sept. 21
San Diego Stadium
San Diego, CA

Pittsburgh Steelers | | | | | San Diego Chargers

	1Q	2Q	3Q	4Q	Total
Steelers	10	10	3	14	37
Chargers	0	0	0	0	0

By RICH EMERT
TIMES Sports Staff

SAN DIEGO — The switch is on.

The Pittsburgh Steelers opened the defense of their Super Bowl title yesterday afternoon at San Diego Stadium in stunning form. And while the Steelers were eating the Chargers 37-0, coach Chuck Noll was eating his words.

It was Noll, after the Steelers finished a horrible exhibition season last weekend with a loss in Dallas, who said that his team just wasn't playing with enough "intensity." And he went on to say that intensity isn't something "you can turn on and off like a switch."

He was wrong.

"I guess I'll have to eat my words," Noll said with a big smile. "They certainly switched on the button today. We played much better than I expected.

"The team proved that you can turn it (intensity) on and off. I guess that makes them very special."

Special enough to dominate the Chargers in every statistical department. Special enough to rack up 443 total yards and hit on 22 of 29 passes. And special enough to not allow San Diego any closer to pay dirt than the Steelers' 41-yard line.

"They did pretty much what they wanted to," Charger coach Tommy Prothro sighed. "They were very, very impressive, and the score ended up a lot worse than I thought it would."

And Noll was a bit stunned by his team's performance.

"I don't think we could have played much better," he stated. "There isn't a whole lot you can say. I didn't notice anything bad... and that's good."

Perhaps the most intense person on the field was quarterback Terry Bradshaw. He cut the Chargers defense into taco meat with a punishing ground game in the first half, and a pin-point passing game in the second half.

Bradshaw went the route and hit on 21 of 28 tosses for 227 yards and two touchdowns. He clicked on nine of 15 third down plays, and was awarded the game ball by his teammates in the locker room.

"We just went out and did what we were supposed to do," Bradshaw explained. "Yeah, I guess we had a little something to prove to oursevles. I guess that's why everybody was pumped up, and after all these are the ones that count."

With Bradshaw going the whole way it might have looked like Noll was trying to rub it in a little, but that wasn't the case. He just didn't want to destroy that intensity.

"Sometimes you get a letdown if you take the man (Bradshaw) out too soon," Noll explained. "And when you get a letdown that's when you get people hurt. Besides, Terry is a strong young man and he can use the work."

However Prothro wasn't sure what to think about the final score.

"What they do is their business," he said rather disgustedly. "All I know is they beat us bad."

And while the biggest part of the reason for the win was Bradshaw and the offense, the defense didn't look too bad either. In fact, it looked, well, super.

Dwight White got to the Chargers' quarterback twice, Jack Ham once and Ernie Holmes once. The "Steeler Curtain" allowed only 145 yards, 87 on the ground, and picked off three passes.

"We had as good a day as you could ask for defensively," linebacker Andy Russell pointed out. "We recorded the shutout and going into every game that's the ultimate goal. But more intense? I'm not too sure about that.

"I think we've played well all along. Whenever the first unit was in on offense or defense they performed well during the exhibition season. So, I don't think we were that much more intense. I think we just realized that they all count now, and we are done experimenting."

The Steelers proved they were done experimenting on the first series of plays. Bradshaw marched Pittsburgh 56 yards in 15 plays with the drive ending in a Roy Gerela field goal of 29 yards.

Not too impressive you say?

Well, the next time Mr. Bradshaw got his hands on the pigskin it took him exactly two plays to go 59 yards for a touchdown. And from there it was a piece of acake.

"We wanted to keep to the ground against them and we had great success running the football in the first half," Bradshaw explained. "But the second half they started playing for the run, so I started throwing those little flairs to the backs.

"Shoot, the protection I had I could have stayed back there all day. I had three and four guys open every play because there was no pressure."

But even though it seemed like all the Steelers were having a great time Bobby Walden even threw a pass for a first down the fun kind of went out of it for some toward the end of the third quarter.

"Oh sure, it was great, but when you are leading 23-0 it's hard to keep fired up," Russell said with a smile. "Besides, I thought we were having a hell of a game and then I looked up at the scoreboard and saw Buffalo had scored 42 points. That kind of took the fun out of it."

The Buffalo Bills are the Steelers opponent Sunday at Three Rivers Stadium. And Russell figures the Bills will be loaded for bear.

"You can bet they'll be out to prove something against us," he stated. They still remember the playoffs last year and how badly we beat them. And after what they did to the Jets, they will be charged up."

Looks like the Steelers will just have to leave the old switch turned on.

		SCORING	PIT	SDG
1st	Steelers	Roy Gerela 29 yard field goal	3	0
	Steelers	Frank Lewis 40 yard pass from Terry Bradshaw (Roy Gerela kick)	10	0
2nd	Steelers	Gerry Mullins fumble recovery in end zone (Roy Gerela kick)	17	0
	Steelers	Roy Gerela 25 yard field goal	20	0
3rd	Steelers	Roy Gerela 38 yard field goal	23	0
4th	Steelers	John Stallworth 38 yard pass from Terry Bradshaw (Roy Gerela kick)	30	0
	Steelers	Mike Collier 7 yard rush (Roy Gerela kick)	37	0

	TEAM STATS	

	PIT	SDG
First downs	24	9
Rush-Yards-TD	45-205-1	23-88-0
Comp-Att-Yards-TD-INT	22-29-246-2-0	12-23-86-0-3
Sacked-Yards	1-8	4-28
Net pass yards	238	58
Total yards	443	146
Fumbles-Lost	3-2	2-1
Turnovers	2	4
Penalties-Yards	4-31	8-54

PASSING, RUSHING and RECEIVING

Steelers

Passing

Terry Bradshaw: 21-of-28, 227 yards, 2 TD, 0 INT
Bobby Walden: 1-of-1, 19 yards

Rushing

Terry Bradshaw: 1 carry for 11 yards
Franco Harris: 17 carries for 78 yards
Frank Lewis: 1 carry for 12 yards
Rocky Bleier: 14 carries for 43 yards
Reggie Harrison: 9 carries for 45 yards
John Fuqua: 2 carries for 9 yards
Mike Collier: 1 carry for 7 yards, 1 TD

Receiving

Franco Harris: 2 catches for 24 yards
Frank Lewis: 4 catches for 69 yards, 1 TD
John Stallworth: 3 catches for 56 yards, 1 TD
Rocky Bleier: 1 catch for 8 yards
Reggie Harrison: 1 catch for 4 yards

John Fuqua: 5 catches for 20 yards
Lynn Swann: 3 catches for 28 yards
Donnie Shell: 1 catch for 19 yards
Larry Brown: 1 catch for 13 yards
Randy Grossman: 1 catch for 5 yards

Chargers

Passing

Dan Fouts: 6-of-13, 36 yards, 0 TD, 1 INT
Virgil Carter: 3-of-5, 24 yards, 0 TD, 1 INT
Jesse Freitas: 3-of-5, 26 yards, 0 TD, 1 INT

Rushing

Dan Fouts: 3 carries for 18 yards
Don Woods: 13 carries for 35 yards
Bo Matthews: 3 carries for 24 yards
Virgil Carter: 2 carries for 11 yards
Sam Scarber: 1 carry for 2 yards
Rickey Young: 1 carry for -2 yards

Receiving

Pat Curran: 6 catches for 42 yards
Don Woods: 1 catch for -3 yards
Bo Matthews: 1 catch for 6 yards
Sam Scarber: 2 catches for 16 yards
Rickey Young: 1 catch for 14 yards
Marlin Briscoe: 1 catch for 11 yards

DEFENSE

Steelers

Interceptions

Glen Edwards: 1 for 0 yards
Donnie Shell: 1 for 29 yards
J.T. Thomas: 1 for 33 yards

KICK RETURNS

Steelers

Punts

Dave Brown: 4 for 30 yards, 7.5 avg.
Glen Edwards: 1 for 13 yards, 13.0 avg.

Chargers

Kickoffs

Mike Fuller: 4 for 107 yards, 26.8 avg.
Rickey Young: 3 for 62 yards, 20.7 avg.

Punts

Mike Fuller: 1 for 2 yards, 2.0 avg.

KICKING and PUNTING

Steelers

Kicking

Roy Gerela: 4-for-4 PAT, 3-for-3 FG

Punting

Bobby Walden: 2 for 88 yards, 44.0 avg.

Chargers

Punting

Dennis Partee: 8 for 304 yards, 38.0 avg.

Week 2

Sept. 28
Three Rivers Stadium
Pittsburgh, PA

Buffalo Bills — Pittsburgh Steelers

	1Q	2Q	3Q	4Q	Total
Bills	0	10	13	7	30
Steelers	0	0	7	14	21

PITTSBURGH (UPI) — O.J. Simpson rushed for 227 yards, including an 88-yard touchdown burst, to direct the Buffalo Bills to an upset 30-21 victory Sunday over the defending Super Bowl champion Pittsburgh Steelers.

Simpson's 227 yards fell 23 short of the NFL single game record of 250 yards he gained in a 1973 contest with the New England Patriots. The Juice carried the ball 28 times in rushing for 100 or more yards for the 26th time in his career.

Joe Ferguson added two touchdown passes and 270-pound defensive tackle Mike Kadish lumbered 26 yards for another TD as the Bills beat the Steelers for the first time in four meetings.

The Bills owned a 3-0 lead on John Leypoldt's 37-yard field goal in the second period when tackle Earl Edwards rushed Bradshaw, picked off his fumble in the air at the Steeler 26 and lateraled to Kadish who rambled for the touchdown.

Ferguson hit Reuben Gant with a seven-yard third period touchdown before Simpson got the Bills out a hole with an 88-yard dash around end after a Bobby Walden punt buried the Bills at their own 3. The extra point failed but Buffalo held a 23-0 lead.

Pittsburgh's Marv Kellum blocked a punt late in the third period and Loren Toews ran the recovery to the six to set up the first Steeler score. Franco Harris bulled over from the two three plays later. But the Bills took the ensuing kick and moved 89 yards in seven plays with Ferguson pitching 28 yards to Bob Chandler making it 30-7.

The Steelers then went 85 yards in seven plays, culminated by Gilliam's 20-yard scoring pass to Randy Grossman and they added another touchdown late in the game on Harris' one-yard plunge through tackle.

The defending Super Bowl champion Steelers, who dropped to 1-1, held Simpson to 49 yards in a 32-14 playoff

(Continued On Page 4D)

victory last year. He is only the second player to gain 100 or more yards at Three Rivers Stadium since Cleveland Leroy Kelly ran for 102 in 1971.

The 30 points were the second highest scored against the Steelers at Three Rivers Stadium since Kansas City's 31-14 victory in 1970.

Terry Bradshaw who completed 21 of 28 passes last week in Pittsburgh's 37-0 conquest of San Diego, completed only 3 of 8 and gave way to Joe Gilliam in the third quarter.

		SCORING	BUF	PIT
2nd	Bills	John Leypoldt 37 yard field goal	3	0
	Bills	Mike Kadish 26 yard fumble return (John Leypoldt kick)	10	0
3rd	Bills	Reuben Gant 7 yard pass from Joe Ferguson (John Leypoldt kick)	17	0
	Bills	O.J. Simpson 88 yard rush (kick failed)	23	0
	Steelers	Franco Harris 2 yard rush (Roy Gerela kick)	23	7
4th	Bills	Bob Chandler 28 yard pass from Joe Ferguson (John Leypoldt kick)	30	7
	Steelers	Randy Grossman 20 yard pass from Joe Gilliam (Roy Gerela kick)	30	14
	Steelers	Franco Harris 1 yard rush (Roy Gerela kick)	30	21

	TEAM STATS	
	BUF	PIT
First downs	21	19
Rush-Yards-TD	46-310-1	30-122-2
Comp-Att-Yards-TD-INT	9-20-129-2-0	14-29-269-1-2

Sacked-Yards	1-5	4-38
Net pass yards	124	231
Total yards	434	353
Fumbles-Lost	3-1	3-3
Turnovers	1	5
Penalties-Yards	7-47	3-30

PASSING, RUSHING and RECEIVING

Bills

Passing

Joe Ferguson: 9-of-20, 129 yards, 2 TD, 0 INT

Rushing

O.J. Simpson: 28 carries for 227 yards, 1 TD
Jim Braxton: 14 carries for 80 yards
Joe Ferguson: 2 carries for 1 yard
Don Calhoun: 2 carries for 2 yards

Receiving

Jim Braxton: 1 catch for 2 yards
Bob Chandler: 3 catches for 59 yards, 1 TD
Reuben Gant: 3 catches for 35 yards, 1 TD
Paul Seymour: 2 catches for 33 yards

Steelers

Passing

Joe Gilliam: 11-of-21, 200 yards, 1 TD, 1 INT
Terry Bradshaw: 3-of-8, 69 yards, 0 TD, 1 INT

Rushing

Franco Harris: 18 carries for 84 yards, 2 TD
Terry Bradshaw: 3 carries for 7 yards

Rocky Bleier: 7 carries for 18 yards
John Fuqua: 2 carries for 13 yards

Receiving

John Stallworth: 3 catches for 103 yards
Franco Harris: 3 catches for 10 yards
Frank Lewis: 2 catches for 63 yards
Lynn Swann: 3 catches for 51 yards
Rocky Bleier: 1 catch for 9 yards
John Fuqua: 1 catch for 13 yards
Randy Grossman: 1 catch for 20 yards, 1 TD

DEFENSE

Bills

Interceptions

Dwight Harrison: 1 for 4 yards
Merv Krakau: 1 for 2 yards

KICK RETURNS

Bills

Kickoffs

John Holland: 1 for 9 yards, 9.0 avg.
Tom Ruud: 1 for 4 yards, 4.0 avg.
Vic Washington: 2 for 41 yards, 20.5 avg.

Punts

Gary Hayman: 2 for 3 yards, 1.5 avg.
John Holland: 1 for 4 yards, 4.0 avg.

Steelers

Kickoffs

Mel Blount: 1 for 12 yards, 12.0 avg.
Dave Brown: 1 for 14 yards, 14.0 avg.
Mike Collier: 2 for 45 yards, 22.5 avg.
Franco Harris: 1 for 27 yards, 27.0 avg.

Punts

Dave Brown: 1 for 20 yards, 20.0 avg.

Glen Edwards: 3 for 5 yards, 1.7 avg.

KICKING and PUNTING

Bills

Kicking

John Leypoldt: 3-for-4 PAT, 1-for-1 FG

Punting

Marv Bateman: 8 for 275 yards, 34.4 avg.

Steelers

Kicking

Roy Gerela: 3-for-3 PAT, 0-for-1 FG

Punting

Bobby Walden: 5 for 210 yards, 42.0 avg.

Week 3

Oct. 5
Municipal Stadium
Cleveland, OH

Pittsburgh Steelers — Cleveland Browns

	1Q	2Q	3Q	4Q	Total
Steelers	7	21	0	14	42
Browns	0	0	0	6	6

By DUANE SCHOOLEY
Blade Sports Writer

CLEVELAND — Greg Pruitt's kickoff return was emblematic

It typified the Cleveland Browns' efforts Sunday in a 42-6 loss to the Pittsburgh Steelers

Pruitt turned his head in disgust in seeking a penalty flag after he had turned on the speed with a 103-yard kick return TD. The run, one of the very few highlights for Browns fans, was wiped out by a clipping penalty

It was certainly an exercise in futility

This one perhaps should have been a first-round TKO. But the Browns, like a punch-drunken brawler, held on in the clinches — then collapsed.

With first Terry Bradshaw, then Jefferson Street Joe Gilliam picking apart the secondary, the Browns were out of it quickly. They had only one first-half possession that lasted more than four plays until after the Steelers had a 21-0 lead.

And even then it took a bit of trickery to sustain the second "extended" as coach Forrest Gregg called for a fake punt on fourth down which Ken Brown turned into a first down.

The statistics bore out just how the Steelers dominated the first 30 minutes.

With a 28-0 lead the Steelers had controlled the ball most of the time as they picked up 274

Statistics

	Steelers	Browns
First downs	23	19
Rushes-yards	40-134	31-122
Passing yards	267	99
Return yards	105	98
Passes	18-23-0	14-31-2
Punts	5-33	8-41
Fumbles-lost	1-0	2-0
Penalties-yards	10-90	7-90

INDIVIDUAL LEADERS
RUSHING—Pittsburgh, Harris 17-57, Bleier 10-37, Fuqua 4-21, Cleveland, Pruitt 14-54, McKinnis 9-46, Pritchett 5-10
RECEIVING—Pittsburgh, Swann 5-126, Stallworth 4-109, Garrett 3-84, Cleveland, Pruitt 6-39, McKinnis 3-17, Miller 2-14.
PASSING—Pittsburgh, Bradshaw, 7-8-0, 151 yards; Gilliam, 11-15-0, 221. Cleveland, Phipps, 16-31-2, 136.

yards, 189 passing, to just 80 yards for the Browns.

The key to the Steeler domination was Bradshaw's third-down conversion rate. Five times in the initial quarter he was faced with a third down and five time he converted.

The first conversion, picked up by a 20 yard pass to Lynn Swann, started the Steelers toward their first touchdown, an 85-yard, 12 play drive. Before the quarter was over Bradshaw had found John Stallworth for a third-down, three-yard touchdown pass and Swann for two more big gainers, 16 and 19 yards, in crucial situations.

"It was just a matter of the things we had been working on for those situations being successful," Bradshaw said. "It wasn't any great play selection, we weren't doing anything unusual."

What the Steelers were doing was frequently beating the Browns secondary which tried all day to rely on basic man to man coverage.

"It is probably easier to throw against the man coverage if they don't have the super speed at the wide spots," Bradshaw said. "We knew where we were going, and they had to try to get there."

The Browns seldom made it. After Bradshaw went to the sidelines when he cut his throwing hand, Gilliam took over. He connected on just one of three first-half tosses, but that was good for 43 yards for a touchdown to Swann.

Then in the second half he completed 10 of 12, one a 45-yard touchdown bomb to Reggie Garrett, before dislocating a finger and giving way to Terry Hanratty.

Turn To Page 21, Col. 1.

Pittsburgh   7 21 0 14—42
Cleveland   0 0 0 6— 6
PIT—Stallworth 3 pass from Bradshaw (Gerela kick).
PIT—Harris 1 run (Gerela kick).
PIT—Collier 1 run (Gerela kick).
PIT—Swann 43 pass from Gilliam (Gerela kick).
CLE—McKinnis 7 run (kick failed).
PIT—Garrett 45 pass from Gilliam (Gerela kick).
PIT—Harrison 3 run (Gerela kick).
A—73,595.

Continued From Page 20.

In the end the Steelers had 501 total yards, 367 on 18 of 23 passing, and continued their excellent third-down efficiency with 8 of 13.

Cleveland quarterback Mike Phipps completed 16 of 31 passes for 136 yards but was dropped four times for losses totalling 37 yards. The Browns finished with just 221 total yards net.

Bradshaw and Gilliam both ran Franco Harris and Rocky Bleier just enough to keep the Browns guessing. Harris picked up 57 yards on 17 carries and Bleier had 37 yards on 10 totes. Greg Pruitt had 54 yards for the Browns and Hugh McKinnis added 46.

The Steelers scored the first three times they had the ball, the first two sustained marches. The first was the 85-yard, 12 play march and the second was an 84-yard, 14-play drive, capped by Harris's run from the one on a fourth down after Bradshaw had suffered his first third down failure.

Then to show a different style the defending Super Bowl champs when 75 yards in four plays for their third score. Bradshaw started it with a 45 yard completion to Stallworth, sent Frenchy Fuqua into the line for one yard, hit Swann for 28 more yards, and let Mike Collier lug it the final yard.

Mel Blount's first interception of the day, and 17 yard return to the Pittsburgh 45, with 36 seconds left in the half set up the fourth score. Fuqua ran for 12 yards and then, after an incomplete pass, Gilliam hit Swann at the Cleveland 19 and he went the rest of the way alone.

The Browns finally got on the board in the fourth quarter when they completed an 82-yard, nine-play drive. Aided by Pittsburgh penalties on five successive plays, three of them after Cleveland had a third and 13 situation at its own 15, the Browns got untracked.

McKinnis capped the drive with a seven-yard run.

Gilliam passed 45 yards to Garrett for the fifth Steeler score and then set up the final TD, a three-yard run by Reggie Harrison, with a 53 yard bomb to Stallworth.

The Browns made one last bid for another score moving from their own 20 across midfield but Blount's second interception at the 3 killed it and certainly fit in with the previous proceedings.

		SCORING	PIT	CLE
1st	Steelers	John Stallworth 3 yard pass from Terry Bradshaw (Roy Gerela kick)	7	0
2nd	Steelers	Franco Harris 1 yard rush (Roy Gerela kick)	14	0
	Steelers	Mike Collier 1 yard rush (Roy Gerela kick)	21	0
	Steelers	Lynn Swann 43 yard pass from Joe Gilliam (Roy Gerela kick)	28	0
4th	Browns	Hugh McKinnis 7 yard rush (kick failed)	28	6
	Steelers	Reggie Garrett 45 yard pass from Joe Gilliam (Roy Gerela kick)	35	6

	Steelers	Reggie Harrison 3 yard rush (Roy Gerela kick)	42	6

	TEAM STATS	
	PIT	CLE
First downs	23	19
Rush-Yards-TD	40-134-3	31-122-1
Comp-Att-Yards-TD-INT	18-23-372-3-0	16-31-136-0-2
Sacked-Yards	1-5	4-37
Net pass yards	367	99
Total yards	501	221
Fumbles-Lost	1-0	2-0
Turnovers	0	2
Penalties-Yards	10-90	7-90

PASSING, RUSHING and RECEIVING

Steelers

Passing

Joe Gilliam: 11-of-15, 221 yards, 2 TD, 0 INT
Terry Bradshaw: 7-of-8, 151 yards, 1 TD, 0 INT

Rushing

Terry Bradshaw: 1 carry for -5 yards
Franco Harris: 17 carries for 57 yards, 1 TD
Rocky Bleier: 10 carries for 37 yards
John Fuqua: 4 carries for 21 yards
Reggie Harrison: 4 carries for 14 yards, 1 TD
Mike Collier: 3 carries for 10 yards, 1 TD
Terry Hanratty: 1 carry for 0 yards

Receiving

Lynn Swann: 5 catches for 126 yards, 1 TD
John Stallworth: 4 catches for 109 yards, 1 TD
Reggie Garrett: 3 catches for 84 yards, 1 TD
Franco Harris: 1 catch for 9 yards
Rocky Bleier: 1 catch for -6 yards
Randy Grossman: 3 catches for 30 yards
Larry Brown: 1 catch for 20 yards

Browns

Passing

Mike Phipps: 16-of-31, 136 yards, 0 TD, 2 INT

Rushing

Greg Pruitt: 14 carries for 54 yards
Mike Phipps: 2 carries for 9 yards
Hugh McKinnis: 9 carries for 46 yards, 1 TD
Billy Pritchett: 5 carries for 10 yards
Ken Brown: 1 carry for 3 yards

Receiving

Greg Pruitt: 6 catches for 30 yards
Hugh McKinnis: 3 catches for 17 yards
Oscar Roan: 1 catch for 31 yards
Reggie Rucker: 1 catch for 15 yards
Willie Miller: 2 catches for 14 yards
Billy Lefear: 1 catch for 14 yards
Ken Brown: 1 catch for 6 yards
Steve Holden: 1 catch for 9 yards

DEFENSE

Steelers

Interceptions

Mel Blount: 2 for 17 yards

KICK RETURNS

Steelers

Punts

Dave Brown: 1 for 23 yards, 23.0 avg.
Mike Collier: 1 for 20 yards, 20.0 avg.

Punts

Dave Brown: 1 for 13 yards, 13.0 avg.
Glen Edwards: 3 for 32 yards, 10.7 avg.

Browns

Kickoffs

Pete Athas: 1 for 5 yards, 5.0 avg.
Eddie Brown: 1 for 27 yards, 27.0 avg.
Ken Brown: 1 for 15 yards, 15.0 avg.
Greg Pruitt: 2 for 35 yards, 17.5 avg.

Punts

Eddie Brown: 2 for 16 yards, 8.0 avg.

KICKING and PUNTING

Steelers

Kicking

Roy Gerela: 6-for-6 PAT

Punting

Bobby Walden: 5 for 165 yards, 33.0 avg.

Browns

Kicking

Don Cockroft: 0-for-1 PAT

Punting

Don Cockroft: 8 for 329 yards, 41.1 avg.

Week 4

Oct. 12
Three Rivers Stadium
Pittsburgh, PA

Denver Broncos vs **Pittsburgh Steelers**

	1Q	2Q	3Q	4Q	Total
Broncos	3	6	0	0	9
Steelers	7	10	0	3	20

PITTSBURGH (UPI) — The Denver Broncos could have used the services of a giant against the Pittsburgh Steelers to block wide receiver Lynn Swann.

Swann made a couple of spectacular leaps in the end zone Sunday, snatching the ball out of the air for two of the finest catches in any recent pro football contests. He was instrumental in the Steelers' 20-9 rout of Denver.

"The first pass I caught (on the goal line between two defenders) was among the top three catches I have made since becoming a pro," Swann said.

Terry Bradshaw agreed saying "Swann jumps like he is on a trampoline." And Coach Chuck Noll simply said the first Swann catch was "the finest I've ever seen."

Bradsaw surpassed the 8,000-yard career passing mark with the first of his two TD passes to Swann, who is a "mere" 5-10. He needed only 29 yards passing, when Swann leaped between two Bronco defenders at the goal line to catch the Steelers quarterback's first pass of the day for a 43-yard touchdown.

After the Steelers held Denver on downs at their own 39 in the next series, Bradshaw found John Stallworth along the left sideline for 29 yards to set up his nine-yard TD pass to Swann on the opening play of the second quarter.

Bradshaw, who finished with 16-of-26 for 191 yards, became the third Steeler quarterback to break the 8,000-yard passing milestone, joining Bobby Layne and Jim Finks.

Franco Harris' 13 yard run in the six-play, second Steeler drive put him over the 3,000 yard career rushing mark.

Denver's only scoring came in the first half on Jim Turner field goals of 23, 40 and 36 yards. Roy Gerela responded with kicks of 39 and 28 yards for the Steelers.

"The Steelers can be expected to throw more often because most teams are keying on Harris and they know what to expect in given situations so we have to mix the run and the pass a little more," Bradshaw explained. "The two passes to Swann could have been interceptions but the son of the gun can jump and he made them good."

Asked if he rated himself a great receiver, Swann said, "There are a lot of receivers who catch the ball well and can be great on any given day but consistency is the key to a great ballplayer."

The Super Bowl champion Steelers, now 3-1, had trailed Denver 0-3-1 in their series before Sunday's game. Denver dropped to 2-2.

Bills 38, Colts 31

Jim Braxton scored three TDs and O.J. Simpson rushed for 159 yards as Buffalo overcame a four-touchdown performance by Lydell Mitchell to defeat Baltimore. Braxton scored on runs of one and three yards and caught a five-yard TD pass from Joe Ferguson. Mitchell scored on runs of six and 11 yards and caught TD passes of 25 and 23 yards from Bert Jones.

		SCORING	DEN	PIT
1st	Broncos	Jim Turner 22 yard field goal	3	0
	Steelers	Lynn Swann 43 yard pass from Terry Bradshaw (Roy Gerela kick)	3	7
2nd	Steelers	Lynn Swann 9 yard pass from Terry Bradshaw (Roy Gerela kick)	3	14
	Steelers	Roy Gerela 39 yard field goal	3	17
	Broncos	Jim Turner 39 yard field goal	6	17
	Broncos	Jim Turner 36 yard field goal	9	17
4th	Steelers	Roy Gerela 28 yard field goal	9	20

	TEAM STATS	
	DEN	PIT
First downs	17	14
Rush-Yards-TD	36-124-0	39-137-0
Comp-Att-Yards-TD-INT	12-36-170-0-3	16-26-191-2-0
Sacked-Yards	2-17	1-1
Net pass yards	153	190

Total yards	277	327
Fumbles-Lost	2-1	4-2
Turnovers	4	2
Penalties-Yards	5-32	13-99

PASSING, RUSHING and RECEIVING

Broncos

Passing

Charley Johnson: 12-of-31, 170 yards, 0 TD, 2 INT
John Hufnagel: 0-of-5, 0 yards, 0 TD, 1 INT

Rushing

Charley Johnson: 2 carries for 6 yards
Riley Odoms: 1 carry for 12 yards
Jon Keyworth: 15 carries for 58 yards
Otis Armstrong: 7 carries for 28 yards
John Hufnagel: 2 carries for 19 yards
Oliver Ross: 9 carries for 1 yard

Receiving

Haven Moses: 4 catches for 81 yards
Riley Odoms: 4 catches for 63 yards
Jon Keyworth: 3 catches for 15 yards
Rick Upchurch: 1 catch for 11 yards

Steelers

Passing

Terry Bradshaw: 16-of-26, 191 yards, 2 TD, 0 INT

Rushing

Terry Bradshaw: 3 carries for 15 yards
Franco Harris: 21 carries for 69 yards
Rocky Bleier: 14 carries for 53 yards
Lynn Swann: 1 carry for 0 yards

Receiving

Franco Harris: 4 catches for 20 yards
Rocky Bleier: 4 catches for 16 yards
Lynn Swann: 2 catches for 52 yards
Frank Lewis: 2 catches for 45 yards
John Stallworth: 3 catches for 31 yards
Larry Brown: 1 catch for 27 yards

DEFENSE

Steelers

Interceptions

Mel Blount: 1 for 0 yards
Jack Lambert: 1 for 11 yards
J.T. Thomas: 1 for 0 yards

KICK RETURNS

Broncos

Kickoffs

Floyd Little: 4 for 76 yards, 19.0 avg.

Punts

Bill Thompson: 2 for 13 yards, 6.5 avg.

Steelers

Kickoffs

Dave Brown: 1 for 21 yards, 21.0 avg.
Mike Collier: 1 for 22 yards, 22.0 avg.
John Fuqua: 1 for 0 yards, 0.0 avg.

Punts

Glen Edwards: 2 for 45 yards, 22.5 avg.
Lynn Swann: 2 for 29 yards, 14.5 avg.

KICKING and PUNTING

Broncos

Kicking

Jim Turner: 3-for-3 FG

Punting

Billy Van Heusen: 4 for 193 yards, 48.3 avg.

Steelers

Kicking

Roy Gerela: 2-for-2 PAT, 2-for-2 FG

Punting

Bobby Walden: 7 for 225 yards, 32.1 avg.

Week 5

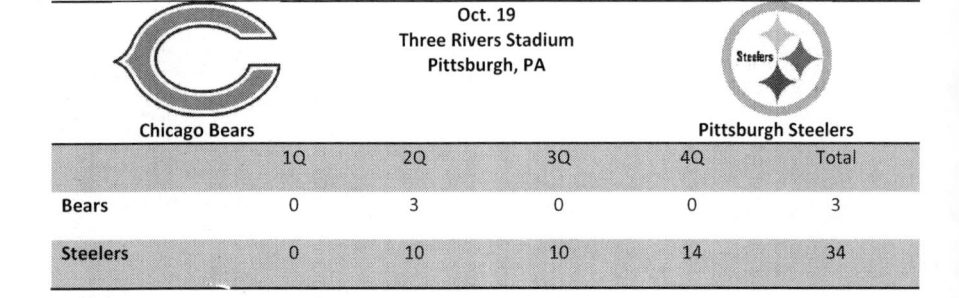

	Oct. 19 Three Rivers Stadium Pittsburgh, PA				
Chicago Bears				Pittsburgh Steelers	
	1Q	2Q	3Q	4Q	Total
Bears	0	3	0	0	3
Steelers	0	10	10	14	34

PITTSBURGH (UPI) — The rebuilding Chicago Bears came into the Pittsburgh Steeler game Sunday with a reputation of not being able to move the ball. And their pass defense was rated the worst in the National Football League.

But for two quarters they played the Steelers to a standstill before Pittsburgh pulled out a 34-3 victory for their fourth win against a single loss.

In the first half, Chicago rushed for 140 yards to a mere 37 for the Steelers. But it was a "different" Steeler team in the second half, according to quarterback Terry Bradshaw. Indeed they were, the Steelers held the Bears to just 56 yards rushing in the second half.

"We just couldn't play ball in the first half," Bradshaw said. "They just smacked up everything we did. We wanted to get points on the board and just couldn't.

"But we really played in the second half and got it together. You just can't take any team lightly."

Apparently the Steelers had taken the Bears too lightly. Pittsburgh punter Bobby Walden felt the Chicago players were "mad" because of some of the press they had received here.

"Some of the things written about them should not have been printed," Walden said, referring to stories that derided the playing ability of the Bears.

The game's leading rusher though, was Chicago's Mike Adamle who ran for 110 yards on 17 carries. The leading Steeler rusher was Rocky Bleier who carried 11 times for

Terry Bradshaw tries to evade Bear

44 yards, while his teammate Franco Harris got only 41 yards in 17 carries.

Linebacker Andy Russell said the Steelers were "overplaying" the Chicago pass plays in the first half which he said permitted the Bears to run the draw so effectively.

"We sure gave up quite a few yards rushing in the first half," Russell said. "But we adjusted in the second half and cut down their runs."

Bradshaw, who hit on 12 of 23 passes, climaxed the Steeler scoring late in the fourth period on a one-yard run. Harris also scored for the Steelers, along with Rocky Bleier and Reggie Harrison, while Roy Gerela contributed a pair of field goals.

The Bears' only score came on the opening play of the second period when Bob Thomas booted a 32-yard field goal to cap a 12-play drive which started at the Chicago 20.

Bradshaw was impressed by the play of Bear defensive

PITTSBURGH (UPI) — Statistics of the Chicago-Pittsburgh football game:

	Chi	Pitt
First downs	16	25
Rushes-yards	30-196	47-192
Passing yards	44	146
Return yards	120	98
Passes	8-22-0	12-23-0
Punts	7-37.1	3-43
Fumbles-lost	1-1	0-0
Penalties-yards	7-109	4-30

tackles Wally Chambers and Roger Stillwell and defensive end Mike Hartenstine.

"They were really something," Bradshaw said. "They all impressed me. Everytime I looked up they were there and it bothered me."

Next week, the Steelers play the Green Bay Packers, who won their first game Sunday with a 19-17 upset victory over Dallas.

134

		SCORING	CHI	PIT
2nd	Bears	Bob Thomas 32 yard field goal	3	0
	Steelers	Roy Gerela 37 yard field goal	3	3
	Steelers	Reggie Harrison 1 yard rush (Roy Gerela kick)	3	10
3rd	Steelers	Roy Gerela 18 yard field goal	3	13
	Steelers	Franco Harris 3 yard rush (Roy Gerela kick)	3	20
4th	Steelers	Rocky Bleier 3 yard rush (Roy Gerela kick)	3	27
	Steelers	Terry Bradshaw 1 yard rush (Roy Gerela kick)	3	34

	TEAM STATS	
	CHI	PIT
First downs	16	25
Rush-Yards-TD	30-196-0	47-157-4
Comp-Att-Yards-TD-INT	8-22-46-0-0	12-23-166-0-0
Sacked-Yards	0-0	2-20
Net pass yards	46	146
Total yards	242	303
Fumbles-Lost	1-1	0-0
Turnovers	1	0
Penalties-Yards	7-109	4-38

PASSING, RUSHING and RECEIVING

Bears

Passing

Gary Huff: 8-of-22, 46 yards

Rushing

Mike Adamle: 17 carries for 110 yards
Roland Harper: 13 carries for 86 yards

Receiving

Mike Adamle: 1 catch for -6 yards
Roland Harper: 4 catches for 10 yards
Bo Rather: 2 catches for 27 yards
Bob Grim: 1 catch for 15 yards

Steelers

Passing

Terry Bradshaw: 11-of-22, 146 yards
Bobby Walden: 1-of-1, 20 yards

Rushing

Terry Bradshaw: 3 carries for 11 yards, 1 TD
John Fuqua: 7 carries for 38 yards
Rocky Bleier: 11 carries for 44 yards, 1 TD
Franco Harris: 17 carries for 41 yards, 1 TD
Mike Collier: 4 carries for 12 yards
Reggie Harrison: 5 carries for 11 yards, 1 TD

Receiving

Lynn Swann: 4 catches for 62 yards
John Fuqua: 1 catch for 11 yards
Franco Harris: 1 catch for 3 yards
Reggie Garrett: 3 catches for 32 yards
Frank Lewis: 1 catch for 21 yards
Donnie Shell: 1 catch for 20 yards
Randy Grossman: 1 catch for 17 yards

KICK RETURNS

Bears

Kickoffs

Bill Knox: 2 for 16 yards, 8.0 avg.
Virgil Livers: 3 for 51 yards, 17.0 avg.
Steve Schubert: 2 for 42 yards, 21.0 avg.

Punts

Virgil Livers: 1 for 11 yards, 11.0 avg.

Steelers

Kickoffs

Mike Collier: 2 for 52 yards, 26.0 avg.

Punts

Dave Brown: 1 for 11 yards, 11.0 avg.
Glen Edwards: 1 for 13 yards, 13.0 avg.
Lynn Swann: 2 for 4 yards, 2.0 avg.

KICKING and PUNTING

Bears

Kicking

Bob Thomas: 1-for-2 FG

Punting

Bob Parsons: 7 for 260 yards, 37.1 avg.

Steelers

Kicking

Roy Gerela: 4-for-4 PAT, 2-for-2 FG

Punting

Bobby Walden: 3 for 129 yards, 43.0 avg.

Week 6

	Oct. 26 County Stadium Milwaukee, WI				
Pittsburgh Steelers				**Green Bay Packers**	
	1Q	2Q	3Q	4Q	Total
Steelers	3	10	0	3	16

| Packers | 0 | 6 | 7 | 0 | 13 |

MILWAUKEE — At last, Rocky Bleier can stop telling war stories.

Now the Vietnam hero can talk about that glorious autumn afternoon when a sellout crowd of 52,815 that included his parents and what seemed to be half the population of his hometown, (Appleton, Wis.) watched him gain a career-high 163 yards on a club-record 35 carries as the Steelers slipped past the feisty Green Bay Packers, 16-13.

"It's a great moment for me," said Bleier, "mainly because we won. If we hadn't won, it would've ruined my day. That's all I could think about while Roy (placekicker Roy Gerela) was kicking the game-winning field goal. I was thinking how miserable it was going to be to have all this success only to see us lose or maybe tie the game."

Gerela's third field goal in four tries — a 29-yarder — did Bleier a favor, not to mention hand the Steelers their fifth victory in six starts.

"There was a tricky and strong wind blowing all day" admitted Gerela. "At the end, it was blowing on an angel against me from my right to over my left shoulder. I cheated a little and hung the ball outside to catch the wind.

"I didn't think it was such a tough kick because I won't let myself think those kind of thoughts. That would only increase the pressure on me. I kick more on instinct and I appreciate the confidence everybody seems to have in me."

That same 10-25 m.p.h. wind dictated much of the Steelers' strategy as they gained their tenth straight win over a National Conference rival and their eighth consecutive road victory (including last season's post-season playoffs).

Quarterback Bradshaw said "That wind was too strong and too tricky to figure out. I was very relieved when Rocky made big gains on the first two plays we ran. That got our running game going and meant I wouldn't have to throw too often.".

Bleier's first two carries each produced seven-yard pickups. By the end of the first quarter he had 75 yards on 14 carries. Most of them (45) came on Pittsburgh's 15-play, 70-yard drive that culminated in Gerela's 19-yard field goal that gave the Steelers a 3-0 lead on the final play of the quarter.

Bleier, who had never gained 100 yards in one game before, had rushed only 56 times for just 195 yards in the Steelers's first five regular-season games.

"But the Packers had shown us on film," said Bradshaw, "that they could take away everything our fullbacks do best. So, even going in, we knew Rocky figured big in our plans. But this big . . . we would've never thought that.

"When we make out a game plan we pick our first four plays. They are plays that check out the defense's reactions. When Rock's two plays worked so well, we just decided to stick with them until they stopped working."

The play which worked best is 84 Special, a variation of the more familiar 84 Trap.

"It's one of our basic plays," said center Ray Mansfield. "Only today we ran the special more than usual. It's different because the fullback takes the end instead of the pulling guard and the tight end takes the linebacker. The pulling guard then takes the first man he sees downfield.

"We haven't run to the strong side that well in a long time, but the way their left end (Clarence Williams) crashed to the inside it was the play to call."

To their credit, the 1-5 Packers retaliated quickly after Gerela's first field goal.

They did so with a 66-yard, 12-play drive aided greatly by four Steeler penalties (one of which was on Coach Chuck Noll for unsportsmanlike conduct). John Brockington's two-yard burst over left guard capped the drive, but Joe Greene blocked the extra point.

Now it was the Steelers turn for instant retaliation, which came in the form of Mike Collier's 94-yard kickoff return. Gerela's second 19-yard field goal made it 13-6 with only 10 seconds left in the first half. Curiously, the Steelers had more penalty yardage (52) at intermission than Green Bay's offensive yardage (48).

The third quarter was spiced by Bobby Walden punts of 55 and 67 yards, Gerela's miss on a 50-yard field-goal attempt, the Packers' John Hadl to Willard Harrell to Steve Odom double reverse that gained 27 yards against a rare Steeler blitz and Hadl's five-yard touchdown pass to Brockington. Now it was 13-all.

Bleier almost spoiled his own day with a pair of fourth-quarter fumbles, but after David Beverly's 51-yard punt and Dave Brown's nine-yard return to the Pittsburgh 27, the Steelers put together their game-winning drive.

Bleier rushed for 29 and Frenchy Fuqua, who went most of the way in place of the ailing Franco Harris (toe, ankle), added, 25, Bradshaw gained seven on the drive's second play but injured his right leg when Fred Carr flipped him.

Joe Gilliam replaced Bradshaw for the remainder of the drive.

"It wasn't the worst spot to come in and face," said Gilliam. "Our line was coming off the ball so well and the backs running so good I knew I probably wouldn't have to pass much."

He didn't, throwing incomplete for Lynn Swann on third and eight from the Packers' 12 on the play preceding Gerela's field goal with 1:07 left.

Trailing, 16-13, the Pack ran a reverse (Odom to Harrell) on the ensuing kickoff and the tiny halfback sped 30 yards to the Green Bay 44 before being bumped out of bounds. On first down, Hadl threw for league-leading receiver Ken Payne, but middle linebacker Jack Lambert picked it off.

Three plays later, time ran out, and Rocky Bleier's smile seemed wider than the state of Wisconsin.

		SCORING	PIT	GNB
1st	Steelers	Roy Gerela 19 yard field goal	3	0
2nd	Packers	John Brockington 2 yard rush (kick failed)	3	6
	Steelers	Mike Collier 94 yard kickoff return (Roy Gerela kick)	10	6
	Steelers	Roy Gerela 19 yard field goal	13	6

| 3rd | Packers | John Brockington 5 yard pass from John Hadl (Joe Danelo kick) | 13 | 13 |
| 4th | Steelers | Roy Gerela 29 yard field goal | 16 | 13 |

	TEAM STATS	
	PIT	GNB
First downs	23	11
Rush-Yards-TD	59-248-0	21-63-1
Comp-Att-Yards-TD-INT	12-23-84-0-0	14-22-128-1-1
Sacked-Yards	0-0	4-30
Net pass yards	84	98
Total yards	332	161
Fumbles-Lost	3-3	2-1
Turnovers	3	2
Penalties-Yards	5-52	1-5

PASSING, RUSHING and RECEIVING

Steelers

Passing

Terry Bradshaw: 12-of-22, 84 yards
Joe Gilliam: 0-of-1, 0 yards

Rushing

Rocky Bleier: 35 carries for 163 yards
Terry Bradshaw: 3 carries for 17 yards
John Fuqua: 13 carries for 52 yards
Franco Harris: 8 carries for 16 yards

Receiving

Rocky Bleier: 2 catches for 7 yards
John Fuqua: 2 catches for 5 yards
Reggie Garrett: 4 catches for 38 yards
Lynn Swann: 3 catches for 25 yards
Larry Brown: 1 catch for 9 yards

Packers

Passing

John Hadl: 14-of-21, 128 yards, 1 TD, 1 INT
Willard Harrell: 0-of-1, 0 yards

Rushing

John Hadl: 2 carries for 5 yards
Steve Odom: 1 carry for 27 yards
John Brockington: 10 carries for 16 yards, 1 TD
Willard Harrell: 7 carries for 12 yards
Barty Smith: 1 carry for 3 yards

Receiving

Steve Odom: 2 catches for 34 yards
John Brockington: 4 catches for 38 yards, 1 TD
Willard Harrell: 4 catches for 28 yards
Ken Payne: 1 catch for 16 yards
Rich McGeorge: 2 catches for 9 yards
Barty Smith: 1 catch for 3 yards

DEFENSE

Steelers

Interceptions

Jack Lambert: 1 for 24 yards

KICK RETURNS

Steelers

Punts

Mel Blount: 1 for 16 yards, 16.0 avg.
Mike Collier: 1 for 94 yards, 94.0 avg., 1 TD

Punts

Dave Brown: 2 for 21 yards, 10.5 avg.
Glen Edwards: 1 for 1 yard, 1.0 avg.

Packers

Kickoffs

Willard Harrell: 1 for 39 yards, 39.0 avg.
Steve Odom: 2 for 48 yards, 24.0 avg.

Punts

Willard Harrell: 1 for 12 yards, 12.0 avg.

KICKING and PUNTING

Steelers

Kicking

Roy Gerela: 1-for-1 PAT, 3-for-4 FG

Punting

Bobby Walden: 4 for 178 yards, 44.5 avg.

Packers

Kicking

Joe Danelo: 1-for-2 PAT

Punting

David Beverly: 8 for 308 yards, 38.5 avg.

Week 7

	Nov. 2 Riverfront Stadium Cincinnati, OH	
Pittsburgh Steelers		**Cincinnati Bengals**

	1Q	2Q	3Q	4Q	Total
Steelers	0	10	13	7	30

| Bengals | 3 | 0 | 0 | 21 | 24 |

"We come alive when the big guy is running like that," said Pittsburgh quarterback Terry Bradshaw Sunday after the Steelers moved into a three-way tie for the American Football Conference Central Division lead.

Fullback Franco Harris erupted for 157 yares, his first 100-yard effort of the season, to key the supercharged Steeler offense, but in the end it was veteran safety Mike Wagner who stole the show.

Pittsburgh dumped the Cincinnati Bengals from the unbeaten ranks with a 30-24 National Football League victory, creating a logjam for first place. Pittsburgh, Cincinnati and Houston each have identical 6-1 records heading into the second half of the season.

"I WAS fortunate to be in the right place at the right time," said Wagner came up with his two interceptions.
douse Cincinnati's comeback hopes. The Steelers, who exploded to a 23-3 lead in the third quarter, were clinging to a tenuous 23-17 advantage when Wagner came up with is two interceptions.

"My job on pass coverage is to be the centerfielder and react to the zone by roaming coverage," said Wagner, whose second interception came with four minutes left. He returned it 65 yards to set up a one-yard plunge by

Bradshaw that enabled the Steelers to open a 13-point bulge.

"Big plays made the difference," said Steeler Coach Chuck Noll. "They turned the game around. Like Lynn Swann's touchdown catch just before the half and Wagner's late interceptions."

BENGALS' Coach Paul Brown pinned the defeat on a critical call as Cincinnati drove to the Pittsburgh 25-yard line.

"There wasn't much difference between the champs and the chumps, except for that 15-yard penalty," he said, referring to a holding infraction called against Cincinnati tight end Bob Trumpy.

One play later, Wagner made the interception that dashed Cincinnati's late bid.

Bradshaw propelled the Steelers to the victory, firing touchdown passes of 37 and 25 yards to wide receiver Swann.

Cincinnati quarterback Ken Anderson, after a dismal first half, finished with 19 completions for 331 yards and keyed the aroused comeback.

		SCORING	PIT	CIN
1st	Bengals	Dave Green 23 yard field goal	0	3
2nd	Steelers	Roy Gerela 42 yard field goal	3	3
	Steelers	Lynn Swann 37 yard pass from Terry Bradshaw (Roy Gerela kick)	10	3
3rd	Steelers	Rocky Bleier 3 yard rush (Roy Gerela kick)	17	3
	Steelers	Lynn Swann 25 yard pass from Terry Bradshaw (kick failed)	23	3
4th	Bengals	Charlie Joiner 34 yard pass from Ken Anderson (Dave Green kick)	23	10

	Bengals	Essex Johnson 3 yard pass from Ken Anderson (Dave Green kick)	23	17
	Steelers	Terry Bradshaw 1 yard rush (Roy Gerela kick)	30	17
	Bengals	Chip Myers 22 yard pass from Ken Anderson (Dave Green kick)	30	24

	TEAM STATS	
	PIT	CIN
First downs	20	17
Rush-Yards-TD	47-239-2	20-69-0
Comp-Att-Yards-TD-INT	13-24-164-2-2	19-43-331-3-3
Sacked-Yards	3-34	4-33
Net pass yards	130	298
Total yards	369	367
Fumbles-Lost	2-2	0-0
Turnovers	4	3
Penalties-Yards	11-85	11-90

PASSING, RUSHING and RECEIVING

Steelers

Passing

Terry Bradshaw: 13-of-24, 164 yards, 2 TD, 2 INT

Rushing

Franco Harris: 27 carries for 157 yards
Terry Bradshaw: 2 carries for 3 yards, 1 TD
Rocky Bleier: 11 carries for 38 yards, 1 TD
Mike Collier: 1 carry for 23 yards
John Fuqua: 4 carries for 11 yards
Reggie Harrison: 2 carries for 7 yards

Receiving

Franco Harris: 2 catches for 0 yards
Lynn Swann: 6 catches for 116 yards, 2 TD
Reggie Garrett: 3 catches for 24 yards
John Fuqua: 1 catch for 11 yards
Larry Brown: 1 catch for 13 yards

Bengals

Passing

Ken Anderson: 19-of-42, 331 yards, 3 TD, 3 INT
John Reaves: 0-of-1, 0 yards

Rushing

Boobie Clark: 13 carries for 56 yards
Essex Johnson: 5 carries for 15 yards
Bruce Coslet: 1 carry for 1 yard
Lenvil Elliott: 1 carry for -3 yards

Receiving

Charlie Joiner: 5 catches for 114 yards, 1 TD
Isaac Curtis: 3 catches for 80 yards
Boobie Clark: 3 catches for 22 yards
Essex Johnson: 5 catches for 54 yards, 1 TD
Chip Myers: 2 catches for 41 yards, 1 TD
Bob Trumpy: 1 catch for 20 yards

DEFENSE

Steelers

Interceptions

Mel Blount: 1 for 6 yards
Mike Wagner: 2 for 83 yards

Bengals

Interceptions

Bernard Jackson: 1 for 0 yards
Ken Riley: 1 for 0 yards

KICK RETURNS

Steelers

Punts

Mel Blount: 1 for 17 yards, 17.0 avg.
Mike Collier: 3 for 74 yards, 24.7 avg.

Punts

Dave Brown: 4 for 13 yards, 3.3 avg.
Glen Edwards: 2 for 22 yards, 11.0 avg.

Bengals

Kickoffs

Bernard Jackson: 3 for 64 yards, 21.3 avg.
Lemar Parrish: 1 for 18 yards, 18.0 avg.

Punts

Lyle Blackwood: 1 for 4 yards, 4.0 avg.
Tommy Casanova: 1 for 6 yards, 6.0 avg.
Lemar Parrish: 3 for 2 yards, 0.7 avg.

KICKING and PUNTING

Steelers

Kicking

Roy Gerela: 3-for-4 PAT, 1-for-1 FG

Punting

Bobby Walden: 6 for 238 yards, 39.7 avg.

Bengals

Kicking

Dave Green: 3-for-3 PAT, 1-for-1 FG

Punting

Dave Green: 8 for 335 yards, 41.9 avg.

Week 8

Nov. 9
Three Rivers Stadium
Pittsburgh, PA

Houston Oilers vs **Pittsburgh Steelers**

	1Q	2Q	3Q	4Q	Total
Oilers	0	7	3	7	17
Steelers	10	7	0	7	24

PITTSBURGH (AP) — Houston Oiler Coach Bum Phillips took a long gulp on a cold beer after swallowing a 24-17 loss to the Pittsburgh Steelers Sunday.

"Terry Bradshaw was the difference," Phillips said after the Pittsburgh quarterback threw three touchdown passes for the Steelers, including a 21-yarder to John Stallworth that snapped a tie with 38 seconds to play.

The victory kept the Steelers tied for first place with Cincinnati in the American Football Conference Central Division. The Steelers, Oilers and Bengals had been in a three-way deadlock.

"I told my coaches that we looked better this year in losing than we did last year up here when we won," said Phillips, referring to Houston's 13-10 victory here last December.

"But Pittsburgh is a much better football team this year because of Bradshaw's poise," he added.

Bradshaw had 17 pass completions in 28 tries for 219 yards. A year ago against Houston, he hit only six of 20 passes.

Bradshaw was spitting tobacco into a Super Bowl mug when told of the complements from Phillips.

"Coach Phillips chews tobacco so he's a pretty good fellow in my book, too. He wears cowboy boots and he's my kind of guy," said Bradshaw.

"But we've got to play them again down in Houston and it will be another tough game. They're a fine football team."

Bradshaw's winning pass capped a 78-yard, six-play drive that began after Houston's Fred Willis plunged one yard for a touchdown, knotting the score 17-17 with 2:18 to play.

A 19-yard end-zone pass interference call against Pittsburgh cornerback Mel Blount had set up the tieing touchdown for Houston, which had trailed the entire game. The Steelers' winning drive was keyed by a 21-yard pass from Bradshaw to John Fuqua on third down and a 26-yard pass to tight end Larry Brown, who had a career high of seven receptions.

Brown fumbled on the play, but teammate Lynn Swann recovered and Bradshaw found Stallworth in the corner of the end zone two plays later.

Bradshaw threw two eight-yard touchdown passes to Swann and Brown in the first half, giving Pittsburgh a 17-7 lead, and the Steelers held on without injured defensive All-Pros Joe Greene and L.C. Greenwood.

Greene spent the day on the sidelines with a groin pull, the first game he's missed as a pro, and Greenwood was sidelined with a first-quarter ankle sprain.

		SCORING	HOU	PIT
1st	Steelers	Roy Gerela 22 yard field goal	0	3
	Steelers	Lynn Swann 8 yard pass from Terry Bradshaw (Roy Gerela kick)	0	10
2nd	Oilers	Ronnie Coleman 3 yard rush (Skip Butler kick)	7	10
	Steelers	Larry Brown 6 yard pass from Terry Bradshaw (Roy Gerela kick)	7	17
3rd	Oilers	Skip Butler 48 yard field goal	10	17
4th	Oilers	Fred Willis 1 yard rush (Skip Butler kick)	17	17

	Steelers	John Stallworth 21 yard pass from Terry Bradshaw (Roy Gerela kick)	17	24

	TEAM STATS	
	HOU	PIT
First downs	18	22
Rush-Yards-TD	29-92-2	40-183-0
Comp-Att-Yards-TD-INT	16-35-231-0-2	17-28-219-3-1
Sacked-Yards	4-25	5-50
Net pass yards	206	169
Total yards	298	352
Fumbles-Lost	1-1	4-1
Turnovers	3	2
Penalties-Yards	4-20	3-38

PASSING, RUSHING and RECEIVING

Oilers

Passing

Dan Pastorini: 15-of-33, 203 yards, 0 TD, 2 INT
Ronnie Coleman: 0-of-1, 0 yards
Lynn Dickey: 1-of-1, 28 yards

Rushing

Dan Pastorini: 1 carry for 1 yard
Ronnie Coleman: 14 carries for 56 yards, 1 TD
Fred Willis: 7 carries for 16 yards, 1 TD
Lynn Dickey: 1 carry for 3 yards
Don Hardeman: 2 carries for 6 yards
Robert Holmes: 3 carries for 8 yards
Willie Rodgers: 1 carry for 2 yards

Receiving

Ken Burrough: 6 catches for 99 yards
Ronnie Coleman: 2 catches for 18 yards
Billy Johnson: 3 catches for 55 yards
John Sawyer: 1 catch for 51 yards
Fred Willis: 3 catches for 5 yards
Don Hardeman: 1 catch for 3 yards

Steelers

Passing

Terry Bradshaw: 17-of-28, 219 yards, 3 TD, 1 INT

Rushing

Terry Bradshaw: 3 carries for 16 yards
Franco Harris: 19 carries for 68 yards
Lynn Swann: 1 carry for 11 yards
Rocky Bleier: 13 carries for 52 yards
John Fuqua: 3 carries for 12 yards
Frank Lewis: 1 carry for 24 yards

Receiving

Larry Brown: 7 catches for 93 yards, 1 TD
Franco Harris: 2 catches for 11 yards
Lynn Swann: 4 catches for 60 yards, 1 TD
Rocky Bleier: 2 catches for 13 yards
John Fuqua: 1 catch for 21 yards
John Stallworth: 1 catch for 21 yards, 1 TD

DEFENSE

Oilers

Interceptions

Bob Atkins: 1 for 1 yard

Steelers

Interceptions

Mel Blount: 1 for 0 yards
Jack Ham: 1 for 2 yards

KICK RETURNS

Oilers

Kickoffs

Ronnie Coleman: 1 for 27 yards, 27.0 avg.
Billy Johnson: 4 for 99 yards, 24.8 avg.

Punts

Billy Johnson: 1 for 14 yards, 14.0 avg.

Steelers

Kickoffs

Mel Blount: 2 for 35 yards, 17.5 avg.
Dave Brown: 1 for 22 yards, 22.0 avg.
Mike Collier: 1 for 14 yards, 14.0 avg.

Punts

Glen Edwards: 4 for 49 yards, 12.3 avg.
Lynn Swann: 1 for 0 yards, 0.0 avg.

KICKING and PUNTING

Oilers

Kicking

Skip Butler: 2-for-2 PAT, 1-for-2 FG

Punting

Dan Pastorini: 6 for 278 yards, 46.3 avg.

Steelers

Kicking

Roy Gerela: 3-for-3 PAT, 1-for-2 FG

Punting

Bobby Walden: 6 for 256 yards, 42.7 avg.

Week 9

Kansas City Chiefs

Nov. 16
Three Rivers Stadium
Pittsburgh, PA

Pittsburgh Steelers

	1Q	2Q	3Q	4Q	Total
Chiefs	0	3	0	0	3
Steelers	0	7	14	7	28

PITTSBURGH (AP) — The margin was slim and maybe temporary, but the Pittsburgh Steelers were alone atop their division for the first time this season after beating the injury-plagued Kansas City Chiefs, 28-3, yesterday

'We weren't flat It just took us a while to get started,' said Terry Bradshaw, who threw a 42-yard touchdown pass to Lynn Swann that put Pittsburgh ahead to stay at 7-3 with seven seconds left before halftime

Bradshaw also led three second-half touchdown drives to secure the Steelers' seventh straight win and give them a one-half game edge with an 8-1 record in the central division of the American Football Conference.

Cincinnati, which was tied for first, can regain a share of the lead by beating Buffalo tonight.

'As long as we keep winning we don't have to worry about other teams,'' said Bradshaw, who also threw a 16-yard touchdown pass to John Stallworth

The Chiefs went into the game without offensive tackle Jim Nicholson, who is nursing a sore knee By game's end knee injuries had also deprived the Chiefs of defensive end Bob Maddox, guard Tom Condon and quarterback Mike Livingston

Maddox was to undergo surgery, while the severity of the other injuries wasn't known, a Chiefs spokesman said.

"I don't want to make excuses: that's not my style," said Chiefs coach Paul Wiggin

"But you start to look around and wonder where it's going to stop,' added Wiggin, whose team also lost defensive end Marv Upshaw earlier this season with a damaged knee

Swann's seventh touchdown catch this season put the Steelers ahead to stay. The Chiefs (4-5) had scored on the first series of the game when Jan Stenerud kicked a 32-yard field goal.

The third quarter began when Stenerud tried to bloop a high onside kick. Steeler rookie John Banaszak grabbed the ball out of the air at the Pittsburgh 49. The Steelers followed with a touchdown drive that ended when Reggie Harrison ran 10 yards.

A series later, Pittsburgh marched 74 yards for another touchdown. It came on a 16-yard pass from Bradshaw to Stallworth.

Steeler cornerback Mel Blount stole two passes, one by Mike Livingston and another by Tony Adams to help shut out Kansas City in the second half.

		SCORING	KAN	PIT
2nd	Chiefs	Jan Stenerud 32 yard field goal	3	0
	Steelers	Lynn Swann 42 yard pass from Terry Bradshaw (Roy Gerela kick)	3	7
3rd	Steelers	Reggie Harrison 10 yard rush (Roy Gerela kick)	3	14
	Steelers	John Stallworth 16 yard pass from Terry Bradshaw (Roy Gerela kick)	3	21
4th	Steelers	Mike Collier 21 yard rush (Roy Gerela kick)	3	28

	TEAM STATS	
	KAN	PIT
First downs	12	23
Rush-Yards-TD	25-78-0	39-239-2
Comp-Att-Yards-TD-INT	13-28-167-0-2	16-24-204-2-1
Sacked-Yards	6-44	2-23

Net pass yards	123	181
Total yards	201	420
Fumbles-Lost	2-0	3-1
Turnovers	2	2
Penalties-Yards	3-25	4-74

PASSING, RUSHING and RECEIVING

Chiefs

Passing

Mike Livingston: 11-of-23, 152 yards, 0 TD, 1 INT
Tony Adams: 2-of-5, 15 yards, 0 TD, 1 INT

Rushing

Ed Podolak: 12 carries for 29 yards
Jeff Kinney: 8 carries for 16 yards
Woody Green: 4 carries for 23 yards
Tony Adams: 1 carry for 10 yards

Receiving

Walter White: 2 catches for 48 yards
Barry Pearson: 3 catches for 48 yards
Ed Podolak: 1 catch for 8 yards
Jeff Kinney: 1 catch for 18 yards
Woody Green: 1 catch for 5 yards
Larry Brunson: 1 catch for 25 yards
MacArthur Lane: 2 catches for 16 yards
Tony Adams: 1 catch for -7 yards
Billy Masters: 1 catch for 6 yards

Steelers

Passing

Terry Bradshaw: 16-of-24, 204 yards, 2 TD, 1 INT

Rushing

Franco Harris: 17 carries for 119 yards
Terry Bradshaw: 1 carry for 2 yards
John Fuqua: 13 carries for 63 yards
Reggie Harrison: 5 carries for 29 yards, 1 TD
Mike Collier: 3 carries for 26 yards, 1 TD

Receiving

Franco Harris: 6 catches for 61 yards
John Fuqua: 2 catches for 36 yards
Lynn Swann: 3 catches for 57 yards, 1 TD
Larry Brown: 2 catches for 24 yards
John Stallworth: 2 catches for 21 yards, 1 TD
Randy Grossman: 1 catch for 5 yards

DEFENSE

Chiefs

Interceptions

Emmitt Thomas: 1 for 0 yards

Steelers

Interceptions

Mel Blount: 2 for 5 yards

KICK RETURNS

Chiefs

Kickoffs

Woody Green: 2 for 28 yards, 14.0 avg.
Jeff Kinney: 2 for 39 yards, 19.5 avg.
Charlie Thomas: 1 for 31 yards, 31.0 avg.

Punts

Reggie Craig: 1 for 1 yard, 1.0 avg.
Ed Podolak: 2 for 13 yards, 6.5 avg.
Charlie Thomas: 2 for 28 yards, 14.0 avg.

Steelers

Kickoffs

Mike Collier: 1 for 19 yards, 19.0 avg.

Punts

Lynn Swann: 1 for 21 yards, 21.0 avg.

KICKING and PUNTING

Chiefs

Kicking

Jan Stenerud: 1-for-2 FG

Punting

Jerrel Wilson: 6 for 263 yards, 43.8 avg.

Steelers

Kicking

Roy Gerela: 4-for-4 PAT

Punting

Bobby Walden: 6 for 226 yards, 37.7 avg.

Week 10

	1Q	2Q	3Q	4Q	Total
Steelers	2	13	3	14	32
Oilers	0	3	0	6	9

Pittsburgh Steelers — Nov. 24, Astrodome, Houston, TX — Houston Oilers

By MICHAEL A. LUTZ
AP Sports Writer

HOUSTON (AP) — The Houston Oilers, sworn to "hold the rope," came unraveled on nationwide television Monday night under the aerial assault of pressure-proof Terry Bradshaw and Pittsburgh's Steel Curtain defense.

Bradshaw flawlessly threaded 13 of 16 passes through the porous Houston Oilers defense to lift the Steelers to a 32-9 victory and give Pittsburgh a one-game lead over Cincinnati in the American Football Conference's Central Division chase.

Coach Chuck Noll was so impressed with his Steelers' handiwork that he pronounced them playoff ready. "Our offense is where it was at the end of last season, moving the ball well and taking the pressure off the defense," Noll said after Bradshaw whipped the Steelers to two touchdowns in a 1:28 span of the second quarter for a commanding 15-3 halftime lead.

"When you get the protection and the blocking from the offensive line that we did tonight, you're bound to move the ball," Noll said.

Despite the motto of "hold the rope" and 49,947 fans cheering them on, the Oilers wilted under the pinpoint passing of Bradshaw and the undeniable runs of Franco Harris, who gained 149 yards and scored two touchdowns.

The Oilers, who dropped to a 7-3 record and third place in the AFC's Central Division, took a 3-2 lead in the second quarter on a 27-yard field goal by Skip Butler but Bradshaw

Guys And Gals

Green Frog and Peacock split 2-2 in Guys-and-Gals Bowling action last week at the local lanes as Rich Pudina rolled a 200 high game and 548 high series to lead Green Frog. Imogene Lucas posted a 198-499 also for Green Frog. For Peacock George Fort had a 191 high game and Jess Beauregard a 530 high series, as Nell Beauregard bowled a 166-452.

Billy Griffin had a 233-589 and Lillian Dail a 156-417 to guide Amoco Oil to a three-game victory over Dixie Concrete. Jesse Boyd posted a 170-452, Billy Boyd a 135 high game, and Carolyn Boyd a 358 high series for Dixie.

Dwight Leatherman rolled a 170 high game and Walter Boyd a 486 high series, with Jannette Boyd bowling a 173-432 to lead the Pinpoppers to a four-game victory over Sand Hill Farms. Bernard Nelson had a 161-432 and Grace Sirmans a 150-427 for Sand Hill.

GAS-O-MAT TOOK three from Pogo Foods as Dennis Walker bowled a 193-488 and Kristie Britt a 181-489 for the winners. Edwin Peacock had a 211-484, Faye Grobsmith a 148 high game, and Judy Peacock a 409 high series for Pogo.

Cotton Beverly rolled a 201-503 and Debbie Walker a 137-396 to lead Team Number 14 to a three-game win over the Tar Babies. Jim O'Steen had a 185-484 and Virginia Tatum a 146-310 for the losing squad.

Climate Controllers and King's Front End Service split 2-2 in had the Steelers ahead 15-3 by the half with a pair of lightning-quick touchdowns in the second quarter.

The Steelers got a safety in the first quarter when Houston quarterback Dan Pastorini was tackled in the end zone after losing the ball from a shotgun formation.

Bradshaw keyed the first of two touchdown runs by Harris with passes of 18 and 10 yards to Lynn Swann in the second quarter. Harris, the first runner to gain 100 yards against Houston's defense this season, bulled four yards for a touchdown with 2:23 to go in the half for a 9-3 Steeler lead.

Cornerback J. T. Thomas returned an interception 11 yards on Houston's next series and Bradshw again went to the air with four straight completions, the last one 18 yards to Swann for a touchdown and the 15-3 halftime lead.

		SCORING	PIT	HOU
1st	Steelers	Safety, White tackled Pastorini in end zone	2	0
2nd	Oilers	Skip Butler 27 yard field goal	2	3
	Steelers	Franco Harris 4 yard rush (Roy Gerela kick)	9	3
	Steelers	Lynn Swann 18 yard pass from Terry Bradshaw (kick failed)	15	3
3rd	Steelers	Roy Gerela 30 yard field goal	18	3
4th	Steelers	John Fuqua 13 yard rush (Roy Gerela kick)	25	3

	Oilers	Ken Burrough 59 yard pass from Dan Pastorini (kick failed)	25	9
	Steelers	Franco Harris 13 yard rush (Roy Gerela kick)	32	9

	TEAM STATS	
	PIT	HOU
First downs	22	13
Rush-Yards-TD	45-228-3	23-126-0
Comp-Att-Yards-TD-INT	13-16-168-1-2	17-32-172-1-2
Sacked-Yards	3-29	4-41
Net pass yards	139	131
Total yards	367	257
Fumbles-Lost	5-3	3-2
Turnovers	5	4
Penalties-Yards	8-70	3-30

PASSING, RUSHING and RECEIVING

Steelers

Passing

Terry Bradshaw: 13-of-16, 168 yards, 1 TD, 2 INT

Rushing

Franco Harris: 21 carries for 149 yards, 2 TD
Terry Bradshaw: 5 carries for 26 yards
John Fuqua: 13 carries for 32 yards, 1 TD
Lynn Swann: 1 carry for 2 yards
Mike Collier: 4 carries for 19 yards
Reggie Harrison: 1 carry for 0 yards

Receiving

Franco Harris: 1 catch for -2 yards
John Fuqua: 4 catches for 27 yards
Lynn Swann: 3 catches for 46 yards, 1 TD
Frank Lewis: 3 catches for 47 yards
John Stallworth: 1 catch for 25 yards
Larry Brown: 1 catch for 25 yards

Oilers

Passing

Dan Pastorini: 17-of-32, 172 yards, 1 TD, 2 INT

Rushing

Ronnie Coleman: 10 carries for 58 yards
Fred Willis: 6 carries for 36 yards
Don Hardeman: 6 carries for 34 yards
Billy Johnson: 1 carry for -2 yards

Receiving

Ronnie Coleman: 4 catches for 23 yards
Ken Burrough: 2 catches for 56 yards, 1 TD
Fred Willis: 5 catches for 16 yards
Nate Hawkins: 1 catch for 32 yards
Emmett Edwards: 1 catch for 18 yards
Mack Alston: 2 catches for 15 yards
Willie Frazier: 1 catch for 9 yards
Billy Johnson: 1 catch for 3 yards

DEFENSE

Steelers

Interceptions

Mel Blount: 1 for 47 yards
J.T. Thomas: 1 for 11 yards

Oilers

Interceptions

Gregg Bingham: 1 for 6 yards
Willie Germany: 1 for 0 yards

KICK RETURNS

Steelers

Punts

Dave Brown: 1 for 26 yards, 26.0 avg.
Mike Collier: 3 for 57 yards, 19.0 avg.

Punts

Dave Brown: 4 for 19 yards, 4.8 avg.
Lynn Swann: 1 for 10 yards, 10.0 avg.

Oilers

Kickoffs

Ronnie Coleman: 1 for 18 yards, 18.0 avg.
Billy Johnson: 4 for 63 yards, 15.8 avg.

Punts

Mark Cotney: 2 for 8 yards, 4.0 avg.
Billy Johnson: 2 for 10 yards, 5.0 avg.

KICKING and PUNTING

Steelers

Kicking

Roy Gerela: 3-for-4 PAT, 1-for-1 FG

Punting

Bobby Walden: 4 for 169 yards, 42.3 avg.

Oilers

Kicking

Skip Butler: 0-for-1 PAT, 1-for-2 FG

Punting

Dan Pastorini: 5 for 211 yards, 42.2 avg.

Week 11

	Nov. 30 Shea Stadium New York, NY	
Pittsburgh Steelers		New York Jets

	1Q	2Q	3Q	4Q	Total
Steelers	0	10	10	0	20
Jets	0	0	0	7	7

NEW YORK (AP) — Terry Bradshaw threw for two touchdowns and Pittsburgh intercepted four Joe Namath passes Sunday to give the Steelers a 20-7 National Football League victory over the New York Jets.

Bradshaw connected on a touchdown strike of 44 yards to running back Franco Harris in the second quarter and hit wide receiver Frank Lewis with an eight-yarder in the third period. Roy Gerela kicked two field goals for the Steelers, from 26 and 19 yards out.

The victory, the Steelers' ninth in a row, raised their record to 10-1 and kept them first in the American Conference's Central Division. The Jets, last in the AFC East, fell to 2-9 with their eighth straight loss.

Cornerback Mel Blount made two of the four interceptions to give him 10 for the season, tying a Pittsburgh club record held by three other players. His first preceded Harris' touchdown catch and the second paved the way to Gerela's 19yard field goal in the third quarter.

New York's only touchdown came with 3:55 to play on Namath's six-yard pass to Jerome Barkum. But by then, the game was out of hand.

Twice earlier, the Jets got within the Steelers' 10-yard line and came away empty.

		SCORING	PIT	NYJ
2nd	Steelers	Roy Gerela 26 yard field goal	3	0
	Steelers	Franco Harris 44 yard pass from Terry Bradshaw (Roy Gerela kick)	10	0
3rd	Steelers	Frank Lewis 8 yard pass from Terry Bradshaw (Roy Gerela kick)	17	0
	Steelers	Roy Gerela 19 yard field goal	20	0
4th	Jets	Jerome Barkum 6 yard pass from Joe Namath (Pat Leahy kick)	20	7

	TEAM STATS	
	PIT	NYJ
First downs	21	16
Rush-Yards-TD	39-213-0	41-141-0
Comp-Att-Yards-TD-INT	9-23-120-2-0	8-21-138-1-4
Sacked-Yards	2-7	1-9

Net pass yards	113	129
Total yards	326	270
Fumbles-Lost	1-0	0-0
Turnovers	0	4
Penalties-Yards	7-41	11-77

PASSING, RUSHING and RECEIVING

Steelers

Passing

Terry Bradshaw: 9-of-22, 120 yards, 2 TD, 0 INT
Bobby Walden: 0-of-1, 0 yards

Rushing

Franco Harris: 14 carries for 61 yards
Terry Bradshaw: 3 carries for 56 yards
Reggie Harrison: 12 carries for 67 yards
John Fuqua: 9 carries for 27 yards
Mike Collier: 1 carry for 2 yards

Receiving

Franco Harris: 3 catches for 59 yards, 1 TD
Frank Lewis: 4 catches for 43 yards, 1 TD
Lynn Swann: 2 catches for 18 yards

Jets

Passing

Joe Namath: 8-of-21, 138 yards, 1 TD, 4 INT

Rushing

John Riggins: 16 carries for 69 yards
Steve Davis: 14 carries for 50 yards
Carl Garrett: 5 carries for 14 yards
Bob Gresham: 2 carries for 6 yards
Emerson Boozer: 4 carries for 2 yards

Receiving

Jerome Barkum: 4 catches for 79 yards, 1 TD
Steve Davis: 1 catch for -4 yards
Eddie Bell: 1 catch for 36 yards
Rich Caster: 2 catches for 27 yards

DEFENSE

Steelers

Interceptions

Jimmy Allen: 1 for 0 yards
Mel Blount: 2 for 32 yards
Glen Edwards: 1 for 47 yards

KICK RETURNS

Steelers

Punts

Mike Collier: 1 for 22 yards, 22.0 avg.

Jets

Kickoffs

Lou Piccone: 5 for 135 yards, 27.0 avg.

Punts

Lou Piccone: 2 for -1 yard, -0.5 avg.

KICKING and PUNTING

Steelers

Kicking

Roy Gerela: 2-for-2 PAT, 2-for-2 FG

Punting

Bobby Walden: 3 for 124 yards, 41.3 avg.

Jets

Kicking

Pat Leahy: 1-for-1 PAT

Punting

Greg Gantt: 2 for 75 yards, 37.5 avg.

Week 12

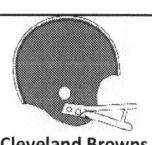

Dec. 7
Three Rivers Stadium
Pittsburgh, PA

Cleveland Browns   Pittsburgh Steelers

	1Q	2Q	3Q	4Q	Total
Browns	3	14	0	0	17
Steelers	7	3	14	7	31

PITTSBURGH (AP) — Coach Forrest Gregg was asked to evaluate the Pittsburgh Steelers after they defeated his Cleveland Browns 31-17 Sunday to secure at least a wild card playoff berth.

"Nobody will ever convince me there will ever be a football team as good as the Green Bay Packers were," said Gregg, who was a player and a coach under the late Vince Lombardi.

"But I'm sure all these Pittsburgh Steelers and these Steeler fans would argue the point. They have a great football team."

The Browns scored a pair of touchdowns within 14 seconds of the first half, but Pittsburgh rallied behind two third-quarter touchdown passes from Terry Bradshaw to Lynn Swann for the National Football League victory.

It was the 10th consecutive victory for the

THE NFL

Steelers, 11-1, who can clinch the Central Division title in the American Football Conference by beating Cincinnati here next Saturday.

"We're not just interested in clinching a playoff spot," said Steeler cornerback Mel Blount, whose 11th interception set up one of Swann's touchdowns. "We want to beat Cincinnati and win the division outright. We don't want to go in the back door."

Cleveland, 2-9, took a 10-7 lead with 2:09 left in the first half when Greg Pruitt ran one yard for a touchdown after a 39-yard drive. Steeler rookie Mike Collier fumbled the ensuing kickoff, and Brown rookie Willie Miller scooped it up and ran 17 yards for another touchdown.

Roy Gerela's 32-yard field goal trimmed the lead to 17-10 at the half, before Bradshaw hit Swann with third-quarter touchdown passes of three and 18 yards.

The second touchdown, snapping a 17-17 tie, came after Steeler cornerback Mel Blount intercepted his 11th pass this season and his eighth in six games.

Blount returned the pass 14 yards. Swann's previous touchdown was set up by a 48-yard punt return by rookie safety Dave Brown.

It was Brown's first-quarter fumble of a punt, however, that paved the way for a 26-yard Don Cockroft field goal.

The Steelers countered on their next series with a three-yard touchdown run by Franco Harris, who also ran eight yards for a fourth-quarter touchdown that gave him more than 1,000 yards rushing for the third time in four seasons.

Harris finished the game with 103 yards on 25 carries. He has 1,002 this season.

		SCORING	CLE	PIT
1st	Browns	Don Cockroft 26 yard field goal	3	0
	Steelers	Franco Harris 3 yard rush (Roy Gerela kick)	3	7
2nd	Browns	Greg Pruitt 1 yard rush (Don Cockroft kick)	10	7
	Browns	Willie Miller 17 yard fumble return (Don Cockroft kick)	17	7
	Steelers	Roy Gerela 32 yard field goal	17	10
3rd	Steelers	Lynn Swann 3 yard pass from Terry Bradshaw (Roy Gerela kick)	17	17
	Steelers	Lynn Swann 18 yard pass from Terry Bradshaw (Roy Gerela kick)	17	24
4th	Steelers	Franco Harris 8 yard rush (Roy Gerela kick)	17	31

	TEAM STATS	
	CLE	PIT

First downs	15	17
Rush-Yards-TD	32-122-1	39-160-2
Comp-Att-Yards-TD-INT	14-37-145-0-3	11-25-135-2-0
Sacked-Yards	3-30	4-37
Net pass yards	115	98
Total yards	237	258
Fumbles-Lost	2-1	2-2
Turnovers	4	2
Penalties-Yards	4-41	7-40

PASSING, RUSHING and RECEIVING

Browns

Passing

Mike Phipps: 14-of-37, 145 yards, 0 TD, 3 INT

Rushing

Greg Pruitt: 19 carries for 85 yards, 1 TD
Mike Phipps: 3 carries for 11 yards
Hugh McKinnis: 8 carries for 20 yards
Billy Pritchett: 2 carries for 6 yards

Receiving

Greg Pruitt: 3 catches for 15 yards
Reggie Rucker: 5 catches for 39 yards
Hugh McKinnis: 2 catches for 17 yards
Steve Holden: 1 catch for 28 yards
Billy Pritchett: 1 catch for 18 yards
Milt Morin: 1 catch for 19 yards
Henry Hynoski: 1 catch for 9 yards

Steelers

Passing

Terry Bradshaw: 11-of-25, 135 yards, 2 TD, 0 INT

Rushing

Franco Harris: 25 carries for 103 yards, 2 TD
Terry Bradshaw: 3 carries for 30 yards
Rocky Bleier: 9 carries for 24 yards
Reggie Harrison: 1 carry for 2 yards
Mike Collier: 1 carry for 1 yard

Receiving

Franco Harris: 2 catches for 15 yards
Lynn Swann: 5 catches for 67 yards, 2 TD
Rocky Bleier: 2 catches for 24 yards
Frank Lewis: 1 catch for 20 yards
Randy Grossman: 1 catch for 9 yards

DEFENSE

Steelers

Interceptions

Jimmy Allen: 1 for 0 yards
Mel Blount: 1 for 14 yards
Mike Wagner: 1 for 1 yard

KICK RETURNS

Browns

Kickoffs

Ken Brown: 1 for 29 yards, 29.0 avg.
Henry Hynoski: 3 for 81 yards, 27.0 avg.
Hugh McKinnis: 1 for 9 yards, 9.0 avg.

Punts

Willie Miller: 3 for 13 yards, 4.3 avg.
Greg Pruitt: 1 for 11 yards, 11.0 avg.

Steelers

Kickoffs

Mel Blount: 1 for 23 yards, 23.0 avg.
Mike Collier: 3 for 51 yards, 17.0 avg.

Punts

Dave Brown: 2 for 52 yards, 26.0 avg.
Glen Edwards: 4 for 53 yards, 13.3 avg.

KICKING and PUNTING

Browns

Kicking

Don Cockroft: 2-for-2 PAT, 1-for-1 FG

Punting

Don Cockroft: 8 for 328 yards, 41.0 avg.

Steelers

Kicking

Roy Gerela: 4-for-4 PAT, 1-for-2 FG

Punting

Bobby Walden: 8 for 333 yards, 41.6 avg.

Week 13

Dec. 13
Three Rivers Stadium
Pittsburgh, PA

Cincinnati Bengals   Pittsburgh Steelers

	1Q	2Q	3Q	4Q	Total
Bengals	0	7	0	7	14
Steelers	14	7	7	7	35

By PHIL MUSICK

Somewhere in the background you kept hearing the tune "We've Only Just Begun," and after it was over and the Cincinnati Bengals had been declawed with almost ridiculous ease, they walked around the subdued locker-room patting one another on the butt and smiling some secret smile like they were part of a great conspiracy.

"The first step," Chuck Noll called it. With a straight face.

There was no champagne, no whooping, nothing to indicate the roller-coaster wasn't still on its way up. The Steelers beat the Bengals like a drum, 35-14, yesterday and then sat back and admired dispassionately their handiwork the way a bricklayer might a half-finished house.

"Last year we thought we could win," said Andy Russell, in the final analysis perhaps the key player in nailing down the AFC Central Division championship for the third time in four years, and along with it the home-field advantage in the playoffs. "This year we thought we should win.

"There's a great deal of difference."

On a day so lovely even the 48,889 partisans at Three Rivers must've been thinking about a picnic, the Steelers had one.

All of the Steelers, Terry Bradshaw and Lynn Swann did a number on Bengal rookie cornerman Marvin Cobb, and it produced a critical first touchdown and another one later. In between, Franco Harris was running for 118 yards and the defense was turning two Cincinnati miscues into touchdowns.

That brought a 28-7 lead only four minutes into the second half. Meanwhile, linebackers Russell and Jack Ham were covering Bengal receiver Isaac Curtis man-for-man in a brilliant defensive scheme and the Steelers were manhandling Cincinnati physically to the point that Bengal Coach Paul Brown later said, "They were Super Bowl champions before today . . . and there's nothing new."

Indeed, the Steelers looked like the NFL's answer to "Jaws." They won their 11th straight game, one which made them the winningest team in the club's 43-year history, and it gave them a 12-1 record, a second consecutive division title and turned next Saturday's game in Los Angeles into a playoff practice. And all without Joe Greene, whose injuries kept him on the bench. Laughing.

It was that sort of game. The Steelers got out of the gate like Secretariat, as Bradshaw and Swann immediately went to work. On Cobb, a rookie replac-

174

ing the injured Lemar Parrish.

"We went after him with inside routes," explained Bradshaw, who threw to Swann for 14, 12 and three yards as the Steelers went 68 yards in 12 plays with the opening kickoff.

Swann was driven out of the end zone by Tommy Casanova after catching the three-yard touchdown pass, but the rule reads a score is recorded if the receiver would've come down in the end zone and the Steelers had a 7-0 lead.

Less than six minutes later, the margin jumped to 14-0 on a superb defensive play involving five Steelers and some luck. The rout had begun and the Steelers were en route to the first AFC Central intra-division sweep ever.

Russell slowed Bengal back Boobie Clark and Dwight White knocked the ball loose at the Cincinnati 42. Mel Blount, named the club's most valuable player after the game, batted it around. Jack Lambert scooped up the ball, ran 21 yards, then leteraled to J.T. Thomas, who ran for 21 more and a touchdown.

The Bengals got one touchdown back, Stan Fritts diving a yard to conclude a 77-yard march powered by Ken Anderson's pahsing, but then they made a second, killing mistake.

Late in the second quarter, Anderson forced one to tight end Bob Trumpy. But Mike Wagner picked it off, his sixth career interception off Anderson, and ran 20 yards to set up a 10-yard scoring sweep by Harris that put the Bengals two touchdowns behind and in the bag.

"They're a great team, you can't give them anything," Brown said of the errors that forced Cincinnati to beat San Diego next week to claim the AFC wild-card berth in the playoffs.

"I was probably out of position," Wagner grinned. "I just lucked out, really."

Chuck Noll, voted the game ball, didn't think so. "A fumble, a TD; an interception, a TD . . . those are tough things for a football team to overcome," he said.

Certainly, they were too tough for the Bengals. Late in the first half the Steelers turned a shanked Bengal punt into a

50-yard touchdown drive, capped by Bradshaw's nine-yard scramble into the end zone, and it was over.

"We were just doing a good job," Noll explained. "Offensively . . . defensively. Especially defensively. Bud Carson's done a good job with the secondary and that's been a big part of it."

Carson, t h e defensive coordinator, didn't do a bad job with the outside linebackers, either. Russell and Ham had man coverage on Curtis until the game was out of reach, and the risky maneuver worked almost to perfection. Curtis caught two passes and wasn't a factor.

"It was a great scheme," Russell said. "We took away what they like to do . . . the patient, short passing game . . . throwing to the backs.

"Everybody plays a three-deep zone on them and lets the short stuff eat them up. We had linebackers on Curtis. I didn't get much sleep all last week. Really. A 9.2 guy on a . . . 13.2 guy."

Regardless of Russell's concern, Curtis was covered, the front four sacked Anderson four times and the Steelers moved inexorably on to a playoff date here Dec. 27 with the AFC East survivor, Miami or Baltimore.

"It doesn't matter which," Noll thought. "We're liable to see the Bengals again. We'll let Fate handle it. She's been pretty good to us."

Maybe, thought Harris, because the Steelers are good to each other. Reporters kept asking about his individual accomplishments—he recorded his fifth 100-yard plus game of the year and the 18th of his career and broke John Henry Johnson's club record with his 28th rushing touchdown—but Harris kept talking about "a team thing."

"Listen, we have a lot of pride. We have a lot of guys who don't get any publicity, but we know what they do for the team. We see that, even if no one else does," he noted.

Somebody mentioned the lack of celebration. Harris smiled.

"Nobody in this room wants to stop here," he said. "It's going to keep on growing. We'll come in here Monday and everyone will get together and feel loose.

"But we'll still be conscious of what we have to do. Nobody wants to end it here."

That is the Steeler secret.

If yesterday is any sort of an indication, the Steelers won't end it until mid-January.

		SCORING	CIN	PIT
1st	Steelers	Lynn Swann 3 yard pass from Terry Bradshaw (Roy Gerela kick)	0	7
	Steelers	J.T. Thomas 21 yard fumble return (Roy Gerela kick)	0	14
2nd	Bengals	Stan Fritts 1 yard rush (Dave Green kick)	7	14
	Steelers	Franco Harris 10 yard rush (Roy Gerela kick)	7	21
3rd	Steelers	Terry Bradshaw 7 yard rush (Roy Gerela kick)	7	28
4th	Steelers	Franco Harris 2 yard rush (Roy Gerela kick)	7	35
	Bengals	Isaac Curtis 1 yard pass from Ken Anderson (Dave Green kick)	14	35

	TEAM STATS	
	CIN	PIT
First downs	16	21
Rush-Yards-TD	26-123-1	38-191-3
Comp-Att-Yards-TD-INT	19-33-236-1-1	13-23-149-1-1
Sacked-Yards	4-42	1-21
Net pass yards	194	128
Total yards	317	319
Fumbles-Lost	1-1	2-0
Turnovers	2	1
Penalties-Yards	8-45	7-48

PASSING, RUSHING and RECEIVING

Bengals

Passing

Ken Anderson: 19-of-32, 236 yards, 1 TD, 1 INT
Stan Fritts: 0-of-1, 0 yards

Rushing

Ken Anderson: 5 carries for 69 yards
Boobie Clark: 7 carries for 21 yards
Lenvil Elliott: 3 carries for 14 yards
Essex Johnson: 10 carries for 18 yards
Stan Fritts: 1 carry for 1 yard, 1 TD

Receiving

Chip Myers: 5 catches for 96 yards
Bob Trumpy: 3 catches for 48 yards
Boobie Clark: 2 catches for 15 yards

Isaac Curtis: 2 catches for 34 yards, 1 TD
Lenvil Elliott: 2 catches for 17 yards
Essex Johnson: 4 catches for 11 yards
Charlie Joiner: 1 catch for 15 yards

Steelers

Passing

Terry Bradshaw: 13-of-23, 149 yards, 1 TD, 1 INT

Rushing

Franco Harris: 20 carries for 118 yards, 2 TD
Terry Bradshaw: 3 carries for 19 yards, 1 TD
Mike Collier: 2 carries for 16 yards
Rocky Bleier: 9 carries for 25 yards
Reggie Harrison: 1 carry for 8 yards
John Fuqua: 3 carries for 5 yards

Receiving

Lynn Swann: 5 catches for 69 yards, 1 TD
John Stallworth: 3 catches for 57 yards
Mike Collier: 1 catch for 7 yards
Larry Brown: 1 catch for 20 yards
Rocky Bleier: 2 catches for -6 yards
John Fuqua: 1 catch for 2 yards

DEFENSE

Bengals

Interceptions

Ken Riley: 1 for 2 yards

Steelers

Interceptions

Mike Wagner: 1 for 20 yards

KICK RETURNS

Bengals

Kickoffs

Lenvil Elliott: 3 for 57 yards, 19.0 avg.
Bernard Jackson: 1 for 8 yards, 8.0 avg.

Punts

Lyle Blackwood: 1 for -2 yards, -2.0 avg.

Steelers

Kickoffs

Mel Blount: 2 for 36 yards, 18.0 avg.
Mike Collier: 1 for 16 yards, 16.0 avg.

Punts

Dave Brown: 1 for 4 yards, 4.0 avg.
Glen Edwards: 2 for 19 yards, 9.5 avg.

KICKING and PUNTING

Bengals

Kicking

Dave Green: 2-for-2 PAT, 0-for-2 FG

Punting

Dave Green: 5 for 190 yards, 38.0 avg.

Steelers

Kicking

Roy Gerela: 5-for-5 PAT

Punting

Bobby Walden: 4 for 170 yards, 42.5 avg.

Week 14

Pittsburgh Steelers	Dec. 20 L.A. Memorial Coliseum Los Angeles, CA	Los Angeles Rams

	1Q	2Q	3Q	4Q	Total
Steelers	3	0	0	0	3
Rams	0	3	0	7	10

LOS ANGELES (UPI) — Ron Jaworski, making his first NFL start, surprised the Pittsburgh defense and scored on a five-yard quarterback draw in the fourth quarter Saturday night as the Los Angeles Rams upset the defending world champion Steelers 10-3 in the regular season finale for both playoff-bound clubs.

Subbing for sore-armed James Harris, Jaworski calmly drove the Rams 60 yards in 13 plays at the beginning of the final period for the only touchdown of the night.

The second-year pro from Youngstown State crossed up the startled Steelers on a third and five situation on the Pittsburgh five and tallied with 9:42 left in the game to break a 3-3 tie.

Winning their sixth straight game, the NFC champion Rams finished their regular season with a 12-2 record. The Steelers had an 11-game skein broken and also wound up with 12-2.

The Rams will play St. Louis in the opening round of the NFL playoffs here next Saturday, while the Steelers will host either Baltimore or Miami the same day.

Jaworski was able to complete only one of six passes for just two yards in the first three quarters, but completed three of four aerials during the Rams' touchdown drive for 48 of their 60 yards. He teamed with Harold Jackson and Willie McGee for 17-yard gainers and passed 14 yards to Ron Jessie.

A defensive holding penalty called on Pittsburgh linebacker Andy Russell gave the Rams a first down and the ball on the Steeler six. Rob Scribner gained one yard and Jaworski missed on a pass to running back Rod Phillips before the Los Angeles touchdown.

Because of injuries, the Rams had only three running backs available for the game, but the Los Angeles defense was enough to offset that handicap.

The Ram defense forced the Steelers to commit four turnovers, three of them interceptions. The Rams also recorded two sacks as the Steelers were held without a touchdown for the first time this season.

		SCORING	PIT	RAM
1st	Steelers	Roy Gerela 20 yard field goal	3	0
2nd	Rams	Tom Dempsey 26 yard field goal	3	3
4th	Rams	Ron Jaworski 5 yard rush (Tom Dempsey kick)	3	10

	TEAM STATS	
	PIT	RAM
First downs	14	14
Rush-Yards-TD	34-177-0	48-171-1
Comp-Att-Yards-TD-INT	5-21-57-0-3	6-13-79-0-1
Sacked-Yards	2-17	2-17
Net pass yards	40	62
Total yards	217	233
Fumbles-Lost	1-1	1-0
Turnovers	4	1
Penalties-Yards	3-20	3-36

PASSING, RUSHING and RECEIVING

Steelers

Passing

Terry Bradshaw: 3-of-10, 28 yards, 0 TD, 1 INT
Joe Gilliam: 2-of-11, 29 yards, 0 TD, 2 INT

Rushing

Franco Harris: 21 carries for 126 yards
Rocky Bleier: 7 carries for 31 yards
Terry Bradshaw: 1 carry for 2 yards
Mike Collier: 1 carry for 8 yards
Reggie Harrison: 3 carries for 8 yards
John Fuqua: 1 carry for 2 yards

Receiving

Franco Harris: 1 catch for 4 yards
Randy Grossman: 3 catches for 49 yards
Lynn Swann: 1 catch for 4 yards

Rams

Passing

Ron Jaworski: 6-of-13, 79 yards, 0 TD, 1 INT

Rushing

Rob Scribner: 19 carries for 67 yards
Rod Phillips: 11 carries for 51 yards
Cullen Bryant: 15 carries for 50 yards
Ron Jaworski: 3 carries for 3 yards, 1 TD

Receiving

Rod Phillips: 2 catches for 10 yards
Harold Jackson: 2 catches for 38 yards
Willie McGee: 1 catch for 17 yards
Ron Jessie: 1 catch for 14 yards

DEFENSE

Steelers

Interceptions

Glen Edwards: 1 for 21 yards

Rams

Interceptions

Ken Geddes: 1 for 4 yards
Monte Jackson: 1 for 3 yards
Eddie McMillan: 1 for 25 yards

KICK RETURNS

Steelers

Kickoffs

Dave Brown: 1 for 20 yards, 20.0 avg.
Mike Collier: 2 for 37 yards, 18.5 avg.

Punts

Dave Brown: 2 for 34 yards, 17.0 avg.
Glen Edwards: 2 for 15 yards, 7.5 avg.

Rams

Kickoffs

Willie McGee: 1 for 21 yards, 21.0 avg.

Punts

Dave Elmendorf: 1 for 8 yards, 8.0 avg.
Rob Scribner: 3 for 23 yards, 7.7 avg.

KICKING and PUNTING

Steelers

Kicking

Roy Gerela: 1-for-1 FG

Punting

Bobby Walden: 6 for 206 yards, 34.3 avg.

Rams

Kicking

Tom Dempsey: 1-for-1 PAT, 1-for-2 FG

Punting

Duane Carrell: 7 for 263 yards, 37.6 avg.

AFC Divisional Playoffs

Baltimore Colts — Dec. 27, Three Rivers Stadium, Pittsburgh, PA — **Pittsburgh Steelers**

	1Q	2Q	3Q	4Q	Total
Colts	0	7	3	0	10
Steelers	7	0	7	14	28

PITTSBURGH (UPI) — Franco Harris blasted Baltimore's Cinderella hopes Saturday by carrying for a playoff record 153 yards, rushing seven yards for one score and setting up the clinching touchdown, to lead the Super Bowl champion Pittsburgh Steelers to a 28-10 victory over the Colts and a berth in the AFC title game next week.

Harris scored Pittsburgh's first touchdown in the first period and set up Terry Bradshaw's one-yard plunge with 6:11 left to play.

Baltimore made it close, moving down to the Steeler three with 2:25 remaining, when Jack Ham deflected a pass and Andy Russell returned it 93 yards for a touchdown.

The victory enabled the Steelers to play host to the winner of today's Oakland-Cincinnati game next Sunday

★★★★★★★★★★★★★★★★★★★

THE YARDSTICK

Pittsburgh (28)		Baltimore (10)
16	First Downs	10
211	Yds. Rushing	62
76	Yds. Passing	72
13	Passes Att.	22
8	Passes Comp.	8
2	Had Int.	2
2	Fumbles Lost	1
4-40	Punts Ave.	9-40
45	Penalties	53

★★★★★★★★★★★★★★★★★★★

for the AFC title and a berth in the Super Bowl.

With Pittsburgh trailing 10-7 and the Colts on the verge of one of the great upsets in NFL history, NFL interception leader Mel Blount picked off sub quarterback Marty Domres' pass and returned it 20 yards to the Colt seven. Rocky Bleier then burst off right tackle on the first play to give Pittsburgh the lead.

Pittsburgh started a 39-yard scoring drive with 9:32 remaining. Bradshaw, who had to be heldped off the field at halftime with a knee injury, hit Larry Brown with a nine-yard pass and then Harris took over, carrying four times for 23 yards to set up Bradshaw's two-yard TD plunge.

Toni Linhart gave the Colts a 10-7 lead in the third quarter when he kicked a 21-yard field goal and Baltimore seemed in control before Pittsburgh's 21-point second half onslaught.

Both quarterbacks suffered injuries in the first half. Baltimore's Bert Jones was hurt on third down on the Colts' first series, suffering a strained arm, and he did not return until the last quarter. Bradshaw was cartwheeled attempting to run for a first down just before the half ended and had to be carried from the field at halftime. He started the second half.

The loss was a bitter one for Baltimore, which capped the greatest comeback by a division winner in NFL history this year by rebounding from a 2-12 record in 1974, the worst record in the league, to 10-4 and the AFC East title in 1975.

The Colts fought to a 7-7 halftime score. Pittsburgh, conservative in its opening series, opened up midway through the first quarter. Taking possession on their own 39, the Steelers needed just four plays to score. Bradshaw threw 34 yards to Frank Lewis, who made a brilliant one-handed leaping catch, and then hit Lynn Swann for 14 more yards. Harris -cracked five yards up the middle and then raced eight yards off left end for the score.

Pittsburgh semed in control when Bradshaw threw directly to Colt cornerback Lloyd Mumphord, who raced down the left sideline 58 yards to the Steeler 19. Lydell Mitchell carried four consecutive times to the five and Domres then rolled right on third down and hit Glenn Doughty, who juggled the ball and finally pulled it in on his knees in the end zone.

Russell's 93-yard run with the fumble was also a playoff record and marked the end for the Colts.

The game was worth only a regular game paycheck to each club.

		SCORING	BAL	PIT
1st	Steelers	Franco Harris 8 yard rush (Roy Gerela kick)	0	7
2nd	Colts	Glenn Doughty 5 yard pass from Marty Domres (Toni Linhart kick)	7	7
3rd	Colts	Toni Linhart 21 yard field goal	10	7
	Steelers	Rocky Bleier 7 yard rush (Roy Gerela kick)	10	14

4th	Steelers	Terry Bradshaw 2 yard rush (Roy Gerela kick)	10	21
	Steelers	Andy Russell 93 yard fumble return (Roy Gerela kick)	10	28

	TEAM STATS	
	BAL	PIT
First downs	10	16
Rush-Yards-TD	41-82-0	43-211-3
Comp-Att-Yards-TD-INT	8-22-100-1-2	8-13-103-0-2
Sacked-Yards	5-28	3-27
Net pass yards	72	76
Total yards	154	287
Fumbles-Lost	2-1	3-3
Turnovers	3	5
Penalties-Yards	6-53	5-45

PASSING, RUSHING and RECEIVING

Colts

Passing

Bert Jones: 6-of-11, 91 yards
Marty Domres: 2-of-11, 9 yards, 1 TD, 2 INT

Rushing

Lydell Mitchell: 26 carries for 63 yards
Bert Jones: 2 carries for 6 yards
Marty Domres: 4 carries for 17 yards
Don McCauley: 3 carries for 3 yards
Bill Olds: 5 carries for 6 yards
Roger Carr: 1 carry for -13 yards

Receiving

Lydell Mitchell: 4 catches for 20 yards
Glenn Doughty: 2 catches for 63 yards, 1 TD
Don McCauley: 1 catch for 9 yards
Jimmie Kennedy: 1 catch for 8 yards

Steelers

Passing

Terry Bradshaw: 8-of-13, 103 yards, 0 TD, 2 INT

Rushing

Franco Harris: 27 carries for 153 yards, 1 TD
Terry Bradshaw: 3 carries for 22 yards, 1 TD
Rocky Bleier: 12 carries for 28 yards, 1 TD
Mike Collier: 1 carry for 8 yards

Receiving

Frank Lewis: 3 catches for 65 yards
Rocky Bleier: 2 catches for 14 yards
Lynn Swann: 2 catches for 15 yards
Larry Brown: 1 catch for 9 yards

DEFENSE

Colts

Sacks

Mike Barnes (1.0), Jim Cheyunski (0.5), Fred Cook (1.0) and John Dutton (0.5)

Interceptions

Lloyd Mumphord: 2 for 67 yards

Steelers

Sacks

Steve Furness (0.5), L.C. Greenwood (1.0), Jack Ham (2.0), Ernie Holmes (0.5) and Dwight White (1.0)

Interceptions

Mel Blount: 1 for 20 yards
Jack Ham: 1 for 6 yards

KICK RETURNS

Colts

Kickoffs

Bruce Laird: 4 for 86 yards, 21.5 avg.
Don McCauley: 1 for 17 yards, 17.0 avg.

Punts

Howard Stevens: 3 for 30 yards, 10.0 avg.

Steelers

Kickoffs

Dave Brown: 2 for 53 yards, 26.5 avg.
Reggie Harrison: 1 for 21 yards, 21.0 avg.

Punts

Dave Brown: 1 for 7 yards, 7.0 avg.
Mike Collier: 1 for 17 yards, 17.0 avg.
Glen Edwards: 2 for 22 yards, 11.0 avg.

KICKING and PUNTING

Colts

Kicking

Toni Linhart: 1-for-1 PAT, 1-for-1 FG

Punting

David Lee: 9 for 361 yards, 40.1 avg.

Steelers

Kicking

Roy Gerela: 4-for-4 PAT

Punting

Bobby Walden: 4 for 159 yards, 39.8 avg.

AFC Championship Game

Jan. 4
Three Rivers Stadium
Pittsburgh, PA

	1Q	2Q	3Q	4Q	Total
Raiders	0	0	0	10	10
Steelers	0	3	0	13	16

PITTSBURGH (AP) — The Pittsburgh Steelers will get a Super Bowl trip to Miami to thaw their numb fingers and toes. But the Oakland Raiders must put their title hopes in the deep freeze—where they've always been—after losing to the Steelers 16-10 Sunday in the American Football Conference title game.

"The weather and the hitting were ferocious," Steelers Coach Chuck Noll said after the two teams lost a total of eight fumbles and five pass interceptions on the frozen field, raked by snow squalls and winds that sent the chill factor to minus 12 degrees.

Quarterback Terry Bradshaw led two second half touchdown drives and middle linebacker Jack Lambert pounced on three Raiders fumbles for the defending Super Bowl champs, who survived five lost fumbles in the second half and three interceptions in the first half.

"We're very disappointed," Coach John Madden said in the subdued locker room of the Raiders, who made their eighth playoff appearance in nine years without ultimate victory—the Super Bowl title.

"When we started out, we thought this was going to be our year," added Madden, whose team was also beaten by Pittsburgh in last year's AFC title game.

Though enjoying the warmth and victory glow in the Steelers locker room, Noll was already thinking ahead to his team's trip to Super Bowl X.

"I can't think of a team that deserves a second Super Bowl more," said Noll, whose team gained the home field advantage in the playoffs by finishing with the best regular season record in the AFC, 12-2.

"These people did everything they had to do," added Noll, six months and 23 games after his team opened training camp with the motto, "Once is not enough."

But before securing victory this day, the Steelers had to hold off a last-second Oakland threat. The Raiders scored on a George Blanda field goal with 12 seconds remaining, recovered the ensuing on-sides kickoff and completed a pass to the Pittsburgh 15 yard line. But the clock ran out on the team that always seems to lose when it counts most.

Vicious hitting and the chilling cold took their toll, especially in the third quarter when both teams lost a pair of fumbles in a span of just over two minutes.

Yet the Steelers, 3-0 leaders at the half on Roy Gerela's 36yard field goal, survived the rash of mistakes. They got the game's first touchdown on the second play of the fourth quarter when Franco Harris bounced outside, broke a tackle by rookie cornerback Neal Colzie and sped untouched down the sidelines on a 25-yard scoring run.

The Raiders countered with a quick drive that was capped by a 14-yard touchdown pass from Ken Stabler to Mike Siani. It cut the Steelers' lead to 10-7.

But then Bradshaw applied the clincher with a 20-yard touchdown pass to John Stallworth. He made the catch with 9:31 to play after Colzie, who seemed in position to intercept in the front corner of the end zone, slipped and fell on the treacherous field. The pass came two plays after Lambert recovered a fumble by Oakland's Marv Hubbard at the Raiders' 20-yard line.

Then with 12 seconds remaining, Blanda kicked a 41-yard field goal to cut the lead to 16-10. The kick, longest of the year for the 48-year-old Blanda, was designed to precede an onsides kickoff.

The Raiders did recover that kickoff on their own 44-yardline. On the game's last play, Stabler hit Cliff Branch with a desperation pass on Pittsburgh's 15, but the clock ran out.

On the first touchdown drive, Bradshaw playing with a sore knee, hit Stallworth with a 10yard pass and the catch was augmented by a 15-yard piling on penalty. Harris caught a 17yard pass from Bradshaw before making his 25-yard scoring run.

Bradshaw had to leave the game with 1:50 to play when he suffered a head injury.

Though Bradshaw threw three first half interceptions, the Steelers shut out the Raiders in the first 30 minutes with the help of All-Pro defensive tackle Joe Greene, who returned to the lineup after being out since mid-season with neck and groin injuries. Greene played the entire game.

Raiders safety Jack Tatum stole two errant Bradshaw passes within a six-minute span of the first quarter, yet the Steelers kept alive their streak of never having allowed a first period touchdown all season.

Tatum's first theft came with 7:18 left in the first quarter. He returned the ball eight yards to the Oakland 35. Stabler then hit Siani with a 22-yard pass and led the Raiders on a drive that stalled at the Steelers' 30-yard line, from where Ray Guy punted out of bounds at the one.

```
Oakland           0  0  0 10—10
Pittsburgh        0  3  0 13—16
Pitt—FG Gerela 36
Pitt—Harris 25 run (Gerela kick)
Oak—Siani 14 pass from Stabler
 (Blanda kick)
Pitt—Stallworth 20 pass from Bradshaw
 (kick failed)
Oak—FG Blanda 41
A—49,103
```

2nd	Steelers	Roy Gerela 36 yard field goal	0	3
4th	Steelers	Franco Harris 25 yard rush (Roy Gerela kick)	0	10
	Raiders	Mike Siani 14 yard pass from Ken Stabler (George Blanda kick)	7	10
	Steelers	John Stallworth 20 yard pass from Terry Bradshaw (kick failed)	7	16
	Raiders	George Blanda 41 yard field goal	10	16

	TEAM STATS	
	OAK	PIT
First downs	18	16
Rush-Yards-TD	32-93-0	39-117-1
Comp-Att-Yards-TD-INT	18-42-246-1-2	15-25-215-1-3
Sacked-Yards	2-18	0-0
Net pass yards	228	215
Total yards	321	332
Fumbles-Lost	4-3	4-4
Turnovers	5	7
Penalties-Yards	4-40	3-32

PASSING, RUSHING and RECEIVING

Raiders

Passing

Ken Stabler: 18-of-42, 246 yards, 1 TD, 2 INT

Rushing

Pete Banaszak: 8 carries for 33 yards
Clarence Davis: 13 carries for 29 yards

Marv Hubbard: 10 carries for 30 yards
Jess Phillips: 1 carry for 1 yard

Receiving

Mike Siani: 5 catches for 80 yards, 1 TD
Dave Casper: 5 catches for 67 yards
Cliff Branch: 2 catches for 56 yards
Pete Banaszak: 2 catches for 12 yards
Clarence Davis: 1 catch for 3 yards
Harold Hart: 1 catch for 16 yards
Bob Moore: 2 catches for 12 yards

Steelers

Passing

Terry Bradshaw: 15-of-25, 215 yards, 1 TD, 3 INT

Rushing

Franco Harris: 27 carries for 79 yards, 1 TD
Terry Bradshaw: 2 carries for 22 yards
Rocky Bleier: 10 carries for 16 yards

Receiving

Franco Harris: 5 catches for 58 yards
Lynn Swann: 2 catches for 45 yards
Randy Grossman: 4 catches for 36 yards
Frank Lewis: 1 catch for 33 yards
John Stallworth: 2 catches for 30 yards, 1 TD
Larry Brown: 1 catch for 13 yards

DEFENSE

Raiders

Interceptions

Monte Johnson: 1 for 11 yards
Jack Tatum: 2 for 8 yards

Steelers

Sacks

Ernie Holmes (1.0) and Andy Russell (1.0)

Interceptions

Mike Wagner: 2 for 34 yards

KICK RETURNS

Raiders

Kickoffs

Pete Banaszak: 1 for 15 yards, 15.0 avg.
Clarence Davis: 3 for 56 yards, 18.7 avg.

Punts

Mike Siani: 1 for 0 yards, 0.0 avg.

Steelers

Kickoffs

Mike Collier: 2 for 57 yards, 28.5 avg.

Punts

Dave Brown: 2 for 28 yards, 14.0 avg.
Mike Collier: 1 for 0 yards, 0.0 avg.

KICKING and PUNTING

Raiders

Kicking

George Blanda: 1-for-1 PAT, 1-for-2 FG

Punting

Ray Guy: 8 for 303 yards, 37.9 avg.

Steelers

Kicking

Roy Gerela: 1-for-2 PAT, 1-for-3 FG

Punting

Bobby Walden: 4 for 154 yards, 38.5 avg.

Super Bowl X

Jan. 18
Orange Bowl
Miami, FL

Dallas Cowboys — **Pittsburgh Steelers**

	1Q	2Q	3Q	4Q	Total
Cowboys	7	3	0	7	17
Steelers	7	0	0	14	21

MIAMI (AP) — They sawed off the shotgun. They out-muscled the flex. They did everything that it takes to make for good, basic, dull football— and it was anything but dull.

The Pittsburgh Steelers, for the second straight year the greatest team in professional football, dealt the wild-card Cowboys of Dallas a fistful of fundamentals Sunday and came away with a 21-17 victory in what was easily the most thrilling Super Bowl game yet played.

And having carved an X on the bad rap these National Football League extravaganzas have carried since their inception, the Steelers immediately began thinking about carving a special niche of their own in the record books by winning a third title in a row.

The Cowboys, with quarterback Roger Staubach passing out of a deep-set shotgun offense and a "flex" defense designed to consternate Pittsburgh, had added a few new wrinkles to this game. But for all their efforts, all they got were furrowed brows. It was blocking and tackling—all there really is to football, when you get down to it—that made the difference.

"I'm a big deal today—but tomorrow we start working for Super Bowl XI," said Reggie Harrison, the bemused, almost embarrassed Steeler whose fourth-quarter blocked punt produced a safety and started Pittsburgh working in earnest toward the triumph in Super Bowl X.

"I think we'll be enjoying this one a lot more than the last one," added running back Franco Harris, a star in the Steelers' Super Bowl IX victory over Minnesota but little more than a bit-part player in this one. "We're No. 1 two times in a row and there's not too many teams that can say that. Now it'll be nice to try for No. 3— and no team can say that yet."

And Jack Lambert, the hyperactive spearhead of the Pittsburgh defense that gave Dallas fits until it was too late to alter the outcome, said simply: "Two is nice...but three would be nicer."

Two was hard to come by. The game was a relatively even one statistically, but those are only cold numbers on a chart. On the field it was as uneven as a manic-depressive, first raising the Cowboys hopes, then dashing them, then doing the same to the Steelers' emotions.

The tempo crashed back and forth, bouncing as crazily as the football that careened into and out of the Dallas end zone after Harrison had collided with it in mid-air, jawbone to pigskin.

It was the Cowboys who got on the scoreboard first. They stampeded into Pittsburgh punter Bobby Walden as he juggled the ball. In one play, a 29-yard touchdown pass from Roger Staubach to a shockingly wide-open Drew Pearson, Dallas bashed a gaping hole in the aura of Pittsburgh's Steel Curtain invincibility, becoming the first team all season to score a first-quarter touchdown against the Steelers.

Was this, then, to be the first tolling of the bell that would ring down that curtain?

It took Pittsburgh less than 4½ minutes to dispel those fears, tying the game on a touchdown pass from Terry Bradshaw to an equally wide-open Randy Grossman.

From then until the fourth minute of the fourth period, it was a war of attrition, a series of missed opportunities. Toni Fritsch kicked a 36-yard field goal 15 seconds into the second period, putting Dallas on top again 10-7. He might have had a shot at another three-pointer later in the period if Pittsburgh's defense hadn't flexed its own muscles, turning a second-and-10 situation on the Pittsburgh 23 into a fourth-and-35 by creaming Staubach on successive pass attempts.

Meanwhile, Pittsburgh was blowing some chances of its own, but doing it more blatantly, compliments of place-kicker Roy Gerela's inaccurate right foot. He lined a 36-yard try of his own to the left of the luminescent yellowgreen uprights in the final minute of the second period, then repeated his act of futility about a third of the way into the third quarter by hooking a 33-yarder.

He had a pretty good excuse, though, for his lack of marksmanship. It seems he was nursing a broken rib. He busted it on the first play of the game by knocking Dallas' Tom Henderson out of bounds, preventing the razzle-dazzle reverse runback from the Super Bowl's first kickoff returned for a touchdown.

So into the fourth quarter these two teams went, the Steelers pounding away at Dallas and coming up empty; the Cowboys cracking away at Pittsburgh and holding, ever so tenuously, their three-point lead.

Something had to give.

Something did. It was, of all things, the Cowboys' punting unit. And what had been an

(Turn to Page 24)

Dallas   7 3 0 7—17
Pittsburgh   7 0 0 14—21
Dal—D. Pearson 29 pass from Staubach (Fritsch kick)
Pitt—Grossman 7 pass from Bradshaw

(Continued from Page 22)
intense, fierce, frustrating game of near-misses became a rollercoaster of scoring, changing the numbers on the scoreboard almost as quickly as the numbers on the big board in the stock exchange.

Harrison, a 1974 midseason acquisition by Pittsburgh after the St. Louis Cardinals cut him adrift, came through the line like a locomotive at full throttle and met the football face first, an instant after punter Mitch Hoopes' foot hit the ball.

"I think I got it with my mouth," he said later, impishly displaying a tongue with a gash up the middle. "I thought I had it with my arm, but after the block I turned around and spat and got nothing but blood, so I guess I took it in the face."

It seemed impossible to some that Harrison wouldn't know where he'd been hit. It was even more incredible that he didn't know how much impact his play had. In fact, it wasn't until he was in the locker room that he found out he'd drawn Pittsburgh within one point of a tie.

"You mean we get points for that!" he said, deadly earnest. "Well, I guess when you're out on the field and your all messed up inside and you're losing when you're supposed to be winning, I guess you don't think about things like that."

He didn't think much about the block itself, either. Both coaches—Chuck Noll of Pittsburgh and Tom Landry of Dallas—and plenty of players on both sides said it was the turning point, the instant the Steelers began smelling blood.

But Harrison brushed it off.

"I don't think it was so important. Heck, there were some really big plays," he said, referring to a Mike Wagner interception that helped the Steelers pad their lead and a 64-yard Lynn Swann touchdown catch that put the game away.

"Those were the big ones. Mine was just lucky. I'd never take credit for winning the game, for doing something as big as that."

But it was big. Hoopes' subsequent free kick travelled 50 yards and came back 25 after Mike Collier caught it. Harris, who finished with 82 yards rushing this time compared to last year's record 158, took turns with Rocky Bleir punching out short gains until it was fourth-and-one at the Dallas 20.

With Gerela's track record, it seemed certain Noll would opt for a shot at a first down. He didn't. He gave Gerela a chance to redeem himself. Gerela did with a perfect 36-yard field goal that put the Steelers ahead for the first time.

"I never looked back at what happened," Gerela said of his two earlier failures—and of two misses in Super Bowl IX. "I never thought about last year's game and I never thought about the two misses. You can't do that. I make it a point never to do that."

		SCORING	DAL	PIT
1st	Cowboys	Drew Pearson 29 yard pass from Roger Staubach (Toni Fritsch kick)	7	0
	Steelers	Randy Grossman 7 yard pass from Terry Bradshaw (Roy Gerela kick)	7	7
2nd	Cowboys	Toni Fritsch 36 yard field goal	10	7
4th	Steelers	Safety, Harrison blocked Hoopes punt through end zone	10	9

Steelers	Roy Gerela 36 yard field goal	10	12
Steelers	Roy Gerela 18 yard field goal	10	15
Steelers	Lynn Swann 64 yard pass from Terry Bradshaw (kick failed)	10	21
Cowboys	Percy Howard 34 yard pass from Roger Staubach (Toni Fritsch kick)	17	21

	TEAM STATS	
	DAL	PIT
First downs	14	13
Rush-Yards-TD	31-108-0	46-149-0
Comp-Att-Yards-TD-INT	15-24-204-2-3	9-19-209-2-0
Sacked-Yards	7-42	2-19
Net pass yards	162	190
Total yards	270	339
Fumbles-Lost	4-0	4-0
Turnovers	3	0
Penalties-Yards	2-20	0-0

PASSING, RUSHING and RECEIVING

Cowboys

Passing

Roger Staubach: 15-of-24, 204 yards, 2 TD, 3 INT

Rushing

Roger Staubach: 5 carries for 22 yards
Robert Newhouse: 16 carries for 56 yards
Preston Pearson: 5 carries for 14 yards
Doug Dennison: 5 carries for 16 yards

Receiving

Robert Newhouse: 2 catches for 12 yards
Preston Pearson: 5 catches for 53 yards
Drew Pearson: 2 catches for 59 yards, 1 TD
Percy Howard: 1 catch for 34 yards, 1 TD
Charley Young: 3 catches for 31 yards
Doug Dennison: 1 catch for 6 yards
Jean Fugett: 1 catch for 9 yards

Steelers

Passing

Terry Bradshaw: 9-of-19, 209 yards, 2 TD, 0 INT

Rushing

Terry Bradshaw: 4 carries for 16 yards
Franco Harris: 27 carries for 82 yards
Rocky Bleier: 15 carries for 51 yards

Receiving

Lynn Swann: 4 catches for 161 yards, 1 TD
Franco Harris: 1 catch for 26 yards
John Stallworth: 2 catches for 8 yards
Larry Brown: 1 catch for 7 yards
Randy Grossman: 1 catch for 7 yards, 1 TD

DEFENSE

Cowboys

Sacks

Randy White (2.0)

Steelers

Sacks

Steve Furness (2.0), L.C. Greenwood (4.0) and Dwight White (1.0)

Interceptions

Glen Edwards: 1 for 35 yards
J.T. Thomas: 1 for 35 yards
Mike Wagner: 1 for 19 yards

KICK RETURNS

Cowboys

Kickoffs

Preston Pearson: 4 for 48 yards, 12.0 avg.

Punts

Golden Richards: 1 for 5 yards, 5.0 avg.

Steelers

Kickoffs

Mel Blount: 3 for 64 yards, 21.3 avg.
Mike Collier: 1 for 25 yards, 25.0 avg.

Punts

Dave Brown: 3 for 14 yards, 4.7 avg.
Glen Edwards: 2 for 17 yards, 8.5 avg.

KICKING and PUNTING

Cowboys

Kicking

Toni Fritsch: 2-for-2 PAT, 1-for-1 FG

Punting

Mitch Hoopes: 6 for 245 yards, 40.8 avg.

Steelers

Kicking

Roy Gerela: 1-for-2 PAT, 2-for-4 FG

Punting

Bobby Walden: 4 for 159 yards, 39.8 avg.

1975 NFL Standings

AFC					
East	W	L	T	PF	PA
Baltimore Colts	10	4	0	395	269
Miami Dolphins	10	4	0	357	222
Buffalo Bills	8	6	0	420	355
New England Patriots	3	11	0	258	358
New York Jets	3	11	0	258	433
Central	W	L	T	PF	PA
Pittsburgh Steelers	12	2	0	373	162
Cincinnati Bengals	11	3	0	340	246
Houston Oilers	10	4	0	293	226
Cleveland Browns	3	11	0	218	372
West	W	L	T	PF	PA
Oakland Raiders	11	3	0	375	255
Denver Broncos	6	8	0	254	307
Kansas City Chiefs	5	9	0	282	341
San Diego Chargers	2	12	0	189	345

NFC					
East	W	L	T	PF	PA
St. Louis Cardinals	11	3	0	356	276
Dallas Cowboys	10	4	0	350	268
Washington Redskins	8	6	0	325	276
New York Giants	5	9	0	216	306
Philadelphia Eagles	4	10	0	225	302
Central	W	L	T	PF	PA
Minnesota Vikings	12	2	0	377	180
Detroit Lions	7	7	0	245	262
Chicago Bears	4	10	0	191	379
Green Bay Packers	4	10	0	226	285
West	W	L	T	PF	PA
Los Angeles Rams	12	2	0	312	135
San Francisco 49ers	5	9	0	255	286
Atlanta Falcons	4	10	0	240	289
New Orleans Saints	2	12	0	165	360

Steelers 1975 Draft Picks

Round 1 (26): Dave Brown, DB, Michigan
Round 2 (51): Bob Barber, DE, Grambling State
Round 3 (78): Walter White, TE, Maryland
Round 4 (104): Harold Evans, LB, Houston
Round 5 (130): Brent Sexton, DB, Elon
Round 6 (156): Marvin Crenshaw, T, Nebraska

Round 8 (182): Wayne Mattingly, T, Colorado
Round 8 (190): Tom Kropp, LB, Kearney State
Round 8 (208): Al Humphrey, DE, Tulsa
Round 9 (222): Eugene Clark, G, UCLA
Round 9 (234): Bruce Reimer, RB, North Dakota State
Round 10 (247): Kirt Heyer, DT, Kearney State
Round 10 (260): Archie Gray, WR, Wyoming
Round 11 (286): Randy Little, TE, West Liberty
Round 12 (312): Greg Murphy, DE, Penn State
Round 13 (337): Bob Gaddis, WR, Mississippi Valley State
Round 14 (364): Mike Collier, RB, Morgan State
Round 15 (371): James Thatcher, WR, Langston
Round 15 (390): Marty Smith, DT, Louisville
Round 16 (415): Miller Bassler, TE, Houston
Round 17 (442): Stan Hegener, G, Nebraska

1978

Season Review

The Steelers lost one game to the Oilers, they lost one game to the Rams, and they spent the rest of the season demonstrating football excellence to the NFL.

The Steel Curtain defense allowed the fewest points in the league. If Joe Greene was dropping off a bit because of age, L.C. Greenwood, Jack Ham, Jack Lambert and Mel Blount still played peerless defense.

The offense began with a sturdy line and had burly Franco Harris for its overland routes.

Quarterback Terry Bradshaw silenced his critics from the past by leading the NFL in touchdown passes, aided in this feat by superb wide receivers Lynn Swann and John Stallworth.

The dynastic mentality of the Steelers kept them on top even while trading off Jim Clack, Ernie Holmes, Glen Edwards and Frank Lewis and losing Bobby Walden to retirement and J.T. Thomas to a blood disorder.

Week 1

	Pittsburgh Steelers		Sept. 3 Rich Stadium Orchard Park, NY			Buffalo Bills
	1Q	2Q	3Q	4Q	Total	
Steelers	0	14	0	14	28	
Bills	0	0	0	17	17	

ORCHARD PARK, N.Y. (AP) — John Stallworth, the unsung hero of Pittsburgh's acrobatic corps of wide receivers, basked in the limelight Sunday following the Steelers' 28-17 victory over the Buffalo Bills in their NFL opener.

"We were putting two guys on the same side," Stallworth said after a sparkling 28-yard touchdown grab and two other long receptions of Terry Bradshaw passes. "They could only put three guys on two and I don't think that is enough. They have a lot of respect for Lynn (Swann), and he deserves it. Now they might have to respect both of us."

Stallworth, Swann and tight end Bennie Cunningham loosened Buffalo's defensive line to spring Steelers' running backs Franco Harris and Sidney Thornton for short-yardage scores which helped the Steelers to a 21-0 lead before the Bills got back on track.

However, 37-year-old quarterback Bill Munson, who came to Buffalo in the last two weeks of training camp, nearly pulled out the game by passing for two touchdowns and driving the Bills within range of Tom Dempsey's 32-yard field goal.

Bills' coach Chuck Knox said he still considers Joe Ferguson, who had a miserable afternoon, the team's No. 1 signal-caller.

"Ferguson has been practicing well and he's got a heck of an arm, but we haven't had a chance to get our timing down," Knox said. "Munson's the kind of guy you rally around because he's been there. He's a veteran."

Ferguson was injured three weeks ago during a preseason game and had not made a game appearance since then.

Munson gobbled up 168 yards, completing 10 of 16 passes — all in the fourth quarter.

He threw a 22-yard scoring strike to ex-Steeler Frank Lewis, set up Dempsey's field goal and capped the scoring with a three-yard toss to Reuben Grant.

Pacing

Bradshaw threw a 28-yard pass to Stallworth and a 15-yard aerial to Theo Bell — the first and last of the Steelers four touchdowns.

Harris slammed in from 1-yard out as the Steelers took a 14-0 halftime lead and Thorton bulled for a score from the 2-yard line early in the fourth period.

Cunningham caught a pair of twin 27-yard passes to set up the rushing touchdowns.

Harris, who entered the game needing 29 yards to surpass the 6,323 yard career rushing total of Denver's Floyd Little, registered 96 for the game, but it was the dazzling play of Stallworth that put the glitter in Pittsburgh's offense.

The Steelers marched 65 yards for their first score after a pass from Ferguson, who hit only three passes for 20 yards in the game, bounced off Gant's hands to Pittsburgh safety Tony Dungy.

Stallworth went up like a basketball forward for A Bradshaw aerial, a 38-yard grab which covered more than half the distance in the drive which gave the Steelers their two-touchdown edge at intermission.

		SCORING	PIT	BUF
2nd	Steelers	John Stallworth 28 yard pass from Terry Bradshaw (Roy Gerela kick)	7	0
	Steelers	Franco Harris 1 yard rush (Roy Gerela kick)	14	0
4th	Steelers	Sidney Thornton 2 yard rush (Roy Gerela kick)	21	0
	Bills	Frank Lewis 22 yard pass from Bill Munson (Tom Dempsey kick)	21	7
	Bills	Tom Dempsey 32 yard field goal	21	10

	Steelers	Theo Bell 15 yard pass from Terry Bradshaw (Roy Gerela kick)	28	10
	Bills	Reuben Gant 3 yard pass from Bill Munson (Tom Dempsey kick)	28	17

	TEAM STATS	
	PIT	BUF
First downs	21	16
Rush-Yards-TD	43-142-2	29-100-0
Comp-Att-Yards-TD-INT	14-19-217-2-1	13-26-191-2-1
Sacked-Yards	0-0	3-27
Net pass yards	217	164
Total yards	359	264
Fumbles-Lost	0-0	0-0
Turnovers	1	1
Penalties-Yards	5-54	9-62

PASSING, RUSHING and RECEIVING

Steelers

Passing

Terry Bradshaw: 14-of-19, 217 yards, 2 TD, 1 INT

Rushing

Franco Harris: 27 carries for 96 yards, 1 TD
Terry Bradshaw: 3 carries for -6 yards
Sidney Thornton: 7 carries for 33 yards, 1 TD
Rocky Bleier: 6 carries for 19 yards

Receiving

Franco Harris: 3 catches for 32 yards
John Stallworth: 3 catches for 86 yards, 1 TD

Bennie Cunningham: 3 catches for 70 yards
Rocky Bleier: 1 catch for 3 yards
Theo Bell: 1 catch for 15 yards, 1 TD
Lynn Swann: 3 catches for 11 yards

Bills

Passing

Bill Munson: 10-of-16, 171 yards, 2 TD, 0 INT
Joe Ferguson: 3-of-10, 20 yards, 0 TD, 1 INT

Rushing

Terry Miller: 20 carries for 60 yards
Dennis D. Johnson: 2 carries for 31 yards
Jim Braxton: 7 carries for 9 yards

Receiving

Terry Miller: 6 catches for 97 yards
Frank Lewis: 2 catches for 46 yards, 1 TD
Dennis D. Johnson: 1 catch for 9 yards
Reuben Gant: 3 catches for 31 yards, 1 TD
Jim Braxton: 1 catch for 8 yards

DEFENSE

Steelers

Interceptions

Tony Dungy: 1 for 0 yards

Bills

Interceptions

Tony Greene: 1 for 0 yards

KICK RETURNS

Steelers

Kickoffs

Larry Anderson: 3 for 49 yards, 16.3 avg.
Gerry Mullins: 1 for 0 yards, 0.0 avg.

Punts

Theo Bell: 4 for 26 yards, 6.5 avg.
Randy Reutershan: 1 for 13 yards, 13.0 avg.

Bills

Kickoffs

Keith Moody: 4 for 109 yards, 27.3 avg.
Leonard Willis: 1 for 0 yards, 0.0 avg.

Punts

Curtis Brown: 1 for 0 yards, 0.0 avg.
Keith Moody: 1 for -10 yards, -10.0 avg.

KICKING and PUNTING

Steelers

Kicking

Roy Gerela: 4-for-4 PAT, 0-for-1 FG

Punting

Craig Colquitt: 4 for 156 yards, 39.0 avg.

Bills

Kicking

Tom Dempsey: 2-for-2 PAT, 1-for-1 FG

Punting

Rusty Jackson: 6 for 258 yards, 43.0 avg.

Week 2

	Sept. 10 Three Rivers Stadium Pittsburgh, PA	
Seattle Seahawks		Pittsburgh Steelers
1Q	2Q	3Q	4Q	Total

Seahawks	0	7	3	0	10
Steelers	0	14	0	7	21

Associated Press

PITTSBURGH — The Pittsburgh Steelers, hit hard by high humidity and the young Seattle Seahawks, sweated out a 21-10 victory Sunday in a National Football League game.

"It's too hot. It's too hot to play football," said Steeler linebacker Jack Lambert, whose face dripped after a game in which he made five tackles, seven assists, a pass interception and a fumble recovery.

"I can't wait until it gets to be about 10 degrees so we can start running again," Lambert added.

Hot or not, the third-year Seahawks kept it close with a surprisingly tough defense that was hurt mainly by Steeler quarterback Terry Bradshaw, who shook off an early hand injury and threw for a pair of touchdowns.

"We scared them last year. But this year we were more prepared to beat them," said Seattle quarterback Jim Zorn, recalling a game here last season in which the Steelers broke a 13-13 tie in the final quarter to beat the Seahawks 30-20.

"Seattle's offense did a heck of a job, and defensively they showed what we thought was improvement," said Steeler Coach Chuck Noll. "There were parts of the game where we were physically outplayed — outhit."

During one third-quarter timeout, the Steeler defenders nearly all sat on their helmets. The Seahawks stood.

"I think we were in better shape today. They seemed to be a little out of shape," said Zorn.

Regardless of how much the Steelers puffed, Bradshaw passed them to victory.

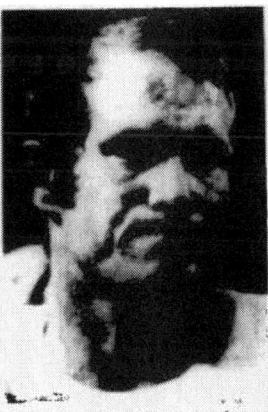

"We made some progress today, but we made some mistakes, too," said Bradshaw. "We did some things you've got to eliminate if you're going to be a championship football team, which we're not yet."

After bruising his throwing hand against a Seattle helmet in the first period, Bradshaw stayed in the game and wound up with 17 completions in 33 attempts for 213 yards, including two touchdown passes.

With Pittsburgh leading by 14-10 early in the final period, Bradshaw also apparently talked Noll into a play that led to another touchdown.

Pittsburgh faced fourth-and-goal at the Seattle 1. Noll sent in placekicker Roy Gerela, but Bradshaw called time and apparently helped sell Noll on a play that led to a 1-yard touchdown by Franco Harris that secured the Steelers' second win in as many games.

After a scoreless first period, Bradshaw threw two touchdown passes in the second quarter. They included a 4-yarder to Lynn Swann and a 20-yarder to running back Sid Thornton.

Seattle (0-2) drove 80 yards for a second-quarter touchdown on a 1-yard run by David Sims. The only Seahawk scoring after that came on Efren Herrera's 20-yard field goal in the third period.

TERRY BRADSHAW
. . . two TD passes.

		SCORING	SEA	PIT
2nd	Steelers	Lynn Swann 4 yard pass from Terry Bradshaw (Roy Gerela kick)	0	7
	Steelers	Sidney Thornton 20 yard pass from Terry Bradshaw (Roy Gerela kick)	0	14
	Seahawks	David Sims 1 yard rush (Efren Herrera kick)	7	14
3rd	Seahawks	Efren Herrera 20 yard field goal	10	14
4th	Steelers	Franco Harris 1 yard rush (Roy Gerela kick)	10	21

	TEAM STATS	
	SEA	**PIT**
First downs	18	26
Rush-Yards-TD	28-93-1	40-151-1
Comp-Att-Yards-TD-INT	11-22-174-0-1	17-33-213-2-0
Sacked-Yards	4-20	2-28
Net pass yards	154	185
Total yards	247	336
Fumbles-Lost	2-2	2-1
Turnovers	3	1
Penalties-Yards	7-52	8-65

PASSING, RUSHING and RECEIVING

Seahawks

Passing

Jim Zorn: 11-of-22, 174 yards, 0 TD, 1 INT

Rushing

Jim Zorn: 1 carry for 1 yard
Al Hunter: 10 carries for 37 yards
David Sims: 9 carries for 20 yards, 1 TD
Don Testerman: 4 carries for 29 yards
Rufus Crawford: 4 carries for 6 yards

Receiving

Steve Largent: 4 catches for 88 yards
Al Hunter: 1 catch for 13 yards
Ron Howard: 1 catch for 42 yards
David Sims: 3 catches for 18 yards

Rufus Crawford: 1 catch for 5 yards
Steve Raible: 1 catch for 8 yards

Steelers

Passing

Terry Bradshaw: 17-of-33, 213 yards, 2 TD, 0 INT

Rushing

Terry Bradshaw: 3 carries for 6 yards
Rocky Bleier: 12 carries for 48 yards
Franco Harris: 18 carries for 64 yards, 1 TD
Sidney Thornton: 5 carries for 13 yards
Rick Moser: 2 carries for 20 yards

Receiving

Rocky Bleier: 2 catches for 30 yards
Franco Harris: 1 catch for 4 yards
Lynn Swann: 6 catches for 65 yards, 1 TD
Bennie Cunningham: 4 catches for 45 yards
John Stallworth: 2 catches for 38 yards
Sidney Thornton: 1 catch for 20 yards, 1 TD
Randy Grossman: 1 catch for 11 yards

DEFENSE

Steelers

Interceptions

Jack Lambert: 1 for 11 yards

KICK RETURNS

Seahawks

Kickoffs

Rufus Crawford: 2 for 39 yards, 19.5 avg.

Punts

John Harris: 3 for 47 yards, 15.7 avg.

Steelers

Kickoffs

Alvin Maxson: 2 for 33 yards, 16.5 avg.

Punts

Randy Reutershan: 2 for 25 yards, 12.5 avg.
Nat Terry: 1 for 8 yards, 8.0 avg.

KICKING and PUNTING

Seahawks

Kicking

Efren Herrera: 1-for-1 PAT, 1-for-2 FG

Punting

Herman Weaver: 3 for 122 yards, 40.7 avg.

Steelers

Kicking

Roy Gerela: 3-for-3 PAT, 0-for-2 FG

Punting

Craig Colquitt: 3 for 125 yards, 41.7 avg.

Week 3

Sept. 17
Riverfront Stadium
Cincinnati, OH

Pittsburgh Steelers vs **Cincinnati Bengals**

	1Q	2Q	3Q	4Q	Total
Steelers	14	7	7	0	28
Bengals	0	3	0	0	3

CINCINNATI (AP) — "Historically speaking," said Pittsburgh Steelers' quarterback Terry Bradshaw, "we've been hot and cold against the '34' defense."

Sunday was one of those hot days.

"We were smoking," said Bradshaw after the Steelers mauled the winless Cincinnati Bengals for 447 yards for a 28-3 National Football League victory to stay unbeaten in three games this season.

The 25-point spread represented the worst beating the Steelers have inflicted on the Bengals since the series began in 1970. Pittsburgh leads the rivalry 12-5, including seven victories in the last eight games.

While Bradshaw befuddled the Bengals' green secondary, hitting 14 of 19 passes for two touchdowns and 242 yards, the Steelers' running game was having a field day, adding 212 yards.

"If you can run the ball like that, you can do anything," said Bradshaw, off to the best start of his career. "It's a quarterback's dream. I just kept mixing it up."

Exploiting every weakness, the Steelers struck swiftly, scoring twice in the first six minutes on runs by Rocky Bleier and Franco Harris. By halftime, Pittsburgh had a 21-3 lead and a 314-97 edge in total yards.

The knockout punch came from 250-pound Benny Cunningham, who is becoming one of the heavyweight tight ends in the NFL.

"In the past I've thrown more to the wide receivers, but Benny is a big target. He's a big hoss," said Bradshaw, the Bayou Bomber who led the Steelers to Super Bowl crowns in 1974 and 1975.

Cunningham caught four passes for 107 yards, including a third-and 12 reception that accounted for 48 yards. Two plays later Bradshaw hit Cunningham on a 28-yard pass play that produced Pittsburgh's third touchdown.

"The two quick scores put 'em in shock, but Cunningham's catches had to hurt 'em," said Bradshaw, who repeatedly threw in the area of first-year cornerback Louis Breeden.

"We wanted to do something on the right side," said Steelers' coach Chuck Noll. "We felt we wanted to see what they could do."

Bradshaw said it was case of going with the odds.

"If I'm going to pick on anyone, it's not going to be Ken Riley (the Bengals' all-time interception leader) I've got 90 career interceptions and he's got about 10 of them."

Swann said the NFL's new "chucking" rule, which cuts down on shoving matches between receivers and defensive backs, has been a boon to the passing game.

"Teams are now more confident in their passing game," said Swann, who had five catches for 78 yards, including a 12-yard TD reception from Bradshaw in the third quarter that capped the scoring.

"It gets people in the pass patterns quicker and you can rid of the ball quicker," said Bradshaw, who has completed 45 of 71 passes after three games for a sizzling .635 completion percentage.

Cincinnati, limited to 56 yards rushing, penetrated Pittsburgh's 30 yard line just twice. Chris Bahr kicked a 33-yard field goal in the second quarter for Cincinnati's only score.

		SCORING	PIT	CIN
1st	Steelers	Rocky Bleier 5 yard rush (Roy Gerela kick)	7	0
	Steelers	Franco Harris 15 yard rush (Roy Gerela kick)	14	0
2nd	Bengals	Chris Bahr 33 yard field goal	14	3
	Steelers	Bennie Cunningham 26 yard pass from Terry Bradshaw (Roy Gerela kick)	21	3
3rd	Steelers	Lynn Swann 12 yard pass from Terry Bradshaw (Roy Gerela kick)	28	3

	TEAM STATS	
	PIT	CIN
First downs	26	9

Rush-Yards-TD	49-212-2	19-56-0
Comp-Att-Yards-TD-INT	14-20-242-2-1	17-36-123-0-2
Sacked-Yards	1-7	0-0
Net pass yards	235	123
Total yards	447	179
Fumbles-Lost	3-3	1-0
Turnovers	4	2
Penalties-Yards	6-56	7-99

PASSING, RUSHING and RECEIVING

Steelers

Passing

Terry Bradshaw: 14-of-19, 242 yards, 2 TD, 1 INT
Mike Kruczek: 0-of-1, 0 yards

Rushing

Terry Bradshaw: 1 carry for 10 yards
Rocky Bleier: 12 carries for 75 yards, 1 TD
Franco Harris: 16 carries for 73 yards, 1 TD
Sidney Thornton: 15 carries for 45 yards
Rick Moser: 2 carries for 7 yards
Alvin Maxson: 2 carries for 5 yards
Mike Kruczek: 1 carry for -3 yards

Receiving

Bennie Cunningham: 4 catches for 107 yards, 1 TD
Rocky Bleier: 1 catch for 8 yards
Lynn Swann: 5 catches for 78 yards, 1 TD
Franco Harris: 1 catch for 4 yards
John Stallworth: 2 catches for 27 yards
Randy Grossman: 1 catch for 18 yards

Bengals

Passing

John Reaves: 16-of-32, 114 yards, 0 TD, 2 INT
Rob Hertel: 1-of-4, 9 yards

Rushing

John Reaves: 1 carry for 10 yards
Pete Johnson: 9 carries for 27 yards
Archie Griffin: 6 carries for 18 yards
Isaac Curtis: 1 carry for 1 yard
Deacon Turner: 2 carries for 0 yards
Rob Hertel: 1 carry for 0 yards

Receiving

Pete Johnson: 5 catches for 31 yards
Archie Griffin: 6 catches for 28 yards
Dennis Law: 1 catch for 19 yards
Billy Brooks: 1 catch for 17 yards
Isaac Curtis: 1 catch for 12 yards
Jim Corbett: 1 catch for 9 yards
Deacon Turner: 2 catches for 7 yards

DEFENSE

Steelers

Interceptions

Tony Dungy: 1 for 17 yards
Ron Johnson: 1 for 0 yards

Bengals

Interceptions

Reggie Williams: 1 for 11 yards

KICK RETURNS

Steelers

Kickoffs

Larry Anderson: 2 for 55 yards, 27.5 avg.

Punts

Randy Reutershan: 4 for 11 yards, 2.8 avg.
Nat Terry: 5 for 62 yards, 12.4 avg.

Bengals

Kickoffs

Ray Griffin: 4 for 106 yards, 26.5 avg.

Punts

Don Bass: 1 for -3 yards, -3.0 avg.

KICKING and PUNTING

Steelers

Kicking

Roy Gerela: 4-for-4 PAT, 0-for-1 FG

Punting

Craig Colquitt: 4 for 175 yards, 43.8 avg.

Bengals

Kicking

Chris Bahr: 1-for-2 FG

Punting

Pat McInally: 10 for 424 yards, 42.4 avg.

Week 4

	Sept. 24 Three Rivers Stadium Pittsburgh, PA					
Cleveland Browns						**Pittsburgh Steelers**
	1Q	2Q	3Q	4Q	OT	Total
Browns	0	6	3	0	0	9
Steelers	3	0	0	6	6	15

PITTSBURGH (AP) — The Pittsburgh Steelers' 15-9 victory over the Cleveland Browns Sunday was a story of sudden death, a slippery football, and a circus play that resulted in the winning touchdown pass by Terry Bradshaw.

"It was one of those plays me and the boys put together in a hayfield one day," Bradshaw said with a grin after Pittsburgh climbed ahead of Cleveland into sole possession into first place in the American Conference Central Division.

"It's called high school right," kidded Steeler Coach Chuck Noll.

"We just put it in. It's called Fake 84 Reverse Gadget Pass," said Steeler tight end Bennie Cunningham, who was on the receiving end of the pass that won the game for the Steelers, 3:43 into sudden death.

Bradshaw called the play himself with the Steelers facing a second-and-nine at the Cleveland 37-yard line on the opening series of sudden death.

While trying for a grip, Bradshaw had to hesitate. That gave Cleveland safety Tom Darden, who had two earlier interceptions, a chance to nearly overtake Cunningham near the goal line.

But Bradshaw lobbed the ball on target. Cunningham made the grab and stepped into the end zone to end the game.

"They couldn't beat us man-to-man," Darden grumbled after the game. Cleveland quarterback Brian Sipe, who had two touchdown passes nullified by penalties in regulation play, took a different view.

"It's a great play. That's what you design those things to do," said Sipe.

"It was a very well executed play," said Browns Coach Sam Rutigliano. "I'm proud of our 45 players and I'm proud of my coaches."

Browns Protest

On the opening sudden death kickoff, the Browns argued in vain that Steeler rookie Larry Anderson had lost the fumble and that it had been recovered at the Pittsburgh 21-yard line by Ricky Feacher.

"He fumbled and I got it," said Feacher. "But they gave it to them and that was the turning point."

"The game was stolen from us," protested Darden. "Feacher definitely fell on it, and when you get a call like that it takes a lot of emotionalism and momentum out of the team."

Cleveland's Don Cockroft and Pittsburgh's Roy Gerela each kicked three field goals in regulation play. Gerela's 36-yard boot with 2:35 left in the last quarter produced the 9-9 tie at the end of regulation time.

Sipe had his first pass of

the game intercepted by Steeler safety Don Shell at the Browns' 36-yard line, setting up a 19-yard field goal by Gerela.

The Browns countered with field goals of 43 and 30 yards by Cockroft in the final seven minutes of the second quarter.

Cockroft's second boot came after Steeler rookie Larry Anderson fumbled a kickoff return and Cleveland's Ron Bolton returned it 13 yards to the Pittsburgh 14-yard line.

After leading 6-3 at halftime, the Browns ran it to 9-3 in the third quarter on a 41-yard field goal by Cockroft, set up by a pass interference penalty.

On the opening play of the final quarter, Gerela kicked a 33-yard field goal after a Steeler drive that featured five straight carries by Franco Harris for 40 yards.

With 2:35 left in the game, Gerela kicked his tying field goal, a 36-yarder that came after Pittsburgh marched from its own 28-yard line to the Browns' 15.

In the coin flip to begin the sudden-death period, Rucker called heads for Cleveland. "You should have called tails," Steeler co-captain Joe Greene said as the coin was in the air.

Greene was right. The Steelers chose to receive and eventually won out.

		SCORING	CLE	PIT
1st	Steelers	Roy Gerela 19 yard field goal	0	3
2nd	Browns	Don Cockroft 43 yard field goal	3	3
	Browns	Don Cockroft 30 yard field goal	6	3
3rd	Browns	Don Cockroft 41 yard field goal	9	3
4th	Steelers	Roy Gerela 33 yard field goal	9	6

	Steelers	Roy Gerela 36 yard field goal	9	9
OT	Steelers	Bennie Cunningham 37 yard pass from Terry Bradshaw	9	15

	TEAM STATS	
	CLE	PIT
First downs	19	18
Rush-Yards-TD	32-97-0	37-139-0
Comp-Att-Yards-TD-INT	14-32-139-0-2	14-32-208-1-2
Sacked-Yards	5-37	1-8
Net pass yards	102	200
Total yards	199	339
Fumbles-Lost	1-0	1-1
Turnovers	2	3
Penalties-Yards	8-68	11-119

PASSING, RUSHING and RECEIVING

Browns

Passing

Brian Sipe: 14-of-32, 139 yards, 0 TD, 2 INT

Rushing

Brian Sipe: 3 carries for 9 yards
Mike Pruitt: 14 carries for 42 yards
Ozzie Newsome: 2 carries for 24 yards
Reggie Rucker: 1 carry for 5 yards
Cleo Miller: 6 carries for 17 yards
Larry Collins: 6 carries for 0 yards

Receiving

Dave Logan: 3 catches for 46 yards
Mike Pruitt: 4 catches for 1 yard
Ozzie Newsome: 2 catches for 19 yards
Reggie Rucker: 2 catches for 37 yards
Cleo Miller: 1 catch for 12 yards
Tom Sullivan: 1 catch for 20 yards
Larry Collins: 1 catch for 4 yards

Steelers

Passing

Terry Bradshaw: 14-of-32, 208 yards, 1 TD, 2 INT

Rushing

Terry Bradshaw: 2 carries for 27 yards
Franco Harris: 26 carries for 84 yards
Rocky Bleier: 9 carries for 28 yards

Receiving

Franco Harris: 3 catches for 9 yards
Lynn Swann: 6 catches for 83 yards
Bennie Cunningham: 2 catches for 69 yards, 1 TD
John Stallworth: 2 catches for 40 yards
Rocky Bleier: 1 catch for 7 yards

DEFENSE

Browns

Interceptions

Thom Darden: 2 for 31 yards

Steelers

Interceptions

Tony Dungy: 1 for 65 yards
Donnie Shell: 1 for 1 yard

KICK RETURNS

Browns

Kickoffs

Larry Collins: 2 for 67 yards, 33.5 avg.
Tom Sullivan: 1 for 24 yards, 24.0 avg.

Punts

Keith Wright: 2 for 2 yards, 1.0 avg.

Steelers

Kickoffs

Larry Anderson: 5 for 116 yards, 23.2 avg.

Punts

Randy Reutershan: 5 for 24 yards, 4.8 avg.
Nat Terry: 1 for 10 yards, 10.0 avg.

KICKING and PUNTING

Browns

Kicking

Don Cockroft: 3-for-4 FG

Punting

Johnny Evans: 6 for 250 yards, 41.7 avg.

Steelers

Kicking

Roy Gerela: 3-for-4 FG

Punting

Craig Colquitt: 6 for 214 yards, 35.7 avg.

Week 5

	1Q	2Q	3Q	4Q	Total
Pittsburgh Steelers					
New York Jets					

Oct. 1
Shea Stadium
New York, NY

Steelers	7	7	14	0	28
Jets	0	10	7	0	17

NEW YORK (AP) — Terry Bradshaw passed for three touchdowns, two to Lynn Swann, and the unbeaten Pittsburgh Steelers staged a pair of goal line stands to beat the New York Jets 28-17 Sunday in the National Football League.

Bradshaw completed 17 of 25 passes for 189 yards before suffering a bruised right knee in the closing minutes. Bradshaw, who was to be x-rayed today, said he'll be back for Sunday's home game against Atlanta.

He hit Swann on a 10-yard scoring pass in the first period, found John Stallworth on a 14-yarder to put Pittsburgh ahead for good in the second quarter, then connected with Swann for 26 yards and a TD early in the third period.

Pittsburgh's other TD came on Sidney Thornton's 1-yard plunge midway in the third period. With the victory, the Steelers, 5-0, remained atop the American Conference's Central Division.

The Jets, 2-3 with Matt Robinson at quarterback in place of injured Richard Todd, scored on a runs of 11 yards by Bruce Harper in the second period and two yards by Kevin Long in the third and Pat Leahy's 47-yard field goal on the last play of the halftime.

But twice the Jets had first downs inside the Pittsburgh 10-yard line, only to be stopped cold. In the first period, with a fourth-and-goal at the one, safety Donnie Shell sacked Robinson for a 9-yard loss. And in the fourth quarter linebacker Loren Toews dropped Robinson for another nine yards on fourth-and-goal at the eight.

```
Pittsburgh        7  7 14  7—28
NY Jets           0 10  7  0—17
Pitt—Swann 10 pass from Bradshaw
  (Gerela kick)
NYJ—Harper 11 run (Leahy kick)
Pitt—Stallworth 14 pass from Bradshaw
  (Gerela kick)
NYJ—FG Leahy 47
Pitt—Swann 26 pass from Bradshaw
  (Gerela kick)
Pitt—Thornton 1 run (Gerela kick)
NYJ—Long 2 run (Leahy kick)
A—52,058.
```

		SCORING	PIT	NYJ
1st	Steelers	Lynn Swann 10 yard pass from Terry Bradshaw (Roy Gerela kick)	7	0
2nd	Jets	Bruce Harper 11 yard rush (Pat Leahy kick)	7	7
	Steelers	John Stallworth 14 yard pass from Terry Bradshaw (Roy Gerela kick)	14	7

	Jets	Pat Leahy 47 yard field goal	14	10
3rd	Steelers	Lynn Swann 26 yard pass from Terry Bradshaw (Roy Gerela kick)	21	10
	Steelers	Sidney Thornton 1 yard rush (Roy Gerela kick)	28	10
	Jets	Kevin Long 2 yard rush (Pat Leahy kick)	28	17

	TEAM STATS	
	PIT	NYJ
First downs	20	18
Rush-Yards-TD	39-138-1	36-155-2
Comp-Att-Yards-TD-INT	17-26-189-3-1	9-23-192-0-1
Sacked-Yards	0-0	5-50
Net pass yards	189	142
Total yards	327	297
Fumbles-Lost	1-1	0-0
Turnovers	2	1
Penalties-Yards	2-7	4-17

PASSING, RUSHING and RECEIVING

Steelers

Passing

Terry Bradshaw: 17-of-25, 189 yards, 3 TD, 1 INT
Franco Harris: 0-of-1, 0 yards

Rushing

Terry Bradshaw: 1 carry for 0 yards
Franco Harris: 20 carries for 67 yards
Rocky Bleier: 6 carries for 22 yards
Sidney Thornton: 8 carries for 29 yards, 1 TD

Rick Moser: 3 carries for 14 yards
Alvin Maxson: 1 carry for 6 yards

Receiving

Lynn Swann: 7 catches for 100 yards, 2 TD
Franco Harris: 1 catch for 7 yards
John Stallworth: 4 catches for 43 yards, 1 TD
Rocky Bleier: 2 catches for 18 yards
Sidney Thornton: 1 catch for 4 yards
Jim Smith: 1 catch for 14 yards
Bennie Cunningham: 1 catch for 2 yards

Jets

Passing

Matt Robinson: 9-of-22, 192 yards, 0 TD, 1 INT
Scott Dierking: 0-of-1, 0 yards

Rushing

Matt Robinson: 4 carries for 33 yards
Wesley Walker: 1 carry for -3 yards
Scott Dierking: 9 carries for 46 yards
Kevin Long: 10 carries for 41 yards, 1 TD
Bruce Harper: 5 carries for 26 yards, 1 TD
Clark Gaines: 7 carries for 12 yards

Receiving

Wesley Walker: 2 catches for 93 yards
Scott Dierking: 3 catches for 27 yards
Kevin Long: 1 catch for 13 yards
Derrick Gaffney: 2 catches for 49 yards
Clark Gaines: 1 catch for 10 yards

DEFENSE

Steelers

Interceptions

Donnie Shell: 1 for 20 yards

Jets

Interceptions

Ed Taylor: 1 for 0 yards

KICK RETURNS

Steelers

Kickoffs

Larry Anderson: 3 for 73 yards, 24.3 avg.

Punts

Randy Reutershan: 4 for 48 yards, 12.0 avg.

Jets

Kickoffs

Bruce Harper: 3 for 62 yards, 20.7 avg.

Punts

Bruce Harper: 1 for 0 yards, 0.0 avg.

KICKING and PUNTING

Steelers

Kicking

Roy Gerela: 4-for-4 PAT

Punting

Craig Colquitt: 2 for 86 yards, 43.0 avg.

Jets

Kicking

Pat Leahy: 2-for-2 PAT, 1-for-1 FG

Punting

Chuck Ramsey: 4 for 167 yards, 41.8 avg.

Week 6

Oct. 8
Three Rivers Stadium
Pittsburgh, PA

Atlanta Falcons | Pittsburgh Steelers

	1Q	2Q	3Q	4Q	Total
Falcons	0	0	0	7	7
Steelers	3	14	7	7	31

By RICH EMERT
TIMES Sports Staff

PITTSBURGH — What do Terry Bradshaw and the Pittsburgh Steelers, and Gen. William Sherman and the Union army have in common?

The answer — they both destroyed Atlanta.

In case you're not a history buff, Gen. Sherman burned Atlanta to the ground during the Civil War. Bradshaw and the Steelers burned the Atlanta Falcons on the ground in NFL warfare yesterday afternoon at chilly Three Rivers Stadium.

Pittsburgh got its running attack geared up for the Falcons and kept its undefeated record (6-0) intact with an easy 31-7 victory over

Beaver County Times
Sports

Atlanta, now 2-4, before 48,202 fans.

Just to show you how much the Steelers were in control, by the end of the third quarter Bradshaw and Lynn Swann were smiling and waving to fans in the stands.

Meanwhile, Franco Harris was rushing for 104 yards, the 20th time he's topped the 100-yard mark. He

averaged 5.2 yards a carry as the Steelers displayed their offensive might against what was touted to be a good Atlanta defense.

The only dark cloud in what was an otherwise bright day for Pittsburgh was the injury to tight end Bennie Cunningham. (See related story) Cunningham will be out at least five to six weeks with a partial tear of the ligaments in his left knee.

"It was a big day for us against a very physical team, except for the injury to Bennie," Steeler head coach Chuck Noll said. "I was most pleased with the way we methodically moved the ball on the ground. The offensive line did an outstanding job in an extremely hard hitting game."

Pittsburgh collected 181 yards on the ground, and out of its 61 offensive plays, 44 were rushes.

"We ran the hell out of 18 and 19 straight," Rocky Bleier said in playbook lingo. "Atlanta was really pursuing, and Franco was just cutting it back inside for big yardage."

Eighteen and 19 straight are Harris' bread-and-butter plays. Franco takes off like he's running a sweep, then cuts inside anytime he wants to.

But Harris wasn't about to take all the glory, and credited the Steeler offensive line.

"When our linemen make up their minds they can do anything," Harris pointed out. "They can keep everybody off Terry, and they can open up the ground game like they did today.

"Webby (center Mike Webster) did a dynamite job on the guy they had over center. But we had the right attitude today to run the football. All week Webby and the guys talked about running the football, and at the start of the game Webby came in the huddle and said, 'let's go 87 yards for the score.' When you got that attitude it's easy to run."

Pittsburgh didn't go 87 yards in that first drive, it went 85 in 18 plays with Roy Gerela kicking a 21-yard field goal. Of those 18 plays, 13 were running attempts.

"That was the thing that really got us started, that first long drive," offensive tackle Jon Kolb explained. "Then we came back a series later and went 80 yards in nine plays for a touchdown and at that point I think we were confident we could do anything we wanted to on offense.

"We usually come into a game and just take what the other team gives us, but today we came in with the idea we were going to run the football and that's exactly what we did. We took what we wanted today."

It wasn't like the Steelers caught the Falcons by surprise either. In fact, Atlanta knew what the Steelers were going to do.

"Pittsburgh is one of the easiest teams in the league to prepare for," Atlanta safety Frank Reed said. "They always do the same thing — they just line up and come at you. They feel so good about what they do they don't have to change from week to week."

Bradshaw hasn't been changing much from week to week and was almost letter perfect again yesterday. He hit on 13 of 18 passes for 231 yards, including an 11-yard scoring strike to John Stallworth, and ran for another TD from six yards out on a broken play.

"I only called about two or three audibles out there all day," Bradshaw said. "Why? Because I didn't have to. I knew what they were doing on defense most of the time.

"I'm not bragging or anything, but we had the right play called pretty much all the time. We were just ready to play football, and maybe they weren't."

The Steelers had better be ready to play football again this Sunday when they take their 6-0 record to Municipal Stadium on the shores of Lake Erie to meet the Cleveland Browns who are now 4-2 after yesterday's 24-16 win over New Orleans.

"It should be another fun one," Joe Greene said with a big grin. "It's nice to come off a big win going into a big game, but I'm not gonna say anything to arouse the natives up there."

Motivation is the last thing the Browns need.... especially after what happened two weeks ago in Pittsburgh.

		SCORING	ATL	PIT
1st	Steelers	Roy Gerela 21 yard field goal	0	3
2nd	Steelers	Rocky Bleier 8 yard rush (Roy Gerela kick)	0	10
	Steelers	Terry Bradshaw 6 yard rush (Roy Gerela kick)	0	17
3rd	Steelers	Rocky Bleier 2 yard rush (Roy Gerela kick)	0	24
4th	Steelers	John Stallworth 11 yard pass from Terry Bradshaw (Roy Gerela kick)	0	31
	Falcons	Wallace Francis 11 yard pass from Steve Bartkowski (Fred Steinfort kick)	7	31

	TEAM STATS	
	ATL	PIT
First downs	20	28
Rush-Yards-TD	34-113-0	44-181-3
Comp-Att-Yards-TD-INT	17-33-188-1-2	13-18-231-1-0
Sacked-Yards	5-44	2-25
Net pass yards	144	206
Total yards	257	387
Fumbles-Lost	3-2	4-3
Turnovers	4	3
Penalties-Yards	4-38	8-74

PASSING, RUSHING and RECEIVING

Falcons

Passing

Steve Bartkowski: 17-of-33, 188 yards, 1 TD, 2 INT

Rushing

Steve Bartkowski: 2 carries for 7 yards
Bubba Bean: 17 carries for 48 yards
Haskel Stanback: 12 carries for 38 yards
Ricky Patton: 3 carries for 20 yards

Receiving

Billy Ryckman: 5 catches for 88 yards
Bubba Bean: 3 catches for 11 yards
Wallace Francis: 4 catches for 58 yards, 1 TD
Ricky Patton: 1 catch for 5 yards
Dennis Pearson: 1 catch for 12 yards
Jim R. Mitchell: 1 catch for 7 yards
Mike Esposito: 2 catches for 7 yards

Steelers

Passing

Terry Bradshaw: 13-of-18, 231 yards, 1 TD, 0 INT

Rushing

Terry Bradshaw: 2 carries for 3 yards, 1 TD
Franco Harris: 20 carries for 104 yards
Rocky Bleier: 13 carries for 46 yards, 2 TD
Sidney Thornton: 8 carries for 30 yards
Alvin Maxson: 1 carry for -2 yards

Receiving

John Stallworth: 6 catches for 114 yards, 1 TD
Lynn Swann: 3 catches for 64 yards
Sidney Thornton: 1 catch for 9 yards
Bennie Cunningham: 2 catches for 28 yards
Randy Grossman: 1 catch for 16 yards

DEFENSE

Steelers

Interceptions

Mel Blount: 1 for 4 yards
Loren Toews: 1 for 12 yards

KICK RETURNS

Falcons

Kickoffs

George Franklin: 3 for 75 yards, 25.0 avg.
Dennis Pearson: 3 for 78 yards, 26.0 avg.

Punts

Billy Ryckman: 1 for 24 yards, 24.0 avg.

Steelers

Kickoffs

Larry Anderson: 1 for 12 yards, 12.0 avg.

Punts

Randy Reutershan: 2 for 15 yards, 7.5 avg.

KICKING and PUNTING

Falcons

Kicking

Fred Steinfort: 1-for-1 PAT, 0-for-2 FG

Punting

John James: 3 for 102 yards, 34.0 avg.

Steelers

Kicking

Roy Gerela: 4-for-4 PAT, 1-for-1 FG

Punting

Craig Colquitt: 2 for 71 yards, 35.5 avg.

Week 7

	Oct. 15 Municipal Stadium Cleveland, OH				
Pittsburgh Steelers				**Cleveland Browns**	
	1Q	2Q	3Q	4Q	Total
Steelers	6	7	14	7	34
Browns	0	7	0	7	14

CLEVELAND (AP) — Larry Anderson has covered 95 yards faster, but the swift Pittsburgh Steelers rookie has never done it at a more opportune time.

Anderson's joyful 95-yard kickoff return Sunday burst the Cleveland Browns' hopeful bubble and sparked the unbeaten Steelers to a 34-14 National Football League victory before 81,302 fans.

The former Louisiana Tech speedster's sparkling touchdown run came with 1:30 left in the first half and erased a 7-6 Cleveland lead put on the scoreboard only 14 seconds earlier on Brian Sipe's 17-yard touchdown pass to Dave Logan.

That 14 seconds was the elapsed time it took Anderson to reach the end zone and prick awake Pittsburgh's slumbering offense. The Steelers dominated the second half as quarterback Terry Bradshaw directed three touchdown marches.

"That runback by Larry really united us," Bradshaw said. "We weren't doing anything offensively and we really needed a break. We hadn't had our special teams return one all year, but you couldn't have asked for it at a better time. It fired us up."

The Steelers, who until Anderson's jaunt had only 67 yards total offense and Roy Gerela field goals of 23 and 44 yards, raised their season mark to 7-0.

Following halftime, Bradshaw hit Lynn Swann for 28 yards and one score. Rocky Bleier added a one-yard touchdown run — giving Pittsburgh a 27-7 lead at the end of three periods — and Bradshaw followed Sipe's 19-yard touchdown pass to Reggie Rucker by combining with John Stallworth for 32 yards and the final score of the game.

"There's no question that the kick return after the (Cleveland) touchdown was the big play of the game. It took the wind out of their sails," said Pittsburgh Coach Chuck Noll. "We've needed a big play from the specialty teams and we think we're growing and getting better in all areas as a football team."

Sipe, who completed 17 of 30 passes for 213 yards, was as disappointed in the outcome as anyone in the Cleveland dressing room.

"We made more mistakes today than they did and that was the difference. They had no turnovers and, if you don't turn the ball over for 60 minutes, you'll win 95 percent of the time.

"I'm very frustrated because we were capable of beating them. We could have put in the kill in the first half, but we let them off."

The Browns fumbled the ball away twice and Sipe had two passes intercepted. The first interception and fumble each led to a Gerela field goal and the second interception — by cornerback Mike Wagner — was the catalyst for Pittsburgh's first sustained drive of the game, early in the third period.

		SCORING	PIT	CLE
1st	Steelers	Roy Gerela 23 yard field goal	3	0
	Steelers	Roy Gerela 44 yard field goal	6	0
2nd	Browns	Dave Logan 17 yard pass from Brian Sipe (Don Cockroft kick)	6	7
	Steelers	Larry Anderson 95 yard kickoff return (Roy Gerela kick)	13	7
3rd	Steelers	Lynn Swann 28 yard pass from Terry Bradshaw (Roy Gerela kick)	20	7
	Steelers	Rocky Bleier 1 yard rush (Roy Gerela kick)	27	7
4th	Browns	Reggie Rucker 18 yard pass from Brian Sipe (Don Cockroft kick)	27	14
	Steelers	John Stallworth 32 yard pass from Terry Bradshaw (Roy Gerela kick)	34	14

	TEAM STATS	
	PIT	CLE
First downs	20	19

Rush-Yards-TD	38-168-1	38-132-0
Comp-Att-Yards-TD-INT	10-21-175-2-0	19-35-252-2-2
Sacked-Yards	3-22	2-24
Net pass yards	153	228
Total yards	321	360
Fumbles-Lost	4-0	3-2
Turnovers	0	4
Penalties-Yards	6-41	10-90

PASSING, RUSHING and RECEIVING

Steelers

Passing

Terry Bradshaw: 10-of-21, 175 yards, 2 TD, 0 INT

Rushing

Terry Bradshaw: 1 carry for 0 yards
Rocky Bleier: 13 carries for 57 yards, 1 TD
Franco Harris: 15 carries for 41 yards
Sidney Thornton: 5 carries for 38 yards
Jack Deloplaine: 3 carries for 34 yards
Mike Kruczek: 1 carry for -2 yards

Receiving

Lynn Swann: 5 catches for 76 yards, 1 TD
John Stallworth: 2 catches for 68 yards, 1 TD
Randy Grossman: 2 catches for 25 yards
Theo Bell: 1 catch for 6 yards

Browns

Passing

Brian Sipe: 17-of-30, 213 yards, 2 TD, 2 INT
Mark Miller: 2-of-5, 39 yards

Rushing

Brian Sipe: 2 carries for 11 yards
Calvin Hill: 10 carries for 42 yards
Mark Miller: 3 carries for 33 yards
Ozzie Newsome: 1 carry for 4 yards
Cleo Miller: 11 carries for 24 yards
Mike Pruitt: 5 carries for 10 yards
Greg Pruitt: 6 carries for 8 yards

Receiving

Reggie Rucker: 4 catches for 95 yards, 1 TD
Calvin Hill: 3 catches for 34 yards
Ozzie Newsome: 3 catches for 47 yards
Dave Logan: 2 catches for 38 yards, 1 TD
Cleo Miller: 3 catches for 11 yards
Mike Pruitt: 3 catches for 19 yards
Greg Pruitt: 1 catch for 8 yards

DEFENSE

Steelers

Interceptions

Mel Blount: 1 for 35 yards
Mike Wagner: 1 for 20 yards

KICK RETURNS

Steelers

Kickoffs

Larry Anderson: 3 for 115 yards, 38.3 avg.

Punts

Theo Bell: 1 for 4 yards, 4.0 avg.
Randy Reutershan: 1 for 7 yards, 7.0 avg.

Browns

Kickoffs

Larry Collins: 1 for 16 yards, 16.0 avg.
Cleo Miller: 1 for 15 yards, 15.0 avg.
Keith Wright: 5 for 111 yards, 22.2 avg.

Punts

Keith Wright: 5 for 24 yards, 4.8 avg.

KICKING and PUNTING

Steelers

Kicking

Roy Gerela: 4-for-4 PAT, 2-for-3 FG

Punting

Craig Colquitt: 5 for 199 yards, 39.8 avg.

Browns

Kicking

Don Cockroft: 2-for-2 PAT

Punting

Johnny Evans: 4 for 125 yards, 31.3 avg.

Week 8

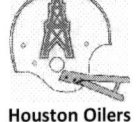

	Oct. 23 Three Rivers Stadium Pittsburgh, PA				
Houston Oilers				**Pittsburgh Steelers**	
	1Q	2Q	3Q	4Q	Total
Oilers	0	10	7	7	24
Steelers	0	10	0	7	17

PITTSBURGH (AP) — The Pittsburgh Steelers, who looked on the bright side after their first loss this season, were also on the bruised side after their first run-in with rookie Earl Campbell.

"I hate to lose, but something good may come out of this," linebacker Jack Lambert said Monday night after Campbell smashed for three touchdowns to lead the Houston Oilers to a 24-17 victory over Pittsburgh.

"There's some possibility that maybe we thought we couldn't be beat. Now we know we can," Lambert added. "That undefeated stuff is over with."

The game capped a weekend of upsets around the National Football League, and the Steelers lost the distinction of being the last NFL team with a perfect record. Now they're 7-1 with the tougher half of their schedule ahead.

The Oilers, who withstood two deep Steeler thrusts in the frantic final four minutes, climbed to 5-3 and now trail Pittsburgh by two games in the American Conference Central Division.

"We'll work hard and hope for the best," said Campbell, who carried 21 times for 89 yards.

His three touchdowns came on short bursts against a Pittsburgh defense that had allowed a total of three rushing touchdowns in seven prior games.

Sooners Maintain Top Spot

By the Associated Press

Alabama, the preseason choice to win college football's national championship, continued its climb toward the top Monday, rising from fourth place to third in The Associated Press ratings, behind front-running Oklahoma and Penn State.

The Oklahoma Sooners held onto the top position for the fifth week in a row by trouncing Iowa State 34-6. Oklahoma received 54 first-place votes and 1,270 of a possible 1,280 points from a nationwide panel of 64 sports writers and broadcasters.

Penn State, a 45-15 winner over Syracuse, re-

The Steelers had also allowed just 77 points through seven games, fewest in the NFL.

"They ran on us like no other team has this year, and a lot of the credit goes to Mr. Campbell," said Lambert.

After the win, the 225-pound Campbell rubbed baby lotion over his massive legs and spread credit around the Oiler locker room.

"I knew before the game that our offensive line could do a great job of blocking and they just did it again tonight," said Campbell.

"And we have another running back in there name Ron Carpenter who did a good job of blocking for me."

Franco Is Checked

The Steelers' Franco Harris, who piled up 149 yards the last time the two teams played, got only 56 in 16 totes this time.

Houston also benefited from the third-down passing of Dan Pastorini, who hit 13 of 19 tries and wasn't sacked.

Pastorini and running back Ron Coleman set the tone early on a 23-yard third-down pass that kept alive an 80-yard drive for a touchdown. It came on Campbell's one-yard run early in the second quarter.

A series later, Terry Bradshaw and Lynn Swann connected on the first of two Steeler touchdown passes, a 25-yarder.

After a fumble recovery, Roy Gerela kicked a 30-yard field goal to give the Steelers the lead. Toni Fritsch countered with a 39-yard Houston field goal six seconds before halftime to make it 10-10.

In the third period, Pastorini hit a pair of third-down passes on a 70-yard drive that ended when Campbell powered three yards.

Early in the last quarter, Pastorini found tight end Mike Barber for 26 yards on third down. Campbell ended the 80-yard march with a one-yard ram and the Oilers led 24-10.

Then Bradshaw went to work. After having a 23-yard touchdown pass to Swann nullified by holding, he hit Swann with a 6-yard scoring toss with 5:20 left.

After a successful onsides kick, Pittsburgh drove to the Houston 15-yard line before a Bradshaw pass was intercepted by safety Kurt Knoff.

After an Oiler punt, Bradshaw led a march to the Oilers' 14-yard line, but it ended when he threw a fourth-down incompletion with 10 seconds left.

		SCORING	HOU	PIT
2nd	Oilers	Earl Campbell 1 yard rush (Toni Fritsch kick)	7	0
	Steelers	Lynn Swann 25 yard pass from Terry Bradshaw (Roy Gerela kick)	7	7
	Steelers	Roy Gerela 30 yard field goal	7	10
	Oilers	Toni Fritsch 39 yard field goal	10	10
3rd	Oilers	Earl Campbell 3 yard rush (Toni Fritsch kick)	17	10

4th	Oilers	Earl Campbell 1 yard rush (Toni Fritsch kick)	24	10
	Steelers	Lynn Swann 6 yard pass from Terry Bradshaw (Roy Gerela kick)	24	17

	TEAM STATS	
	HOU	PIT
First downs	22	21
Rush-Yards-TD	43-169-3	31-113-0
Comp-Att-Yards-TD-INT	13-19-160-0-0	17-33-226-2-1
Sacked-Yards	0-0	1-11
Net pass yards	160	215
Total yards	329	328
Fumbles-Lost	2-1	2-0
Turnovers	1	1
Penalties-Yards	6-51	7-53

PASSING, RUSHING and RECEIVING

Oilers

Passing

Dan Pastorini: 13-of-19, 160 yards

Rushing

Earl Campbell: 21 carries for 89 yards, 3 TD
Dan Pastorini: 2 carries for -1 yard
Rob Carpenter: 12 carries for 42 yards
Rich Caster: 2 carries for 22 yards
Ronnie Coleman: 4 carries for 12 yards
Tim Wilson: 2 carries for 5 yards

Receiving

Rob Carpenter: 4 catches for 23 yards
Rich Caster: 2 catches for 30 yards
Mike Barber: 3 catches for 47 yards
Ronnie Coleman: 1 catch for 23 yards
Mike Renfro: 1 catch for 16 yards
Tim Wilson: 1 catch for 8 yards
Ken Burrough: 1 catch for 13 yards

Steelers

Passing

Terry Bradshaw: 17-of-33, 226 yards, 2 TD, 1 INT

Rushing

Terry Bradshaw: 2 carries for 26 yards
Franco Harris: 16 carries for 56 yards
Rocky Bleier: 12 carries for 31 yards
Sidney Thornton: 1 carry for 0 yards

Receiving

Randy Grossman: 9 catches for 116 yards
Franco Harris: 2 catches for 15 yards
John Stallworth: 2 catches for 55 yards
Rocky Bleier: 1 catch for 8 yards
Lynn Swann: 3 catches for 32 yards, 2 TD

DEFENSE

Oilers

Interceptions

Kurt Knoff: 1 for 6 yards

KICK RETURNS

Oilers

Kickoffs

Johnnie Dirden: 1 for 22 yards, 22.0 avg.
Billy Johnson: 1 for 15 yards, 15.0 avg.

Punts

Billy Johnson: 2 for 22 yards, 11.0 avg.

Steelers

Kickoffs

Larry Anderson: 3 for 81 yards, 27.0 avg.

Punts

Theo Bell: 3 for 39 yards, 13.0 avg.

KICKING and PUNTING

Oilers

Kicking

Toni Fritsch: 3-for-3 PAT, 1-for-1 FG

Punting

Cliff Parsley: 4 for 162 yards, 40.5 avg.

Steelers

Kicking

Roy Gerela: 2-for-2 PAT, 1-for-2 FG

Punting

Craig Colquitt: 3 for 124 yards, 41.3 avg.

Week 9

Oct. 29
Three Rivers Stadium
Pittsburgh, PA

Kansas City Chiefs   **Pittsburgh Steelers**

	1Q	2Q	3Q	4Q	Total
Chiefs	3	0	14	7	24
Steelers	7	13	7	0	27

By MIKE BODURA
Sports Editor

PITTSBURGH -- Whoever named the offense the Kansas City Chiefs employed against the Steelers yesterday at Three Rivers Stadium was way off base.

They call it the Wing-T. The word wing connotes flight. The airwaves. Flying footballs. Such is not the case with the Wing-T, an offense that only a Woody Hayes could love.

There is certainly no love lost between the Steelers and the Wing-T as Chuck Noll's team was able to cling to a 27-24 victory over the Chiefs despite almost having their wings clipped by the offense which is as subtle as a steelworker's tattoo.

"What you have is two running backs in the backfield and a 220-pound running back in motion leading on every play," Steelers' linebacker Jack Ham said in describing the Wing-T. "He can either get the football or take care of the linebacker. He can crack down on you and has a great angle to do it. Obviously, we didn't play it too well."

Ham shook his head when told the Steelers surrendered 186 yards rushing to the Chiefs. The Houston Oilers had similar success last Monday night against a Steeler defense which has the reputation for being tougher to run against than quicksand.

"I wish I knew what was wrong," Ham said. "We have been playing better running teams but we didn't play very well. Almost 190 yards today — it was like a track meet out there. We're going to have to look at the films and see what we're doing wrong. I hope New Orleans doesn't come out in a Wing-T next week."

Donnie Shell shares those feelings.

"I hope I never see it again," Shell said. "How would you like to have three guys coming at you to block you when your trying to support your family?"

Shell was able to survive the blocking onslaught of the Chiefs' offensive line and the slashing of backs Tony Reed, Ted McKnight, Arnold Morgado and company to make the game's big play.

The Steelers were nursing a tenuous 20-17 lead at the time. They had squandered a 20-3 halftime lead allowing Reed two touchdowns. To make matters worse, a bruised right elbow was preventing quarterback Terry Bradshaw from doing much more than handing off and fumbling, like he did to set up the touchdown which brought the Chiefs within three points.

With time running out in the third quarter and the Chiefs on their own 12-yard line, Horace Belton fumbled when belted by the Steelers' Robin Cole. Shell gathered in the loose football and trotted 17 yards down the right sideline for his first pro touchdown and a 27-17 Steeler lead.

"I saw a flag on the play and thought we were offsides," Shell said.

They weren't. The touchdown provided the margin of victory as the Chiefs scored in the fourth quarter on a run by Morgado with less than two minutes remaining. Ham fell on the ensuing onside kick to preserve the Steelers' eighth victory against one loss. It gives them a three-game lead in the AFC Central Division again thanks to Cincinnati's upset of Houston.

"We're very fortunate," Noll said. "We feel fortunate to get out of that thing alive. I was impressed by their offense and the way they ran the ball. We were fortunate to come up with the big plays. Of course the one by Shell was the biggest."

Noll also pointed to Ham's recovery of the onside kick and his interception plus the interception and fine all around play of rookie cornerback Ron Johnson as other factors in the win.

"It was a great effort on their part and they were getting an extra effort from their runners but we didn't have much pursuit," Noll said. "We pretty much figured they'd run left (where Loren Toews got hurt, Mel Blount didn't start and Dwight White was subpar). Houston was successful going left. Under the circumstances, a lot of guys played well."

Bradshaw wasn't one of them. He injured his elbow in the first half but remained in the game throughout the third quarter despite being unable to throw the ball effectively. Noll finally replaced him with Mike Kruczek at the start of the fourth quarter.

"The big thing was I knew I couldn't throw," Bradshaw said. "They knew in the second half that we were going to run the ball and adjusted their defense to stop us

"I couldn't throw. I shouldn't have been in the game but the doctors at halftime let it up to me. I was hoping things would go well and that we'd get another touchdown early in the third quarter and I could come out. I didn't want to abandon my team. But I didn't want to lose it for them either so I decided to come out."

He didn't lose it for them but the Wing-T almost did.

		SCORING	KAN	PIT
1st	Chiefs	Jan Stenerud 25 yard field goal	3	0
	Steelers	Franco Harris 1 yard rush (Roy Gerela kick)	3	7
2nd	Steelers	Franco Harris 11 yard rush (Roy Gerela kick)	3	14

	Steelers	John Stallworth 23 yard pass from Terry Bradshaw (kick failed)	3	20
3rd	Chiefs	Ted McKnight 14 yard rush (Jan Stenerud kick)	10	20
	Chiefs	Tony Reed 16 yard rush (Jan Stenerud kick)	17	20
	Steelers	Donnie Shell 17 yard fumble return (Roy Gerela kick)	17	27
4th	Chiefs	Arnold Morgado 2 yard rush (Jan Stenerud kick)	24	27

	TEAM STATS	
	KAN	PIT
First downs	20	17
Rush-Yards-TD	39-181-3	40-135-2
Comp-Att-Yards-TD-INT	15-28-148-0-2	8-15-119-1-2
Sacked-Yards	1-7	4-39
Net pass yards	141	80
Total yards	322	215
Fumbles-Lost	2-1	1-1
Turnovers	3	3
Penalties-Yards	10-114	9-65

PASSING, RUSHING and RECEIVING

Chiefs

Passing

Mike Livingston: 15-of-28, 148 yards, 0 TD, 2 INT

Rushing

Mike Livingston: 3 carries for 17 yards
Ted McKnight: 8 carries for 70 yards, 1 TD
Tony Reed: 6 carries for 19 yards, 1 TD

Arnold Morgado: 19 carries for 74 yards, 1 TD
Horace Belton: 2 carries for 1 yard

Receiving

Ted McKnight: 1 catch for 14 yards
Tony Reed: 6 catches for 64 yards
Arnold Morgado: 1 catch for 8 yards
Henry Marshall: 2 catches for 31 yards
Walter White: 3 catches for 20 yards
Horace Belton: 1 catch for 5 yards
MacArthur Lane: 1 catch for 6 yards

Steelers

Passing

Terry Bradshaw: 7-of-13, 109 yards, 1 TD, 2 INT
Mike Kruczek: 1-of-2, 10 yards

Rushing

Franco Harris: 25 carries for 90 yards, 2 TD
Lynn Swann: 1 carry for 7 yards
Terry Bradshaw: 1 carry for 6 yards
Rocky Bleier: 9 carries for 23 yards
Sidney Thornton: 4 carries for 9 yards

Receiving

Lynn Swann: 5 catches for 80 yards
Rocky Bleier: 1 catch for 6 yards
John Stallworth: 1 catch for 23 yards, 1 TD
Randy Grossman: 1 catch for 10 yards

DEFENSE

Chiefs

Interceptions

Tim Collier: 1 for 23 yards
Gary Green: 1 for 0 yards

Steelers

Interceptions

Jack Ham: 1 for 0 yards
Ron Johnson: 1 for 21 yards

KICK RETURNS

Chiefs

Kickoffs

Horace Belton: 1 for 31 yards, 31.0 avg.
Eddie Payton: 2 for 54 yards, 27.0 avg.

Punts

Larry Dorsey: 1 for 3 yards, 3.0 avg.
Eddie Payton: 2 for 6 yards, 3.0 avg.

Steelers

Kickoffs

Larry Anderson: 3 for 52 yards, 17.3 avg.

Punts

Randy Reutershan: 1 for 5 yards, 5.0 avg.
Jim Smith: 1 for 12 yards, 12.0 avg.

KICKING and PUNTING

Chiefs

Kicking

Jan Stenerud: 3-for-3 PAT, 1-for-2 FG

Punting

Zenon Andrusyshyn: 4 for 155 yards, 38.8 avg.

Steelers

Kicking

Roy Gerela: 3-for-4 PAT

Punting

Craig Colquitt: 4 for 173 yards, 43.3 avg.

Week 10

	Nov. 5 Three Rivers Stadium Pittsburgh, PA				
New Orleans Saints					Pittsburgh Steelers
	1Q	2Q	3Q	4Q	Total
Saints	0	7	0	7	14
Steelers	3	0	10	7	20

By RICH EMERT
TIMES Sports Staff

PITTSBURGH — Harry Houdini would have been proud of the way the Pittsburgh Steelers performed the last two weeks.

For the second straight game the Steelers made like escape artists and slipped away with a victory, defeating the upset-minded New Orleans Saints 20-14 yesterday afternoon before 48,525 nervous fans at Three Rivers Stadium.

Rocky Bleier and Terry Bradshaw set the Steelers free from the Saints' straightjacket with 1:51 left when they hooked up on a 24-yard touchdown pass, and Bleier's first reception for a score in a regular season game in his 10-year career.

"It was just a brilliant call," Bleier said with a chuckle as he pointed at Bradshaw. "Sure, we had discussed it right before the play. Yeah, we knew it would work."

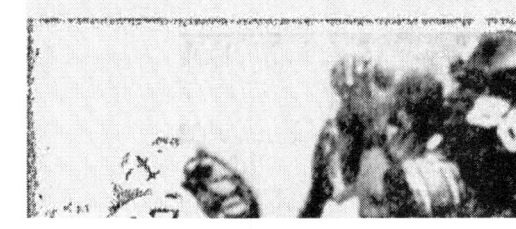

Of course, Bleier (See related story) was just kidding. All Bradshaw wanted was seven yards and a first down, but the Saints ran a delayed blitz and New Orleans' safety Tom Myers took a gamble and tried to knock the pass down. Myers missed, and Bleier hot-footed it into the end zone.

"I saw the blitz coming at the line when I called signals and knew Rock would be open in the flat," Bradshaw explained after packing his cheek with tobacco. "I saw the safety coming, but I didn't think he could get to the ball 'cause I threw it low and to the outside."

"It was a real quick call by

Bradshaw, and I didn't play it right, that's all," Myers said dejectedly. "We had the blitz on and I was just trying to tip the ball away, but I never touched it."

"Tommy wasn't beat on the play, he just gambled and lost," Saints' head man Dick Nolan said quietly. "We've played this way all year. We're fighters, and we've battled all year long."

The Saints, now 5-5, showed they will be a team to reckon with in the very near future by rolling up 421 yards total offense against Pittsburgh. New Orleans quarterback Archie Manning was unreal, and hit on 22 of 32 passes for 344 yards, the most yards passing against the Steelers since Ken Stabler threw for 396 back in 1976.

The 14 points the Saints got is misleading too, since they were at the Pittsburgh 23 and five yard lines in the second quarter but came up empty due to a Jack Lambert interception and a fumble by Manning. Even if New Orleans only kicks field goals on those drives, it's a different game.

"We didn't put any pressure on him (Manning) and he had all day to throw," Steelers' head coach Chuck Noll said. "Late in the game we tried to go after him with the blitz, but he picked it up and hurt us. We're lucky he didn't burn us more."

The Steelers went into the game expecting the Saints to try and ram the ball down their throat with running backs Chuck Muncie and Tony Galbreath, and the Pittsburgh defense held New Orleans to just 81 yards rushing.

"We closed down the parkway, but they opened up the airport," Joe Greene said with a grin. "It's always good to win, but when you look back on what happened out there today you've got to wonder a bit.

"People have been playing their best against us lately. Is that because they respect us so much, or are we making these guys look good?"

"We could have just as easily lost this game," said Lambert, who had an outstanding game with 13 solo tackles along with the interception. "A lot of teams are losing this year that aren't supposed to be losing. I'm kind of disillusioned by the fact we haven't played better the last three games."

Lambert was also surprised that New Orleans didn't try to move the ball on the ground more.

"A lot of our guys were jacked up to stop the run," he said. "I thought sure they'd try and run it down our throat."

While the Steelers' defense was having its problems, Bradshaw and Company didn't encounter much resistance from the Saints. Pittsburgh collected 345 yards, and only had to punt once. However, the Steelers didn't get their hands on the football much.

"We only had three possessions the first half, when usually we have five or six," Bradshaw drawled. "They (New Orleans) did a good job hangin' on to the ball. We moved against them all day though, and they never stopped us . . . we stopped ourselves.

"That's why I wasn't too worried at the end. It wasn't like we were trying things and they weren't goin' anywhere. Shoot, if we'd have had the ball a couple more times we'd have scored more points."

Even though it wasn't a classic, the Steelers are now 9-1 and will face 8-2 Los Angeles, a 26-23 winner over Tampa Bay yesterday, Sunday at 9 p.m. in the Coliseum. More importantly, Pittsburgh still holds a three-game edge over Houston, a 14-7 winner over Cleveland, in the AFC Central Division.

"We played well enough to get it done," Noll said with a sly grin.

But barely Chuck. . barely.

Rich Emert
TIMES Sports Staff

		SCORING	NOR	PIT
1st	Steelers	Roy Gerela 27 yard field goal	0	3
2nd	Saints	Rich Mauti 5 yard pass from Archie Manning (Steve Mike-Mayer kick)	7	3
3rd	Steelers	Lynn Swann 6 yard pass from Terry Bradshaw (Roy Gerela kick)	7	10
	Steelers	Roy Gerela 21 yard field goal	7	13
4th	Saints	Tony Galbreath 5 yard rush (Steve Mike-Mayer kick)	14	13
	Steelers	Rocky Bleier 24 yard pass from Terry Bradshaw (Roy Gerela kick)	14	20

	TEAM STATS	
	NOR	PIT

First downs	23	20
Rush-Yards-TD	32-81-1	34-145-0
Comp-Att-Yards-TD-INT	22-32-344-1-1	16-23-200-2-1
Sacked-Yards	1-4	0-0
Net pass yards	340	200
Total yards	421	345
Fumbles-Lost	1-1	2-1
Turnovers	2	2
Penalties-Yards	7-75	7-48

PASSING, RUSHING and RECEIVING

Saints

Passing

Archie Manning: 22-of-32, 344 yards, 1 TD, 1 INT

Rushing

Archie Manning: 2 carries for -1 yard
Chuck Muncie: 15 carries for 39 yards
Tony Galbreath: 13 carries for 38 yards, 1 TD
Mike Strachan: 2 carries for 5 yards

Receiving

Chuck Muncie: 3 catches for 58 yards
Henry Childs: 6 catches for 94 yards
Tony Galbreath: 5 catches for 54 yards
Ike Harris: 4 catches for 75 yards
Wes Chandler: 2 catches for 39 yards
Tinker Owens: 1 catch for 19 yards
Rich Mauti: 1 catch for 5 yards, 1 TD

Steelers

Passing

Terry Bradshaw: 16-of-23, 200 yards, 2 TD, 1 INT

Rushing

Rocky Bleier: 17 carries for 84 yards
Terry Bradshaw: 2 carries for 4 yards
Franco Harris: 15 carries for 57 yards

Receiving

Rocky Bleier: 3 catches for 46 yards, 1 TD
Franco Harris: 4 catches for 37 yards
Randy Grossman: 3 catches for 44 yards
Lynn Swann: 3 catches for 40 yards, 1 TD
John Stallworth: 3 catches for 33 yards

DEFENSE

Saints

Interceptions

Clarence Chapman: 1 for -4 yards

Steelers

Interceptions

Jack Lambert: 1 for 6 yards

KICK RETURNS

Saints

Kickoffs

Wes Chandler: 2 for 42 yards, 21.0 avg.
Clarence Chapman: 1 for 9 yards, 9.0 avg.
Don Schwartz: 1 for 15 yards, 15.0 avg.

Steelers

Kickoffs

Larry Anderson: 3 for 97 yards, 32.3 avg.

Punts

Theo Bell: 1 for 12 yards, 12.0 avg.

KICKING and PUNTING

Saints

Kicking

Steve Mike-Mayer: 2-for-2 PAT, 0-for-2 FG

Punting

Tom Blanchard: 2 for 120 yards, 60.0 avg.

Steelers

Kicking

Roy Gerela: 2-for-2 PAT, 2-for-3 FG

Punting

Craig Colquitt: 1 for 28 yards, 28.0 avg.

Week 11

Nov. 12
L.A. Memorial Coliseum
Los Angeles, CA

Pittsburgh Steelers vs. Los Angeles Rams

	1Q	2Q	3Q	4Q	Total
Steelers	0	0	7	0	7
Rams	0	0	3	7	10

United Press International

LOS ANGELES — Pat Haden rolled right and threw a 10-yard touchdown pass to Willie Miller between two Pittsburgh defenders with 5:27 left Sunday night to lift the Los Angeles Rams to a 10-7 mud-splattered, mistake-filled victory over the Steelers.

On an unseasonably cold Southern California night with the temperatures in the 40s, the Rams pulled out the game with a 56-yard, eight-play drive that was highlighted by a 26-yard run by John Cappelletti. The burst came on a 3rd-and-1 on the Pittsburgh 36. The former Heisman Trophy winner appeared stopped at the line of scrimmage but bounced off to his left and went to the Steeler 10 before being bumped out of bounds.

After Lawrence McCutcheon ran up the middle for no gain, Haden fired on the run to Miller, who caught the ball between Steelers Mike Wagner and Donnie Shell.

Pittsburgh took a 7-0 lead on Terry Bradshaw's 14-yard touchdown pass to Lynn Swann in the third period and the Rams trimmed that to 7-3 when Frank Corral kicked a 37-yard field goal.

The victory gave the Rams a 9-2 record and allowed them to keep a two-game lead over Atlanta in the NFC West. Pittsburgh, which entered the game with the best record in pro football, also fell to 9-2 and had its lead over Houston in the AFC Central cut to two games.

The game was played under horrendous conditions. The Coliseum natural grass turf was chewed up badly Saturday during the Southern California-Washington college football game and it was virtually impossible for the Steelers and Rams to run outside toward the sidelines.

The game was marred by frequent penalties and even was extended one play when the Rams' Pat Thomas was called for interfernce on Bradshaw's despeation pass to Swann as time ran out. Roy Gerela's 53-yard attempt for a tying field goal attempt with no time showing on the clock was well short of the goalline.

Los Angeles intercepted Bradshaw three times, twice in the opening quarter and the third time by Rod Perry that gave the Rams the ball on their own 40 with 2:28 left.

After a scoreless opening half, the Steelers took the second-half kickoff and went 70 yards in eight plays for a 7-0 lead. Bradshaw hit a leaping Swann in the end zone over Thomas for a 14-yard TD pass with 3:53 gone in the second half.

It was Bradshaw's 19th TD pass — a career high. On the drive, he completed passes of 26 and 15 yards to tight end Randy Grossman.

The Rams came right back and went 55 yards in 14 plays to position Corral for a 37-yard field goal at 10:44 of the third quarter. The Rams had to settle for the three points after Haden, on a 3rd-and 7 from the Steeler 9, was sacked for an 11-yard loss by a blitzing Wagner.

The Rams, who have been stymied by their own mistakes frequently this season, had three holding penalties in their previous drive before their touchdown march. But they didn't make any mistakes during their TD drive.

Cappelletti, the five-year pro from Penn State, gained 106 in 20 carries, only the third time that he has gained 100 yards in an NFL game. Haden completed 13-of-26 passes for 132 yards.

Bradshaw connected on 11-of-25 for 125 yards and Franco Harris got the ball 22 times for 50 yards.

In the second period, Corrall missed a 25-yard field goal 6:56 before halftime and a 31-yard Gerela field goal attempt was wide with 38 seconds left in the first half.

		SCORING	PIT	RAM
3rd	Steelers	Lynn Swann 14 yard pass from Terry Bradshaw (Roy Gerela kick)	7	0
	Rams	Frank Corral 37 yard field goal	7	3
4th	Rams	Willie Miller 10 yard pass from Pat Haden (Frank Corral kick)	7	10

		TEAM STATS	

	PIT	RAM
First downs	12	14
Rush-Yards-TD	25-59-0	44-192-0
Comp-Att-Yards-TD-INT	11-25-125-1-3	14-27-140-1-0
Sacked-Yards	1-10	2-19
Net pass yards	115	121
Total yards	174	313
Fumbles-Lost	2-0	3-2
Turnovers	3	2
Penalties-Yards	5-48	9-115

PASSING, RUSHING and RECEIVING

Steelers

Passing

Terry Bradshaw: 11-of-25, 125 yards, 1 TD, 3 INT

Rushing

Terry Bradshaw: 1 carry for 2 yards
Franco Harris: 22 carries for 50 yards
Rocky Bleier: 2 carries for 7 yards

Receiving

Randy Grossman: 4 catches for 44 yards
John Stallworth: 2 catches for 44 yards
Lynn Swann: 3 catches for 25 yards, 1 TD
Theo Bell: 2 catches for 12 yards

Rams

Passing

Pat Haden: 13-of-26, 132 yards, 1 TD, 0 INT
Vince Ferragamo: 1-of-1, 8 yards

Rushing

John Cappelletti: 20 carries for 106 yards
Pat Haden: 4 carries for 33 yards
Lawrence McCutcheon: 19 carries for 48 yards
Charle Young: 1 carry for 5 yards

Receiving

John Cappelletti: 3 catches for 29 yards
Lawrence McCutcheon: 1 catch for 2 yards
Charle Young: 3 catches for 34 yards
Billy Waddy: 1 catch for 30 yards
Terry Nelson: 2 catches for 15 yards
Ron Jessie: 2 catches for 15 yards
Willie Miller: 1 catch for 10 yards, 1 TD
Preston Dennard: 1 catch for 5 yards

DEFENSE

Rams

Interceptions

Rod Perry: 1 for 0 yards
Bill Simpson: 1 for 14 yards
Pat Thomas: 1 for 27 yards

KICK RETURNS

Steelers

Kickoffs

Larry Anderson: 2 for 41 yards, 20.5 avg.
Rick Moser: 1 for 8 yards, 8.0 avg.

Punts

Theo Bell: 2 for 13 yards, 6.5 avg.

Rams

Kickoffs

Jim Jodat: 1 for 18 yards, 18.0 avg.
Doug C. Smith: 1 for 8 yards, 8.0 avg.

Punts

Billy Waddy: 3 for 24 yards, 8.0 avg.
Jackie Wallace: 3 for 18 yards, 6.0 avg.

KICKING and PUNTING

Steelers

Kicking

Roy Gerela: 1-for-1 PAT, 0-for-2 FG

Punting

Craig Colquitt: 7 for 290 yards, 41.4 avg.

Rams

Kicking

Frank Corral: 1-for-1 PAT, 1-for-2 FG

Punting

Glen Walker: 7 for 189 yards, 27.0 avg.

Week 12

Nov. 19
Three Rivers Stadium
Pittsburgh, PA

Cincinnati Bengals — Pittsburgh Steelers

	1Q	2Q	3Q	4Q	Total
Bengals	3	3	0	0	6
Steelers	0	7	0	0	7

The Pittsburgh Steelers, who gave the Cincinnati Bengals one good beating early this season, settled for a one-point victory in yesterday's rematch.

"They've made tremendous improvement," quarterback Terry Bradshaw said after the Steelers won 7-6 with an offense that netted just 154 yards.

"Either that, or we're going the opposite way – and I don't believe that," added Bradshaw, who was intercepted four times.

Though Cincinnati fell to 1-11, it limited the 10-2 Steelers to a short touchdown plunge by Rocky Bleier in the second period.

"We played as hard as a football team can play," said Bengal coach Homer Rice.

"Usually, when you play the way we have, you win," said rookie Bengal cornerback Louis Breeden.

Breeden, who had two interceptions, helped hold Steeler receiver Lynn Swann to no receptions. It was an abrupt reversal from the first Steeler game, in which Breeden was beaten often.

Breeden's effort helped the Bengals keep it close, despite the absence of wide receivers Isaac Curtis and Billy Brooks due to injuries.

"We have an awful lot of respect for Cincinnati," said Pittsburgh coach Chuck Noll. "Without Curtis and Brooks, the rest of them just gutted it up. They wanted it very badly. They showed a lot of character."

Bradshaw, who hit just 12 of 30 passes for 117 yards, threw all four of his interceptions in the first half.

However, the Steelers managed a 7-6 lead at halftime on the strength of a 1-yard touchdown run by Bleier that capped a 64-yard scoring drive early in the second quarter.

Chris Bahr kicked a 29-yard field goal in the first quarter for Cincinnati and added a 48-yarder 14 seconds before halftime. His latter kick was set up by Breeden's second interception.

In the scoreless second half, the Steelers came up with two key defensive plays.

Midway in the final quarter, defensive tackle Gary Dunn stopped Pete Johnson short on a third-and-1 play at the Steelers' 34-yard line and the Bengals had to punt.

With 48 seconds left and the Bengals at the Steeler 47-yard line, linebacker Jack Ham recovered a fumble by Cincinnati quarterback Ken Anderson, who was slammed hard on a blitz by safety Mike Wagner.

In the first quarter, Bradshaw led Pittsburgh to the Cincinnati 36-yard line before his pass into the end zone was intercepted by Breeden, who made a masterful catch running stride for stride with Swann.

The ensuing 49-yard pass completion from Anderson to tight end Pat McInally gave Cincinnati a first down at the Pittsburgh 5-yard line. But linebacker Jack Lambert sacked Anderson for a 7-yard loss, and Cincinnati had to settle for Bahr's 29-yard field goal.

The Steelers followed with a touchdown drive that included a pair of 21-yard receptions by John Stallworth and ended with Bleier's 1-yard run.

On the next Steeler series, defensive tackle Wilson Whitley sacked Bradshaw, knocking loose a fumble that Whitley recovered himself at the Pittsburgh 13-yard line. But three plays later Steeler tackle Joe Greene recovered a fumble by Anderson.

		SCORING	CIN	PIT
1st	Bengals	Chris Bahr 29 yard field goal	3	0
2nd	Steelers	Rocky Bleier 1 yard rush (Roy Gerela kick)	3	7
	Bengals	Chris Bahr 48 yard field goal	6	7

	TEAM STATS	
	CIN	PIT
First downs	15	14
Rush-Yards-TD	31-97-0	34-70-1
Comp-Att-Yards-TD-INT	14-29-164-0-2	12-30-117-0-4
Sacked-Yards	3-15	2-33
Net pass yards	149	84
Total yards	246	154
Fumbles-Lost	4-3	4-1
Turnovers	5	5
Penalties-Yards	5-44	2-34

PASSING, RUSHING and RECEIVING

Bengals

Passing

Ken Anderson: 14-of-29, 164 yards, 0 TD, 2 INT

Rushing

Ken Anderson: 3 carries for 24 yards
Deacon Turner: 17 carries for 45 yards
Pete Johnson: 10 carries for 27 yards
Tony Davis: 1 carry for 1 yard

Receiving

Pat McInally: 4 catches for 85 yards
Deacon Turner: 3 catches for 12 yards
Pete Johnson: 2 catches for 16 yards
Don Bass: 2 catches for 22 yards
Jim Corbett: 2 catches for 16 yards
Dennis Law: 1 catch for 13 yards

Steelers

Passing

Terry Bradshaw: 12-of-30, 117 yards, 0 TD, 4 INT

Rushing

Franco Harris: 22 carries for 64 yards
Terry Bradshaw: 1 carry for -3 yards
Rocky Bleier: 9 carries for 10 yards, 1 TD
Rick Moser: 1 carry for 0 yards
Sidney Thornton: 1 carry for -1 yard

Receiving

Randy Grossman: 6 catches for 66 yards
Franco Harris: 1 catch for -2 yards
John Stallworth: 3 catches for 52 yards
Rocky Bleier: 2 catches for 1 yard

DEFENSE

Bengals

Interceptions

Louis Breeden: 2 for 7 yards
Jim LeClair: 1 for 11 yards
Ken Riley: 1 for 3 yards

Steelers

Interceptions

Mel Blount: 2 for 16 yards

KICK RETURNS

Bengals

Kickoffs

Ray Griffin: 2 for 50 yards, 25.0 avg.

Punts

Tony Davis: 2 for 13 yards, 6.5 avg.
Dick Jauron: 1 for 15 yards, 15.0 avg.
Dennis Law: 1 for -8 yards, -8.0 avg.

Steelers

Kickoffs

Larry Anderson: 2 for 52 yards, 26.0 avg.
Sidney Thornton: 1 for 37 yards, 37.0 avg.

Punts

Theo Bell: 1 for 7 yards, 7.0 avg.
Donnie Shell: 1 for 6 yards, 6.0 avg.
Jim Smith: 1 for 0 yards, 0.0 avg.

KICKING and PUNTING

Bengals

Kicking

Chris Bahr: 2-for-3 FG

Punting

Chris Bahr: 1 for 24 yards, 24.0 avg.
Pat McInally: 5 for 184 yards, 36.8 avg.

Steelers

Kicking

Roy Gerela: 1-for-1 PAT, 0-for-1 FG

Punting

Craig Colquitt: 7 for 264 yards, 37.7 avg.

Week 13

	Pittsburgh Steelers	Nov. 27 Candlestick Park San Francisco, CA			San Francisco 49ers
	1Q	2Q	3Q	4Q	Total
Steelers	3	14	0	7	24
49ers	0	0	7	0	7

SAN FRANCISCO — Terry Bradshaw and Lynn Swann are the National Football League's No. 1 passing combination, and the load carried by the Pittsburgh Steelers' defense seems considerably lighter today.

"I think we're all starting to play better," said linebacker Jack Ham, who intercepted two passes in last night's 24-7 victory over the San Francisco 49ers.

But only on offense had the Steelers been struggling, scoring one touchdown in each of their previous two games. Bradshaw was intercepted four times and Swann caught no passes in last week's 7-6 decision over Cincinnati.

"We passed well and ran the ball, too, which is what we have to do," said Swann after catching two touchdown passes and totaling 134 yards on eight receptions against the 49ers.

The victory was over a team that lost, 31-28, a week earlier to the Los Angeles Rams, who held the Steelers to 59 yards rushing two weeks ago.

"The Steelers are a great football team," said Fred O'Connor, 0-4 since becoming San Francisco's head coach. "We have three teams coming up (New Orleans, Tampa Bay and Detroit) that we can compete against."

If the 49ers, 1-12 after eight straight defeats, lose their final three games they'll set an NFL record for losses in one season.

"I got my confidence back tonight," said Bradshaw, who took the NFL lead in touchdown passes with his 22nd, an 11-yard pass to John Stallworth in the fourth period.

A request was made that the game be postponed because of the City Hall assassinations of San Francisco Mayor George Moscone and Supervisor Harvey Milk, but the NFL decided the nationally televised game would go on as scheduled.

Pittsburgh made its record 11-2, best in the NFL, and has a two-game lead over the Houston Oilers in the American Football Conference Central Division. The Steelers play in Houston on Sunday and can clinch the title with a victory.

"We'd better be ready for Houston; they'll be ready for us," said Bradshaw. "But right now, I'm enjoying this."

Bradshaw threw a first-period interception, his eighth in three weeks, in the first period after teammate Roy Gerela had kicked a 42-yard field goal.

Then the quarterback, who called his recent games embarrassing, completed 9 of 11 passes for 137 yards on two second-period touchdown drives.

Swann caught scoring passes of 22 and 25 yards, raising his NFL-leading total to 11 touchdown receptions. He has a career-high 57 receptions this season and is tied with Seattle's Steve Largent for the AFC lead.

"The first touchdown pass was Terry's all the way. He threw a perfect pass," said Swann, who made an over-the-head catch of the pass deep in the end zone.

Swann eluded two defenders on the next touchdown play, and Bradshaw said, "He's just a great competitor. He improvised on that one."

Bob Jury, one of the defensive backs faked out by Swann on the second touchdown, said, "He does everything so smoothly, and he's got great speed, too."

O'Connor said, "We covered him very well at times, and he still made the catches."

The 49ers cut Pittsburgh's lead to 17-7 in the third quarter on Paul Hofer's two-yard touchdown run, but Steelers coach Chuck Noll said, "As far as I'm concerned, we had a defensive shutout. We gave them a gift."

Bradshaw is sacked by Mark Nichols

		SCORING	PIT	SFO
1st	Steelers	Roy Gerela 42 yard field goal	3	0
2nd	Steelers	Lynn Swann 22 yard pass from Terry Bradshaw (Roy Gerela kick)	10	0
	Steelers	Lynn Swann 25 yard pass from Terry Bradshaw (Roy Gerela kick)	17	0
3rd	49ers	Paul Hofer 2 yard rush (Ray Wersching kick)	17	7
4th	Steelers	John Stallworth 11 yard pass from Terry Bradshaw (Roy Gerela kick)	24	7

	TEAM STATS	
	PIT	SFO
First downs	22	12
Rush-Yards-TD	53-212-0	29-67-1
Comp-Att-Yards-TD-INT	13-21-195-3-1	10-28-113-0-5
Sacked-Yards	2-27	4-39
Net pass yards	168	74
Total yards	380	141
Fumbles-Lost	5-3	0-0
Turnovers	4	5
Penalties-Yards	13-102	1-5

PASSING, RUSHING and RECEIVING

Steelers

Passing

Terry Bradshaw: 13-of-21, 195 yards, 3 TD, 1 INT

Rushing

Terry Bradshaw: 6 carries for 6 yards
Franco Harris: 12 carries for 61 yards
Rick Moser: 15 carries for 63 yards
Rocky Bleier: 13 carries for 58 yards
Sidney Thornton: 7 carries for 24 yards

Receiving

Lynn Swann: 8 catches for 134 yards, 2 TD
Franco Harris: 1 catch for 11 yards
John Stallworth: 2 catches for 26 yards, 1 TD
Randy Grossman: 2 catches for 24 yards

49ers

Passing

Scott Bull: 10-of-28, 113 yards, 0 TD, 5 INT

Rushing

Scott Bull: 3 carries for 16 yards
Paul Hofer: 16 carries for 35 yards, 1 TD
Bob Ferrell: 8 carries for 17 yards
Freddie Solomon: 1 carry for -7 yards
Dave Williams: 1 carry for 6 yards

Receiving

Paul Hofer: 1 catch for 20 yards
Paul Seal: 3 catches for 38 yards
Bob Ferrell: 3 catches for 16 yards
Kenny Harrison: 2 catches for 21 yards
Freddie Solomon: 1 catch for 18 yards

DEFENSE

Steelers

Interceptions

Tony Dungy: 1 for 13 yards
Jack Ham: 2 for 7 yards
Ron Johnson: 1 for 3 yards
Donnie Shell: 1 for 0 yards

49ers

Interceptions

Chuck Crist: 1 for 25 yards

KICK RETURNS

Steelers

Kickoffs

Larry Anderson: 2 for 38 yards, 19.0 avg.

Punts

Theo Bell: 1 for 9 yards, 9.0 avg.
Jim Smith: 3 for 21 yards, 7.0 avg.

49ers

Kickoffs

Greg Boykin: 1 for 0 yards, 0.0 avg.
Paul Hofer: 3 for 65 yards, 21.7 avg.
Mark R. Nichols: 1 for 16 yards, 16.0 avg.

Punts

Jack Steptoe: 1 for 28 yards, 28.0 avg.

KICKING and PUNTING

Steelers

Kicking

Roy Gerela: 3-for-3 PAT, 1-for-1 FG

Punting

Craig Colquitt: 3 for 127 yards, 42.3 avg.

49ers

Kicking

Ray Wersching: 1-for-1 PAT, 0-for-1 FG

Punting

Mike Connell: 5 for 199 yards, 39.8 avg.

Week 14

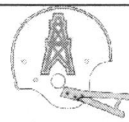

	Pittsburgh Steelers	Dec. 3 Astrodome Houston, TX		Houston Oilers	
	1Q	2Q	3Q	4Q	Total
Steelers	3	0	3	7	13
Oilers	0	3	0	0	3

Pittsburgh's defense decked Earl Campbell and alertly grabbed six Houston turnovers Sunday as the Steelers cooled off the Oilers 13-3 and wrapped up the American Conference's Central Division title.

Campbell, the NFL's leading rusher, crumpled to the Astroturf after a 10-yard gain in the first quarter. He left the game before a hushed record crowd of 54,261 and did not return.

The former Heisman Trophy winner suffered bruised ribs, but Oiler coach O.A. (Bum) Phillips said Campbell should be ready next week.

"We didn't have enough bandages," Phillips said, referring to Houston's string of injuries that included quarterback Dan Pastorini, receivers Mike Barber and Mike Renfro, middle guard Curly Culp and cornerback Willie Alexander.

"I said it would be that kind of game," Phillips added. "In my 31 years of coaching, I've never seen a game that was hammer and tong like that one. It was also the best one I've ever seen played defensively."

The Steelers intercepted three Pastorini passes and recovered three Oiler fumbles. Two of Houston's miscues led to field goals of 41 and 23 yards by Roy Gerela.

That gave Pittsburgh a 6-3 lead in the third quarter, and Terry Bradshaw hit John Stallworth with a five-yard touchdown pass to ice the game with 3:42 left to play.

Bradshaw agreed with Phillips' assessment.

"I've never played a game so hard and so intense in my life," Bradshaw said. "Both teams wanted to win so bad and played so hard that the defenses were as tight as a drum. We played awesome on defense, and the Houston Oiler defense was incredible."

Bradshaw said losing Campbell didn't hurt the Oiler offense. However, Pittsburgh coach Chuck Noll said, "I'm sure it had some effect on their football team. It really came down to a defensive game and the ability to make the right play at the right time."

Pittsburgh ran its record to 12-2, tying its best performance ever.

		SCORING	PIT	HOU
1st	Steelers	Roy Gerela 41 yard field goal	3	0
2nd	Oilers	Toni Fritsch 37 yard field goal	3	3
3rd	Steelers	Roy Gerela 23 yard field goal	6	3
4th	Steelers	John Stallworth 5 yard pass from Terry Bradshaw (Roy Gerela kick)	13	3

	TEAM STATS	
	PIT	HOU
First downs	17	9
Rush-Yards-TD	48-177-0	26-81-0
Comp-Att-Yards-TD-INT	11-24-97-1-1	10-27-91-0-3
Sacked-Yards	2-23	1-8
Net pass yards	74	83
Total yards	251	164
Fumbles-Lost	1-1	4-3
Turnovers	2	6
Penalties-Yards	7-60	5-35

PASSING, RUSHING and RECEIVING

Steelers

Passing

Terry Bradshaw: 11-of-24, 97 yards, 1 TD, 1 INT

Rushing

Franco Harris: 27 carries for 102 yards
Rocky Bleier: 13 carries for 66 yards
Terry Bradshaw: 3 carries for -3 yards
Sidney Thornton: 4 carries for 12 yards
Rick Moser: 1 carry for 0 yards

Receiving

Franco Harris: 4 catches for 20 yards
John Stallworth: 2 catches for 39 yards, 1 TD
Randy Grossman: 4 catches for 36 yards
Jim Smith: 1 catch for 2 yards

Oilers

Passing

Dan Pastorini: 10-of-27, 91 yards, 0 TD, 3 INT

Rushing

Ronnie Coleman: 15 carries for 45 yards
Earl Campbell: 7 carries for 41 yards
Ken Burrough: 1 carry for -3 yards
Tim Wilson: 3 carries for -2 yards

Receiving

Ronnie Coleman: 1 catch for 11 yards
Mike Barber: 2 catches for 37 yards
Conrad Rucker: 1 catch for 22 yards
Ken Burrough: 3 catches for 19 yards
Mike Renfro: 2 catches for 3 yards
Tim Wilson: 1 catch for -1 yard

DEFENSE

Steelers

Interceptions

Jack Lambert: 2 for 24 yards
Mike Wagner: 1 for 14 yards

Oilers

Interceptions

C.L. Whittington: 1 for 6 yards

KICK RETURNS

Steelers

Kickoffs

Larry Anderson: 1 for 20 yards, 20.0 avg.
Jim Smith: 1 for 16 yards, 16.0 avg.

Punts

Jim Smith: 4 for 32 yards, 8.0 avg.

Oilers

Kickoffs

Brian Duncan: 2 for 38 yards, 19.0 avg.
Robert Woods: 1 for 24 yards, 24.0 avg.

Punts

Robert Woods: 3 for 28 yards, 9.3 avg.

KICKING and PUNTING

Steelers

Kicking

Roy Gerela: 1-for-1 PAT, 2-for-4 FG

Punting

Craig Colquitt: 5 for 201 yards, 40.2 avg.

Oilers

Kicking

Toni Fritsch: 1-for-2 FG

Punting

Cliff Parsley: 5 for 239 yards, 47.8 avg.

Week 15

Dec. 9
Three Rivers Stadium
Pittsburgh, PA

Baltimore Colts vs **Pittsburgh Steelers**

	1Q	2Q	3Q	4Q	Total
Colts	0	7	6	0	13
Steelers	7	14	7	7	35

PITTSBURGH (UPI) — Baltimore Colts Coach Ted Marchibroda said he thought the steady snow that covered the field of Three Rivers Stadium would be an "equalizer."

Pittsburgh Steelers Coach Chuck Noll thought the snow might enable his team to pass well against the Colts.

Marchibroda was wrong; Noll was right.

Terry Bradshaw riddled the Colts' secondary for 240 yards and three touchdowns passing Saturday to lead Pittsburgh to a 35-13 victory that pushed the Steelers' record to a league-best 13-2 and assured them a home field advantage through the AFC playoffs.

"We figured everybody would have a tough time with footing and we felt the Colts would have people who couldn't come off the ball well, who couldn't cut and run," said Noll. "We felt our passing game would be successful."

Marchibroda admitted Noll's pre-game assessment was correct.

"The slippery conditions hampered our defense on the pass rush," Marchibroda said.

Bradshaw said that despite the freezing temperatures, he enjoyed the weather conditions.

"We threw everything at them. I came out and decided to just keep throwing at them and see what happened," Bradshaw said. "I had a lot of time. The snow was a luxury, really. The footing was bad, and the Colts couldn't get in."

Bradshaw, who left the game early in the fourth quarter, increased his league-leading TD pass total to 26 with a 31-yard scoring pass to John Stallworth, a 12-yarder to Randy Grossman and a 29-yarder to Jim Smith.

Grossman's reception was his first score of the season and Smith's TD catch was the first of his career. Stallworth was forced to leave the game in the second period due to a stomach virus.

The steady snow and freezing temperatures probably contributed to eight turnovers in the game. Bradshaw lost a fumble and was intercepted twice, and Colts' quarterback Bill Troup lost two fumbles and threw two interceptions. Baltimore running back Joe Washington fumbled once.

Franco Harris scored the Steelers' other two touchdowns on plunges of 3 and 2 yards in the second quarter.

Baltimore got its two TDs when Troup hit Roger Carr with a 5-yard scoring pass late in the second period and Derrel Luce recovered a Bradshaw fumble and returned it 44 yards for a score in the third period. Toni Linhart's second point-after attempt bounced off the left upright and was no good.

The Steelers dominated the first half, gaining 221 total yards while holding the Colts — badly missing injured quarterback Bert Jones — to just 66 yards.

Bradshaw got 87 of those yards by completing three passes to Lynn Swann, who was forced to leave the game in the second period with a head injury.

Steelers' second-year defensive back Tony Dungy, making his first pro start in place of injured safety Mike Wagner, intercepted his fifth pass of the season — the Steelers' season high. Rookie Ron Johnson also intercepted a pass, while veterans L.C. Greenwood, Steve Furness and Dwight White each recovered a fumble.

		SCORING	BAL	PIT
1st	Steelers	John Stallworth 31 yard pass from Terry Bradshaw (Roy Gerela kick)	0	7
2nd	Steelers	Franco Harris 3 yard rush (Roy Gerela kick)	0	14
	Steelers	Franco Harris 2 yard rush (Roy Gerela kick)	0	21
	Colts	Roger Carr 5 yard pass from Bill Troup (Toni Linhart kick)	7	21
3rd	Colts	Derrel Luce 44 yard fumble return (kick failed)	13	21
	Steelers	Randy Grossman 12 yard pass from Terry Bradshaw (Roy Gerela kick)	13	28
4th	Steelers	Jim Smith 29 yard pass from Terry Bradshaw (Roy Gerela kick)	13	35

	TEAM STATS	
	BAL	PIT
First downs	12	20
Rush-Yards-TD	27-86-0	48-139-2
Comp-Att-Yards-TD-INT	8-19-62-1-2	12-21-247-3-2
Sacked-Yards	2-19	2-13
Net pass yards	43	234
Total yards	129	373
Fumbles-Lost	5-3	1-1
Turnovers	5	3
Penalties-Yards	6-50	6-35

PASSING, RUSHING and RECEIVING

Colts

Passing

Bill Troup: 8-of-18, 62 yards, 1 TD, 1 INT
Mike Kirkland: 0-of-1, 0 yards, 0 TD, 1 INT

Rushing

'oe Washington: 18 carries for 48 yards
Don Hardeman: 8 carries for 33 yards
Don McCauley: 1 carry for 5 yards

Receiving

Joe Washington: 1 catch for 5 yards
Don Hardeman: 3 catches for 19 yards
Reese McCall: 1 catch for 17 yards
Glenn Doughty: 1 catch for 16 yards
Roger Carr: 1 catch for 5 yards, 1 TD
Don McCauley: 1 catch for 0 yards

Steelers

Passing

Terry Bradshaw: 11-of-18, 240 yards, 3 TD, 2 INT
Mike Kruczek: 1-of-3, 7 yards

Rushing

Terry Bradshaw: 3 carries for 15 yards
Rocky Bleier: 13 carries for 48 yards
Franco Harris: 17 carries for 52 yards, 2 TD
Sidney Thornton: 1 carry for 0 yards
Rick Moser: 8 carries for 15 yards
Jack Deloplaine: 6 carries for 9 yards

Receiving

Lynn Swann: 3 catches for 87 yards
Rocky Bleier: 1 catch for 32 yards
Jim Smith: 2 catches for 36 yards, 1 TD
John Stallworth: 1 catch for 31 yards, 1 TD
Sidney Thornton: 1 catch for 24 yards
Theo Bell: 2 catches for 20 yards
Randy Grossman: 2 catches for 17 yards, 1 TD

DEFENSE

Colts

Interceptions

Lloyd Mumphord: 1 for 19 yards
Norm Thompson: 1 for 31 yards

Steelers

Interceptions

Tony Dungy: 1 for 0 yards
Ron Johnson: 1 for 0 yards

KICK RETURNS

Colts

Kickoffs

Don McCauley: 3 for 58 yards, 19.3 avg.
Joe Washington: 2 for 71 yards, 35.5 avg.

Punts

Joe Washington: 1 for 17 yards, 17.0 avg.

Steelers

Kickoffs

Larry Anderson: 2 for 81 yards, 40.5 avg.
Jack Deloplaine: 1 for 19 yards, 19.0 avg.

Punts

Theo Bell: 3 for 21 yards, 7.0 avg.

KICKING and PUNTING

Colts

Kicking

Toni Linhart: 1-for-2 PAT

Punting

David Lee: 6 for 224 yards, 37.3 avg.

Steelers

Kicking

Roy Gerela: 5-for-5 PAT

Punting

Craig Colquitt: 4 for 131 yards, 32.8 avg.

Week 16

Dec. 16
Mile High Stadium
Denver, CO

Pittsburgh Steelers | | | | | Denver Broncos

	1Q	2Q	3Q	4Q	Total
Steelers	7	14	0	0	21
Broncos	0	0	7	10	17

Terry Bradshaw, dissecting Denver's defense with a razor-sharp passing attack, threw for two touchdowns and set up another with key third-down passes to John Stallworth, sparking the Pittsburgh Steelers to a 21-17 victory Saturday.

The victory enabled the playoff-bound Steelers to end their regular season 14-2. Denver, also headed for the playoffs, finished at 10-6, despite a furious second-half rally.

Bradshaw's TD aerials of 25 yards to Stallworth and 10 yard to Jim Smith gave him 28 for the season – tops in the NFL since the pro football merger in 1970.

The Steelers, who jumped out to a 21-0 halftime lead, opened the scoring late in the first quarter. Bradshaw kept the drive alive with third-down tosses of 17 and 20 yards to Stallworth, and Franco Harris plunged the final yard.

After a Denver fumble at the Bronco 42, Stallworth promptly caught a 17-yarder from Bradshaw and on the next play, with Bradshaw rolling out and throwing on the run, Stallworth outwrestled two Broncos in the end zone for a 25-yard scoring pass.

Pittsburgh got one more crack in the closing minutes of the half. Bradshaw, again scrambling to escape Denver's pass rush, found Smith wide open in the rear of the end zone for the score.

Denver's Norris Weese, taking over for Craig Morton in the second half, threw touchdown passes to Haven Moses and Riley Odoms, and Jim Turner kicked a 45-yard field goal. But Denver's rally fell short when Lonnie Perrin was stopped for no gain at the 1-yard line on the game's final play.

Weese breathed new life into the Broncos with a 25-yard scoring pass to Moses midway through the third quarter.

Interceptions helped set up two Denver scores in the fourth period. Linebacker Tom Jackson picked off a Mike Kruczek pass at the Bronco 49 and Weese threw 22 yards to Moses, setting the stage for the Turner field goal that pulled Denver within 21-10 with 9:04 left.

With 4:08 remaining, cornerback Louis Wright's interception gave Denver possession at the Bronco 24. Ten plays later, Weese lofted a pass to Odoms for a 30-yard scoring play with 1:17 left.

An onside kick failed, but the Steelers couldn't retain possession and Denver mounted a desperation rally in the closing seconds. The key play was a face-guarding penalty against Steeler cornerback Ray Oldham in the end zone, which moved Denver from the 50 to the 1-yard line with seven seconds left.

But on the final play of the game, Perrin was stopped short of the goal line by linebacker Jack Lambert and tackle Joe Greene.

In the first half, Pittsburgh generated 196 total yards to the Broncos' 42. But Weese fired up Denver's offense in the second half, and the Broncos finished with a 300-251 edge in total yards.

		SCORING	PIT	DEN
1st	Steelers	Franco Harris 1 yard rush (Roy Gerela kick)	7	0
2nd	Steelers	John Stallworth 25 yard pass from Terry Bradshaw (Roy Gerela kick)	14	0
	Steelers	Jim Smith 10 yard pass from Terry Bradshaw (Roy Gerela kick)	21	0
3rd	Broncos	Haven Moses 25 yard pass from Norris Weese (Jim Turner kick)	21	7
4th	Broncos	Jim Turner 45 yard field goal	21	10
	Broncos	Riley Odoms 30 yard pass from Norris Weese (Jim Turner kick)	21	17

	TEAM STATS	
	PIT	DEN
First downs	14	19
Rush-Yards-TD	38-116-1	26-74-0

Comp-Att-Yards-TD-INT	13-19-160-2-2	15-26-274-2-1
Sacked-Yards	2-16	6-48
Net pass yards	144	226
Total yards	260	300
Fumbles-Lost	2-0	2-1
Turnovers	2	2
Penalties-Yards	6-82	10-72

PASSING, RUSHING and RECEIVING

Steelers

Passing

Terry Bradshaw: 10-of-14, 131 yards, 2 TD, 0 INT
Mike Kruczek: 3-of-5, 29 yards, 0 TD, 2 INT

Rushing

Sidney Thornton: 5 carries for 32 yards
Rick Moser: 10 carries for 34 yards
Franco Harris: 12 carries for 21 yards, 1 TD
Mike Kruczek: 3 carries for 12 yards
Rocky Bleier: 6 carries for 11 yards
Jack Deloplaine: 2 carries for 6 yards

Receiving

John Stallworth: 4 catches for 79 yards, 1 TD
Sidney Thornton: 1 catch for 9 yards
Rick Moser: 1 catch for -1 yard
Jim Smith: 2 catches for 31 yards, 1 TD
Franco Harris: 1 catch for 7 yards
Randy Grossman: 1 catch for 21 yards
Rocky Bleier: 2 catches for 9 yards
Lynn Swann: 1 catch for 5 yards

Broncos

Passing

Norris Weese: 12-of-17, 228 yards, 2 TD, 0 INT
Craig Morton: 3-of-6, 46 yards, 0 TD, 1 INT

Rushing

Norris Weese: 2 carries for 7 yards
Dave Preston: 5 carries for 36 yards
Jon Keyworth: 7 carries for 14 yards
Lonnie Perrin: 3 carries for 9 yards
Larry Canada: 2 carries for 0 yards
Otis Armstrong: 2 carries for 6 yards
Rob Lytle: 5 carries for 2 yards

Receiving

Haven Moses: 5 catches for 116 yards, 1 TD
Riley Odoms: 4 catches for 83 yards, 1 TD
Dave Preston: 3 catches for 40 yards
Jon Keyworth: 1 catch for 10 yards
Jack Dolbin: 1 catch for 16 yards
Larry Canada: 1 catch for 9 yards

DEFENSE

Steelers

Interceptions

Tony Dungy: 1 for 0 yards

Broncos

Interceptions

Tom Jackson: 1 for 0 yards
Louis Wright: 1 for 2 yards

KICK RETURNS

Steelers

Kickoffs

Larry Anderson: 2 for 48 yards, 24.0 avg.

Punts

Theo Bell: 5 for 21 yards, 4.2 avg.

Broncos

Kickoffs

Jon Keyworth: 1 for 11 yards, 11.0 avg.
Chris Pane: 1 for 29 yards, 29.0 avg.
Lonnie Perrin: 1 for 26 yards, 26.0 avg.
Dave Preston: 1 for 32 yards, 32.0 avg.

Punts

Dave Preston: 2 for -11 yards, -5.5 avg.
Charlie West: 1 for 3 yards, 3.0 avg.

KICKING and PUNTING

Steelers

Kicking

Roy Gerela: 3-for-3 PAT, 0-for-1 FG

Punting

Craig Colquitt: 6 for 278 yards, 46.3 avg.

Broncos

Kicking

Jim Turner: 2-for-2 PAT, 1-for-1 FG

Punting

Bucky Dilts: 6 for 254 yards, 42.3 avg.

AFC Divisional Playoffs

		Dec. 30 Three Rivers Stadium Pittsburgh, PA			
Denver Broncos				**Pittsburgh Steelers**	
	1Q	2Q	3Q	4Q	Total

Broncos	3	7	0	0	10
Steelers	6	13	0	14	33

From Wire Service Reports

PITTSBURGH (AP) — Lyle Alzado, who jolted Terry Bradshaw with a late hit during the game, gave him a lusty compliment after he quarterbacked the Pittsburgh Steelers to a 33-10 victory over the Denver Broncos Saturday in the American Football Conference Divisional playoffs.

"Terry Bradshaw was incredible. We knew if he got hot we'd be in trouble. And he got hot," said Alzado, the 250-pound end and defensive heart of the Broncos.

Bradshaw, in his most potent post-season display ever, hit 16 of 29 passes for 272 yards and a pair of fourth-quarter touchdown bombs.

"I had a lot of room and I just kept firing away at them," said Bradshaw, who will lead the Steelers into the Jan. 7 AFC championship game here against today's Houston-New England winner.

Bradshaw's passing, which included 10 receptions by wide receiver John Stallworth, was coupled with 105 yards rushing and a pair of touchdowns by Franco Harris as the Steelers displayed the all-around offensive clout that helped them to a 14-2 regular-season record, best in the National Football League.

"That was the best offensive performance against us in the last two years," said Alzado, who drew a 15-yard penalty early in the third quarter for roughing Bradshaw.

"They're a better football team, and they'll probably win the whole thing," said Alzado. "They just kicked our butts and they beat the crap out of us. I don't know what else to tell you."

Stallworth's 10 catches were an NFL record for a divisional playoff. That excludes the conference championship games and the Super Bowl.

"We went into the game figuring they were going to take away Lynn Swann by double covering him," said Bradshaw. "So we intended from the start to get the ball to John (Stallworth). I keep saying he's as good a receiver as Swann, and he showed it today."

The AFC-West champion Broncos, who booted Pittsburgh from the playoffs a year ago, took a 3-0 lead with 5:50 left in the opening quarter on a 37-yard field goal by Jim Turner.

But with Steeler fans waving their yellow "Terrible Towels" at packed Three Rivers Stadium, Pittsburgh took command with the kind of offensive power for which the Steelers are known, and its famed defense — the Steel Curtain — bent a couple of times, but never folded as the Steelers got to Denver quarterback six times in the game.

And Denver's one-year reign as AFC champion ended abruptly.

"We won this time because we have a really great team, and because we really wanted to beat them," said Harris. "We had some embarrassing moments against them last year, and I guess people were beginning to think we couldn't beat Denver, so we had to prove them wrong."

Harris, typically primed for the playoffs, dove 1 yard for a touchdown with 2:33 left in the first quarter to put Pittsburgh ahead to stay 7-3. He added an 18-yard touchdown sweep early in the second quarter. His two TDs gave him the NFL record for touchdowns in playoff competition with 12.

Harris carries the reputation of getting tough when the steelers need a victory the most, and explained why.

"I guess it's just because it's a win-or-die situation. There's no second chance. It's just a thing when I let everything go," he continued. "It's not a 16-game schedule — when I can pace myself and look at next week."

Craig Morton, Denver's ineffective starting quarterback, was relieved in the second quarter by Norris Weese, who directed a touchdown drive that closed the gap to 19-10 by halftime.

After a scoreless third quarter, Bradshaw put the game away on a 45-yard touchdown pass to Stallworth, who made a leaping catch at the end of the end zone, and a series later Bradshaw found Swann at the goal line on a 38-yard touchdown toss.

In the first half, Harris rushed for 57 yards on 14 carries, while Bradshaw hit 10 of 18 passes for 120 yards. His 22-yard pass play to Stallworth early in the second quarter set up Harris's sweep for a touchdown.

After Weese led the Broncos on a 49-yard touchdown drive that ended with a 3-yard run by Dave Preston. Gerela added a 27-yard field goal with seven seconds left before halftime.

Weese got the Broncos moving on their first drive of the third quarter.

He opened with a 24-yard pass completion to tight end Riley Odoms and later added a 10-yard run after winding up with the ball on a flea-flicker play.

The march stalled at the Steelers' 14-yard line, and Jim Turner's 29-yard field goal attempt was blocked by Steeler defensive tackle Joe Greene.

"The block was a big point in the game," said Denver Coach Red Miller. "I thought we could still come back. That made a big difference."

		SCORING	DEN	PIT
1st	Broncos	Jim Turner 37 yard field goal	3	0
	Steelers	Franco Harris 1 yard rush (kick failed)	3	6
2nd	Steelers	Franco Harris 18 yard rush (Roy Gerela kick)	3	13
	Steelers	Roy Gerela 24 yard field goal	3	16
	Broncos	Dave Preston 3 yard rush (Jim Turner kick)	10	16
	Steelers	Roy Gerela 27 yard field goal	10	19
4th	Steelers	John Stallworth 45 yard pass from Terry Bradshaw (Roy Gerela kick)	10	26
	Steelers	Lynn Swann 38 yard pass from Terry Bradshaw (Roy Gerela kick)	10	33

	TEAM STATS	
	DEN	PIT

First downs	15	24
Rush-Yards-TD	27-87-1	40-153-2
Comp-Att-Yards-TD-INT	12-22-168-0-0	16-29-272-2-1
Sacked-Yards	6-37	0-0
Net pass yards	131	272
Total yards	218	425
Fumbles-Lost	2-2	4-1
Turnovers	2	2
Penalties-Yards	8-104	11-88

PASSING, RUSHING and RECEIVING

Broncos

Passing

Norris Weese: 8-of-16, 118 yards
Craig Morton: 3-of-5, 34 yards
Bucky Dilts: 1-of-1, 16 yards

Rushing

Norris Weese: 4 carries for 43 yards
Dave Preston: 4 carries for 14 yards, 1 TD
Lonnie Perrin: 6 carries for 6 yards
Jon Keyworth: 6 carries for 12 yards
Rob Lytle: 5 carries for 6 yards
Otis Armstrong: 1 carry for 3 yards
Larry Canada: 1 carry for 3 yards

Receiving

Jack Dolbin: 4 catches for 77 yards
Dave Preston: 2 catches for 19 yards
Haven Moses: 2 catches for 33 yards
Riley Odoms: 1 catch for 24 yards

Lonnie Perrin: 2 catches for 16 yards
Rob Lytle: 1 catch for -1 yard

Steelers

Passing

Terry Bradshaw: 16-of-29, 272 yards, 2 TD, 1 INT

Rushing

Terry Bradshaw: 2 carries for 4 yards
Franco Harris: 24 carries for 105 yards, 2 TD
Rocky Bleier: 8 carries for 26 yards
Rick Moser: 2 carries for 6 yards
Sidney Thornton: 2 carries for 4 yards
Jack Deloplaine: 1 carry for 4 yards
Jim Smith: 1 carry for 4 yards

Receiving

John Stallworth: 10 catches for 156 yards, 1 TD
Randy Grossman: 4 catches for 64 yards
Lynn Swann: 2 catches for 52 yards, 1 TD

DEFENSE

Broncos

Interceptions

Bob Swenson: 1 for 4 yards

KICK RETURNS

Broncos

Kickoffs

Jon Keyworth: 1 for 5 yards, 5.0 avg.
Chris Pane: 1 for 0 yards, 0.0 avg.
Lonnie Perrin: 1 for 18 yards, 18.0 avg.
Rick Upchurch: 3 for 47 yards, 15.7 avg.

Punts

Rick Upchurch: 2 for 30 yards, 15.0 avg.

Steelers

Kickoffs

Larry Anderson: 2 for 57 yards, 28.5 avg.
Sidney Thornton: 1 for 8 yards, 8.0 avg.

Punts

Theo Bell: 3 for 7 yards, 2.3 avg.
Jack Deloplaine: 1 for 21 yards, 21.0 avg.

KICKING and PUNTING

Broncos

Kicking

Jim Turner: 1-for-1 PAT, 1-for-2 FG

Punting

Bucky Dilts: 6 for 204 yards, 34.0 avg.

Steelers

Kicking

Roy Gerela: 3-for-4 PAT, 2-for-2 FG

Punting

Craig Colquitt: 2 for 72 yards, 36.0 avg.

AFC Championship Game

Jan. 7
Three Rivers Stadium
Pittsburgh, PA

Houston Oilers — Pittsburgh Steelers

	1Q	2Q	3Q	4Q	Total
Oilers	0	3	2	0	5
Steelers	14	17	3	0	34

PITTSBURGH — Terry Bradshaw passed through icy rain for two touchdowns Sunday and Pittsburgh busted free from the shackles of its own errors to hydroplane past the Houston Oilers 34-5 into Super Bowl XIII.

The Steelers (16-2) had squeezed little from a volume of first-half opportunities when Pittsburgh suddenly about-faced an Oiler drive and scored 17 points in 48 astonishing seconds to turn the American Conference finals into a landslide.

Thus, Pittsburgh and Dallas, winner over Los Angeles in the NFC finals, will have a chance to become the first three-time Super Bowl winner. Also, it will be a rematch of their 1976 Super Bowl game, won 21-17 by the Steelers in Miami's Orange Bowl, site of XIII Jan. 21.

It was a day of meteorological misery at Three Rivers Stadium, rain and 26 degrees dancing on an artificial turf ringed by the snows of the night before.

Weather sacked both sides.

TWELVE TIMES they fumbled, six times apiece. Seven interceptions didn't make it any more glamorous. But no matter what the elements were to be, Pittsburgh was clearly king.

Franco Harris ran seven yards for the first score, Rocky Bleier sped 17 for the second. But it was the passing by Bradshaw that put it away, a 29-yard gem to Lynn Swann and a 17-yarder to John Stallworth for touchdowns.

It was that frantic final first-half minute that totally eradicated upstart Houston (12-7) from continuing its playoff fantasy. A 14-3 lead became, quicker than you can say the names of Pittsburgh's front four, a 31-3 halftime runaway.

Dan Pastorini, Houston's quarterback, had the Oilers moving even on a day when he would throw five interceptions and be sacked four times. He ripped a 12-yard pass to running back Ronnie Coleman, seeking to whittle Pittsburgh's lead from 14-3 to a more 14-10.

COLEMAN WAS crushed at the Steeler 31, the slippery football squirted away and Pittsburgh linebacker Jack Ham recovered. Only 1:23 remained in the half, but four plays and 31 seconds later Bradshaw was hooking with Swann for a touchdown. The score became 21-3.

On came the avalanche.

Rookie Robert Woods from Grambling fumbled, without nary a Steeler touching him, on the next kickoff and rookie Rick Moser recovered for Pittsburgh at the Houston 17. Harris ran once for no gain, but then Bradshaw looped the 17-yard touchdown pass to Stallworth.

It was 28-3 now, 33 seconds to go in the half.

The Oilers were falling apart by now. On their first play after still another Steeler kickoff, Coleman fumbled again and Steve Furness recovered for Pittsburgh at the Houston 24. That led to a 37-yard Roy Gerela field goal that made the Steeler lead 31-3 with 0:04 on the clock.

THEY PLAYED the second half, but it didn't mean much. Houston was too far gone to threaten a defense of the Steeler caliber. The game had ended, for all purposes, in that 17-point flurry at the tail of the second quarter.

Earl Campbell ran 22 times for 62 yards, but was thoroughly handled by Pittsburgh. Pastorini was 12-of-26 passing for 96 yards, but again was no problem for the men of steel.

Bradshaw completed 11 of 19 for 200 yards. He defeated the rain and cold and the field loaded with so many frigid puddles. The 30-year-old quarterback from Louisiana Tech has reached new highs in performance in his eighth NFL season.

AFC from 1-C

"We busted loose after fouling up three or four great scoring chances," Bradshaw said, still shivering in the Steeler dressing room. "We were down close so often, and we weren't getting anything. Then came the explosion."

A 34-yard Bradshaw pass to Swann was the major weapon in Pittsburgh's drive for a 7-0 lead, Harris scoring with a quick move around right end with 10:02 left in the first quarter.

PITTSBURGH GOT quickly back to the Houston 19, but Willie Alexander stepped in front of Swann and intercepted a Bradshaw throw. Two other times the Steelers were threatening and Harris fumbled the ball.

"Lousy weather like this is okay for the defense," Harris said. "Our defense probably even enjoys this. But it is murder on running backs. The ball is like holding a greased pig."

Bleier made one of his better runs of the season to raise the Steeler lead to 14-0 late in the first quarter, sprinting right and finally diving into a wet end zone.

Houston's only points came on Toni Fritsch's 19-yard field goal that made it 14-3, plus a safety in the third period when Bleier was tackled in the end zone by linebacker Russ Washington.

Pittsburgh led in total offense 379 yards to 168. The Steelers made 21 first downs to Houston's 10. The score could have been worse. The Oilers were proud, not of Sunday but for getting so far in the playoffs, but they were clobbered.

"I hope the Oilers don't get too discouraged," said Steeler defensive tackle Joe Greene. "They are like we were in 1972, young and promising and getting killed by Miami. But I do think Houston realizes that it got beat by a better team today."

		SCORING	HOU	PIT
1st	Steelers	Franco Harris 7 yard rush (Roy Gerela kick)	0	7
	Steelers	Rocky Bleier 15 yard rush (Roy Gerela kick)	0	14
2nd	Oilers	Toni Fritsch 19 yard field goal	3	14
	Steelers	Lynn Swann 29 yard pass from Terry Bradshaw (Roy Gerela kick)	3	21
	Broncos	John Stallworth 17 yard pass from Terry Bradshaw (Roy Gerela kick)	3	28
	Steelers	Roy Gerela 37 yard field goal	3	31
3rd	Steelers	Roy Gerela 22 yard field goal	3	34
	Oilers	Safety, Washington tackled Bleier in end zone	5	34

	TEAM STATS	
	HOU	PIT
First downs	10	21
Rush-Yards-TD	26-72-0	47-179-2
Comp-Att-Yards-TD-INT	12-26-96-0-5	11-19-200-2-2
Sacked-Yards	4-26	0-0
Net pass yards	70	200
Total yards	142	379
Fumbles-Lost	6-4	6-3
Turnovers	9	5
Penalties-Yards	5-48	4-32

PASSING, RUSHING and RECEIVING

Oilers

Passing

Dan Pastorini: 12-of-26, 96 yards, 0 TD, 5 INT

Rushing

Earl Campbell: 22 carries for 62 yards
Tim Wilson: 2 carries for 6 yards
Ronnie Coleman: 1 carry for -5 yards
Robert Woods: 1 carry for 9 yards

Receiving

Earl Campbell: 1 catch for 4 yards
Rich Caster: 5 catches for 44 yards
Tim Wilson: 5 catches for 33 yards
Ronnie Coleman: 1 catch for 15 yards

Steelers

Passing

Terry Bradshaw: 11-of-19, 200 yards, 2 TD, 2 INT

Rushing

Terry Bradshaw: 7 carries for 29 yards
Rocky Bleier: 10 carries for 45 yards, 1 TD
Franco Harris: 20 carries for 51 yards, 1 TD
Jack Deloplaine: 3 carries for 28 yards
Sidney Thornton: 3 carries for 22 yards
Rick Moser: 3 carries for 7 yards
Mike Kruczek: 1 carry for -3 yards

Receiving

Lynn Swann: 4 catches for 98 yards, 1 TD
Rocky Bleier: 4 catches for 42 yards
Randy Grossman: 2 catches for 43 yards
John Stallworth: 1 catch for 17 yards, 1 TD

DEFENSE

Oilers

Interceptions

Willie Alexander: 1 for 0 yards
Greg Stemrick: 1 for 0 yards

Steelers

Interceptions

Mel Blount: 1 for 16 yards
Jack Ham: 1 for 0 yards
Ron Johnson: 1 for 34 yards
Donnie Shell: 1 for 5 yards
Loren Toews: 1 for 35 yards

KICK RETURNS

Oilers

Kickoffs

Johnnie Dirden: 3 for 72 yards, 24.0 avg.
Brian Duncan: 1 for 17 yards, 17.0 avg.

Guido Merkens: 2 for 57 yards, 28.5 avg.
Robert Woods: 2 for 33 yards, 16.5 avg.

Steelers

Kickoffs

Larry Anderson: 1 for 15 yards, 15.0 avg.
Jack Deloplaine: 1 for 21 yards, 21.0 avg.

Punts

Theo Bell: 6 for 91 yards, 15.2 avg.

KICKING and PUNTING

Oilers

Kicking

Toni Fritsch: 1-for-1 FG

Punting

Cliff Parsley: 6 for 237 yards, 39.5 avg.

Steelers

Kicking

Roy Gerela: 4-for-4 PAT, 2-for-4 FG

Punting

Craig Colquitt: 1 for 53 yards, 53.0 avg.

Super Bowl XIII

Pittsburgh Steelers vs **Dallas Cowboys**
Jan. 21
Orange Bowl
Miami, FL

	1Q	2Q	3Q	4Q	Total
Steelers	7	14	0	14	35
Cowboys	7	7	3	14	31

Miami, Fla. — As Super Bowls go, the one played Sunday on real grass in the Orange Bowl was the best one ever played.

The score was Pittsburgh 35, Dallas 31, and it seemed that if the Cowboys had had a few more minutes at the end, they would have walked off with the professional football championship.

Instead, the Steelers hung on to win. Actually, they had the Cowboys on the ropes, leading, 35-17, with less than 7 minutes to play.

Then Roger Staubach got hot and directed an incredible fourth quarter comeback. Staubach's 7 yard touchdown pass to Billy Joe DuPree capped an 8 play, 89 yard drive. And following the recovery of an onside kickoff, Staubach hit Butch Johnson on a four yard strike with 22 seconds left in the first rematch in Super Bowl history.

As good as the Cowboys were, the Steelers had more gifted receivers in Lynn Swann and John Stallworth. And certainly they had the superior quarterback in Terry Bradshaw, who was named the game's most valuable player.

Bradshaw had his best day ever as a pro. He completed 17 of 30 passes for 318 yards, and he threw four touchdown passes. There were two to Stallworth and one to Rocky Bleier in the first half, and another one to Swann in the fourth quarter.

At halftime, Bradshaw had completed 11 of 18 passes for 253 yards which broke Green Bay Packer Bart Starr's record of 250 yards in the first Super Bowl game in 1967. Starr's feat, of course, was for the entire game.

The interesting thing about Bradshaw's performance is that the Cowboys wanted to get him into long passing situations. Dallas blitzed Bradshaw most of the game, and the Cowboys wound up sacking him four times.

Bradshaw suffered a bruised left shoulder in the second quarter when he was hit by Cowboy linebackers Thomas Henderson and Mike Hegman. In the collision, Hegman stole the ball from the dazed Bradshaw and lumbered 37 yards for a touchdown and a 14-7 Dallas lead.

"My shoulder really hurt," Bradshaw said in a jammed interview room after the game. "I was sick to my stomach, and I was scared to death because when they first checked the injury they said it was a separation. But it was only a bad strain."

Bradshaw certainly didn't show any evidence of the injury. Right after the Dallas touchdown, he hit the speedy Stallworth. And when Stallworth spun away from Dallas defender Aaron Kyle, it resulted in the biggest gain of the game — 75 yards and a Pittsburgh touchdown.

"I never threw well against Dallas until today," said Bradshaw, answering questions while sticking a handful of Red Man chewing tobacco into his mouth. "I was relaxed. I was having fun. I was kind of lackasdaisical. Maybe I had something to prove."

Whatever it was, Dallas couldn't do much about it. Swann, who caught 7 passes for 124 yards, and Stallworth, who snared 3 for

115 yards, were like waterbugs as they darted in, out and away from the Cowboys' secondary.

There were two plays, however, that did an awful lot to keep the Cowboys from winning.

The first occurred midway through the third quarter when Staubach moved the Cowboys into scoring position on the Pittsburgh 10 yard line. On third down from the 10, Staubach fired a quick pass over the middle to Jackie Smith. Smith was alone in the end zone and on his knees when the ball came to him.

But he dropped it, and Dallas had to settle for a 27 yard field goal by Rafael Septien.

The second critical play for Dallas came in the fourth quarter when the Steelers were hanging onto a 21-17 lead. The Steelers had a second down on their 43, and Bradshaw threw a long pass to Swann.

Benny Barnes was the Dallas defender,

Continued From Page 1

and when Swann came close to him it looked as if Swann had pushed off on Barnes. But the officials called an interference penalty on Barnes, and it was a big one — 33 yards to the Dallas 23.

Four plays later, Bradshaw handed the ball off to Franco Harris. The Cowboys were fooled completely by the trap play, and Harris scored on a 22 yard run up the middle to give Pittsburgh a 28-17 lead.

"Swann ran right up my back," Barnes complained later. "When I saw the flag I knew it was on him."

Referee Pat Haggerty said it was a judgment call. "The two players bumped before the ball was even close to them, perhaps before the ball was thrown," said Haggerty.

"They were both looking back, and the defender went to the ground. The Pittsburgh receiver, in trying to get to the ball, was tripped by the back trying to get to the ball. It was coming back to him in that direction, and I threw the flag for pass interference."

The Steelers dominated the Cowboys in the first half, outgaining them 271 yards to 102. Dallas stayed close because Staubach, under heavy pressure, was able to connect with Tony Hill on a dandy 39 yard touchdown play and because Hegman stole the ball and ran 37 yards untouched for another score.

In the second half the Cowboys began to contain Bradshaw much more effectively. But Staubach's receivers — Hill and Drew Pearson — weren't in the same class with Pittsburgh's Swann and Stallworth. So Staubach ended up completing more passes to Dorsett (five) than anyone else.

How They Scored

	Pittsburgh	Dallas
First downs	19	20
Rushes-yards	24-66	32-141

Dorsett emerged as the game's leading ground gainer with 96 yards on 25 carries. "I felt we could run on them," he said. "I was going well early in the game, and then I wasn't getting the ball. What can I say?"

Dorsett added that the Steelers showed some class. He told about one play in the second half, on an incomplete pass, when Steeler linebacker Jack Lambert grabbed him by the face mask.

"He (Lambert) said, 'Hey, I'm sorry,'" Dorsett said. "That's the sign of a champion. But on the next play, I told myself that I'd better button my chin strap because he's not going to go easy on me."

In beating the Cowboys, the Steelers became the first three time winner in the Super Bowl game. Three years ago, Pittsburgh defeated Dallas, 21-17, in this spectacle.

Super Bowl XIII, played before a crowd of 78,656, produced a lot of records, including most points by both teams (65), most touchdowns by both teams (9), most touchdown passes by both teams (7), and most yards passing by both teams (467).

But Pittsburgh had Bradshaw and he WAS the difference.

		SCORING	PIT	DAL
1st	Steelers	John Stallworth 28 yard pass from Terry Bradshaw (Roy Gerela kick)	7	0

	Cowboys	Tony Hill 39 yard pass from Roger Staubach (Rafael Septien kick)	7	7
2nd	Cowboys	Mike Hegman 37 yard fumble return (Rafael Septien kick)	7	14
	Steelers	John Stallworth 75 yard pass from Terry Bradshaw (Roy Gerela kick)	14	14
	Steelers	Rocky Bleier 7 yard pass from Terry Bradshaw (Roy Gerela kick)	21	14
3rd	Cowboys	Rafael Septien 27 yard field goal	21	17
4th	Steelers	Franco Harris 22 yard rush (Roy Gerela kick)	28	17
	Steelers	Lynn Swann 18 yard pass from Terry Bradshaw (Roy Gerela kick)	35	17
	Cowboys	Billy Joe DuPree 7 yard pass from Roger Staubach (Rafael Septien kick)	35	24
	Cowboys	Butch Johnson 4 yard pass from Roger Staubach (Rafael Septien kick)	35	31

	TEAM STATS	
	PIT	DAL
First downs	19	20
Rush-Yards-TD	24-66-1	32-154-0
Comp-Att-Yards-TD-INT	17-30-318-4-1	17-30-228-3-1
Sacked-Yards	4-27	5-52
Net pass yards	291	176
Total yards	357	330
Fumbles-Lost	2-2	3-2
Turnovers	3	3
Penalties-Yards	5-35	9-89

PASSING, RUSHING and RECEIVING

Steelers

Passing

Terry Bradshaw: 17-of-30, 318 yards, 4 TD, 1 INT

Rushing

Terry Bradshaw: 2 carries for -5 yards
Franco Harris: 20 carries for 68 yards, 1 TD
Rocky Bleier: 2 carries for 3 yards

Receiving

Lynn Swann: 7 catches for 124 yards, 1 TD
John Stallworth: 3 catches for 115 yards, 2 TD
Franco Harris: 1 catch for 22 yards
Randy Grossman: 3 catches for 29 yards
Theo Bell: 2 catches for 21 yards
Rocky Bleier: 1 catch for 7 yards, 1 TD

Cowboys

Passing

Roger Staubach: 17-of-30, 228 yards, 3 TD, 1 INT

Rushing

Roger Staubach: 4 carries for 37 yards
Tony Dorsett: 16 carries for 96 yards
Preston Pearson: 1 carry for 6 yards
Scott Laidlaw: 3 carries for 12 yards
Robert Newhouse: 8 carries for 3 yards

Receiving

Tony Dorsett: 5 catches for 44 yards
Drew Pearson: 4 catches for 73 yards
Tony Hill: 2 catches for 49 yards, 1 TD
Butch Johnson: 2 catches for 30 yards, 1 TD
Preston Pearson: 2 catches for 15 yards
Billy Joe DuPree: 2 catches for 17 yards, 1 TD

DEFENSE

Steelers

Sacks

John Banaszak (1.0), Steve Furness (1.0), Joe Greene (1.0), L.C. Greenwood (1.0) and Dwight White (1.0)

Interceptions

Mel Blount: 1 for 13 yards

Cowboys

Sacks

Mike Hegman (1.0), Thomas Henderson (1.0), Harvey Martin (1.0) and Randy White (1.0)

Interceptions

D.D. Lewis: 1 for 21 yards

KICK RETURNS

Steelers

Kickoffs

Larry Anderson: 3 for 45 yards, 15.0 avg.

Punts

Theo Bell: 4 for 27 yards, 6.8 avg.

Cowboys

Kickoffs

Larry Brinson: 2 for 41 yards, 20.5 avg.
Butch Johnson: 3 for 63 yards, 21.0 avg.
Randy White: 1 for 0 yards, 0.0 avg.

Punts

Butch Johnson: 2 for 33 yards, 16.5 avg.

KICKING and PUNTING

Steelers

Kicking

Roy Gerela: 5-for-5 PAT, 0-for-1 FG

Punting

Craig Colquitt: 3 for 129 yards, 43.0 avg.

Cowboys

Kicking

Rafael Septien: 4-for-4 PAT, 1-for-1 FG

Punting

Danny White: 5 for 198 yards, 39.6 avg.

1978 NFL Standings

AFC

East	W	L	T	PF	PA
Miami Dolphins	11	5	0	372	254
New England Patriots	11	5	0	358	286
New York Jets	8	8	0	359	364
Baltimore Colts	5	11	0	239	421
Buffalo Bills	5	11	0	302	354

Central	W	L		PF	PA
Pittsburgh Steelers	14	2	0	356	195
Houston Oilers	10	6	0	283	298
Cleveland Browns	8	8	0	334	356
Cincinnati Bengals	4	12	0	252	284

West	W	L		PF	PA
Denver Broncos	10	6	0	282	198
San Diego Chargers	9	7	0	355	309
Oakland Raiders	9	7	0	311	283
Seattle Seahawks	9	7	0	345	358
Kansas City Chiefs	4	12	0	243	327

NFC

East	W	L	T	PF	PA
Dallas Cowboys	12	4	0	384	208
Philadelphia Eagles	9	7	0	270	250
Washington Redskins	8	8	0	273	283
New York Giants	6	10	0	264	298
St. Louis Cardinals	6	10	0	248	296

Central	W	L	T	PF	PA
Minnesota Vikings	8	7	1	294	306
Green Bay Packers	8	7	1	249	269
Detroit Lions	7	9	0	290	300
Chicago Bears	7	9	0	253	274
Tampa Bay Buccaneers	5	11	0	241	259

West	W	L	T	PF	PA
Los Angeles Rams	12	4	0	316	245
Atlanta Falcons	9	7	0	240	290
New Orleans Saints	7	9	0	281	298
San Francisco 49ers	2	14	0	219	350

Steelers 1978 Draft Picks

Round 1 (22): Ron Johnson, DB, Eastern Michigan
Round 2 (49): Willie Fry, DE, Notre Dame
Round 3 (76): Craig Colquitt, P, Tennessee
Round 4 (101): Larry Anderson, DB, Louisiana Tech
Round 6 (160): Randy Reutershan, WR, Pittsburgh
Round 7 (187): Mark Dufresne, TE, Nebraska
Round 8 (208): Rick Moser, RB, Rhode Island
Round 8 (214): Andre Keys, WR, Cal Poly-San Luis Obispo

Round 9 (241): Lance Reynolds, T, BYU
Round 10 (268): Doug Becker, LB, Notre Dame
Round 10 (276): Tom Jurich, K, Northern Arizona
Round 11 (279): Nat Terry, DB, Florida State
Round 11 (300): Tom Brzoza, C, Pittsburgh
Round 12 (327): Brad Carr, LB, Maryland

1979

Season Review

With four victories to open the season, the Steelers reasserted their dominance in the AFC.

Occasional lapses, however, demonstrated their humanity and made them struggle to hold off challengers to their perch.

Losses to the Eagles, Bengals and Chargers dropped them into a first-place tie with Houston at 9-3.

On November 25, they hosted the rising Cleveland Browns and went into overtime to take a 33-30 decision.

One week later, they beat Cincinnati while the Oilers were losing.

The Steelers thus took a one-game lead into the Astrodome for a Monday night confrontation on December 10.

The physical Oilers outmuscled the Steelers and won the game 20-17, creating another tie going into the final weekend.

The veteran Steelers geared up for the visiting Buffalo Bills.

With habitual winners named Greene, Bradshaw, Harris, Swann, Stallworth, Greenwood, Lambert, Shell and Webster on the job, the Steelers throttled Buffalo 28-0 to retain first place for another year.

Week 1

Sept. 3
Schaefer Stadium
Foxborough, MA

Pittsburgh Steelers vs **New England Patriots**

	1Q	2Q	3Q	4Q	OT	Total
Steelers	0	6	0	7	3	16
Patriots	7	6	0	0	0	13

FOXBORO, Mass. (AP) — You can play perfect football for 59 minutes, but make one mistake against the Pittsburgh Steelers and you can pack it up and go home with a loss.

That's what makes them champions. That's what the New England Patriots have to live with.

They played well — very well — against Terry Bradshaw's passing game virtually all night. But a mistake here, a slip-up there, and the noose began to tighten.

They clamped down on Franco Harris' pile driver running, but when they paused to take a breath, he and Sidney Thornton ran by them like locomotives.

They reveled in Matt Bahr's erratic right foot, but when they tried to rattle the rookie once too often, he just shrugged and kicked their teeth in.

"In a situation like that, the tough guys just naturally come out," said Bradshaw, whose 21-yard touchdown pass to Thornton tied the game with 4:09 to go in regulation play Monday night and whose canny play-calling put Bahr in position to win it 16-13 at 5:10 of overtime with a 41-yard field goal.

"We just made up our minds and did it," added Bradshaw, one of those "tough guys" who played most of the game with a painfully sprained toe but who still managed to complete 15 of 26 passes for 221 yards.

Bahr, the rookie from Penn State who started his pro career raggedly when his first extra point attempt after Thornton had scored the Steelers' first TD on a 2-yard run was just plain bad, left Pittsburgh trailing 7-6.

And his first try at a pro field goal, a 43-yarder with Pittsburgh trailing 13-6 in the third period, was equally poor, short and off line.

But when it mattered, when he had to prove that the Steelers' decision to hand Roy Gerela his walking papers was a sound one, he came through perfectly.

His kick was dead-center and easily 10 yards longer than it had to be, this despite a timeout called by the Patriots in an attempt to build the already awesome pressure.

"Nobody's ever done that to me before," Bahr said. "I could hear the noise (60,978 fans can create a lot of it) but it just gave me a little more time."

The noise the fans created then was nothing compared to the shattering roar of a tribute they gave to Darryl Stingley in the second period.

The Patriots' former wide receiver, paralyzed in a preseason collision a year ago, returned to Schaefer Stadium for the first time since the accident and the fans stood for more than five minutes, delaying the game with their applause, shouts and chants. So caught up in the frenzy were they that when the Patriots attempted to run a play they showered boos down upon the team they had come to cheer.

If it can be said that one good kick won it for the Steelers, it is equally true that one bad one lost it for the Patriots.

Eddie Hare, like Bahr a rookie, had been booming punts all night, 50 yards and more. But with five minutes to play in the fourth period and the Pats still clinging to their 13-6 lead, the kid from Tulsa shanked one, driving it a measly 14 yards to the New England 34.

"The kicking game was pretty good - except for one. It's the best kicking we've had in this stadium in a long time, but " and New England Coach Ron Erhardt's voice trailed off.

It had cost him his first victory as a head coach in the National Football League. Instead, it had given Chuck Noll of the Steelers his 100th.

"I don't have the words to express how I feel about this team being able to hang in there," Noll said of the players who have given him three Super Bowl rings, something no other coach has. "We were less than efficient but we gutted it out."

That is the essence of the Steelers, the way they can lay back and wait for the other team to make the mistake, then call on some inner reserve for the plays, the yards, the victories.

"The game was ours for the asking," said John Hannah, the Patriots' All-Pro guard. "We just didn't take it. The game should have been ours. But every time we did something big, we got penalized." Like when his illegal motion penalty wiped out a 39-yard Steve Grogan pass that would have put the ball on the Steeler 5-yard line. Or Sam Cunningham's 31-yard run to the Pittsburgh 15 killed by a clip.

In the overtime, after the Pats went nowhere with the kickoff and Hare punted 40 yards to the Steeler 31, Harris and Thornton took turns taking Bradshaw handoffs and chewing up the yards, 17 of them in one chunk by Thornton, 11 by Harris in a sweep. Finally the ball was on the Patriots' 24, and then it was through the uprights.

"We should have won the game," said Patriots safety Tim Fox. "We won it five times — and lost it six times."

Schonert Lands Marlin As No Broadbill Caught

It turned out to be a dry tournament.

But 17-year-old Ernie Schonert Jr., was as happy as a lark.

In the eighth annual Channel Islands Invitational Broadbill Tournament, 140 anglers participated and there were 30 sightings of broadbill reported. Schonert won the award for

Broadbill president Ed Weigel said, "I don't know if some these fish are ever going to show up."

Weigel, who went out and came back empty of broadbill, said, "The Floridans can have the night fishing. It won't be done by me."

Monday marked the broadbill awards banquet of

		SCORING	PIT	NWE
1st	Patriots	Russ Francis 4 yard pass from Steve Grogan (John Smith kick)	0	7
2nd	Steelers	Sidney Thornton 2 yard rush (kick failed)	6	7
	Patriots	John Smith 31 yard field goal	6	10
	Patriots	John Smith 32 yard field goal	6	13
4th	Steelers	Sidney Thornton 21 yard pass from Terry Bradshaw (Matt Bahr kick)	13	13
OT	Steelers	Matt Bahr 41 yard field goal	16	13

	TEAM STATS	
	PIT	NWE
First downs	20	16
Rush-Yards-TD	38-118-1	37-162-0
Comp-Att-Yards-TD-INT	15-29-221-1-0	11-33-123-1-2
Sacked-Yards	4-30	5-41

Net pass yards	191	82
Total yards	309	244
Fumbles-Lost	2-2	1-0
Turnovers	2	2
Penalties-Yards	6-50	7-58

PASSING, RUSHING and RECEIVING

Steelers

Passing

Terry Bradshaw: 15-of-26, 221 yards, 1 TD, 0 INT
Mike Kruczek: 0-of-3, 0 yards

Rushing

Franco Harris: 26 carries for 74 yards
Sidney Thornton: 12 carries for 44 yards, 1 TD

Receiving

John Stallworth: 5 catches for 95 yards
Franco Harris: 3 catches for 14 yards
Sidney Thornton: 3 catches for 41 yards, 1 TD
Bennie Cunningham: 2 catches for 40 yards
Lynn Swann: 1 catch for 19 yards
Randy Grossman: 1 catch for 12 yards

Patriots

Passing

Steve Grogan: 11-of-33, 123 yards, 1 TD, 2 INT

Rushing

Steve Grogan: 4 carries for 38 yards
Sam Cunningham: 17 carries for 62 yards
Andy Johnson: 12 carries for 42 yards
Horace Ivory: 4 carries for 20 yards

Receiving

Sam Cunningham: 2 catches for 9 yards
Andy Johnson: 2 catches for 19 yards
Russ Francis: 5 catches for 53 yards, 1 TD
Stanley Morgan: 1 catch for 33 yards
Harold Jackson: 1 catch for 9 yards

DEFENSE

Steelers

Interceptions

Jack Lambert: 1 for 4 yards
Dwayne Woodruff: 1 for 31 yards

KICK RETURNS

Steelers

Kickoffs

Anthony Anderson: 1 for 13 yards, 13.0 avg.
Larry Anderson: 3 for 85 yards, 28.3 avg.

Punts

Lynn Swann: 1 for -1 yard, -1.0 avg.

Patriots

Kickoffs

Allan Clark: 3 for 64 yards, 21.3 avg.
Rick Sanford: 1 for 17 yards, 17.0 avg.

Punts

Mike Haynes: 1 for 4 yards, 4.0 avg.
Stanley Morgan: 1 for 3 yards, 3.0 avg.

KICKING and PUNTING

Steelers

Kicking

Matt Bahr: 1-for-2 PAT, 1-for-2 FG

Punting

Craig Colquitt: 7 for 281 yards, 40.1 avg.

Patriots

Kicking

John Smith: 1-for-1 PAT, 2-for-2 FG

Punting

Eddie Hare: 9 for 357 yards, 39.7 avg.

Week 2

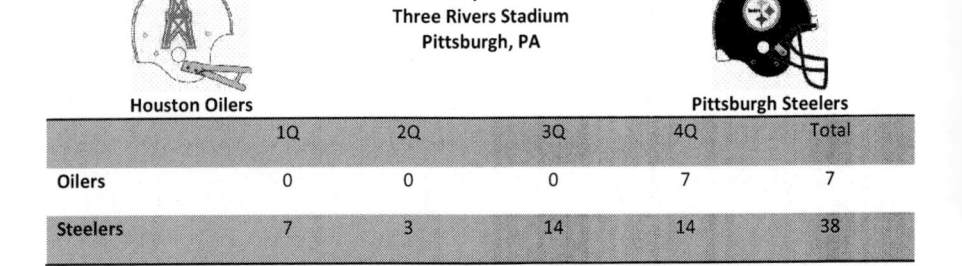

Sept. 9
Three Rivers Stadium
Pittsburgh, PA

Houston Oilers — Pittsburgh Steelers

	1Q	2Q	3Q	4Q	Total
Oilers	0	0	0	7	7
Steelers	7	3	14	14	38

The Pittsburgh Steelers beat Houston 38-7 behind a gang-tackling defensive effort that left Oilers quarterback Dan Pastorini with his arm in a sling and Earl Campbell with his lowest rushing total in the NFL.

"They did everything that got them to the Super Bowl," said Houston coach Bum Phillips, who also watched Terry Bradshaw pass for two Steelers touchdowns and running back Sidney Thornton score tow more.

The Steelers beat Houston 34-5 in Pittsburgh on Jan. 7 in the AFC title game, played in steady, freezing rain.

The footing was fine and the sky was clear on this day. It was anything but a perfect football afternoon for a Houston offense that was limited to 124 net yards – 22 passing and 102 rushing.

"We just played a good football team today. We just couldn't get nothing going," said Campbell, the second-year pro who was limited to 36 yards rushing on 16 carries.

Pastorini left the game in the third quarter with a jammed right arm sustained on a play in which he threw his third interception. Sacked five times, he finished with four completions in 16 pass attempts for 16 yards.

"It was a devastating effort, the kind of effort that can take the life out of a football team," said Steelers defensive tackle Joe Greene.

"Defensively, we've played some great games over the years. This is one of the better ones," said linebacker Jack Lambert.

"You ought to win a football game when you've got a defense playing like ours did," said Bradshaw.

Yet the Steelers also stressed that it was just the second game of the season, and Campbell was preaching a similar message in the Houston locker room.

"Cheer up. What happened, somebody die?" said Campbell. "What does Lou Rawls sing, 'The sun's gonna come up tomorrow.'"

Nonetheless, the Oilers left town with two big question marks – the severity of Pastorini's arm injury and the seriousness of a knee injury sustained in the fourth quarter by Billy "White Shoes" Johnson.

X-rays taken at the stadium of Pastorini's arm were negative, but there was no immediate word on possible muscle damage.

On a third-quarter play, Pastorini was hit while passing by linebacker Loren Toews and the ball fluttered into the air.

End John Banaszak made the interception, and Pastorini hurt his arm while tackling the 250-pounder at the Houston 8-yard line.

Banaszak's interception set up an eight-yard scoring touchdown run by rookie Greg Hawthorne.

Houston backup quarterback Gifford Nielsen later had a pass intercepted by Steelers linebacker Dennis "Dirt" Winston and returned 41 yards for the final Pittsburgh touchdown. With Pittsburgh leading 38-0 Nielsen averted a shutout with a nine-yard touchdown pass to Guido Merkens.

"They played like the Super Bowl champions they are," said Houston offensive tackle Leon Gray. "We didn't execute at all."

Pittsburgh improved to 2-0 and Houston fell to 1-1 in the matchup of AFC Central division rivals.

Thornton, making his second start in the Steelers' backfield, gave Pittsburgh a 7-0 lead with a one-yard touchdown run midway through the first period. The score capped a 45-yard drive that the Steelers managed despite two costly penalties which wiped out a pair of pass completions totaling 58 yards.

		SCORING	HOU	PIT

1st	Steelers	Sidney Thornton 1 yard rush (Matt Bahr kick)	0	7
2nd	Steelers	Matt Bahr 45 yard field goal	0	10
3rd	Steelers	Sidney Thornton 16 yard pass from Terry Bradshaw (Matt Bahr kick)	0	17
	Steelers	Greg Hawthorne 8 yard rush (Matt Bahr kick)	0	24
4th	Steelers	Jim Smith 18 yard pass from Terry Bradshaw (Matt Bahr kick)	0	31
	Steelers	Dirt Winston 41 yard interception return (Matt Bahr kick)	0	38
	Oilers	Guido Merkens 9 yard pass from Gifford Nielsen (Toni Fritsch kick)	7	38

	TEAM STATS	
	HOU	PIT
First downs	12	17
Rush-Yards-TD	39-102-0	29-82-2
Comp-Att-Yards-TD-INT	8-27-57-1-5	12-29-198-2-2
Sacked-Yards	5-35	3-24
Net pass yards	22	174
Total yards	124	256
Fumbles-Lost	4-1	5-0
Turnovers	6	2
Penalties-Yards	10-64	8-74

PASSING, RUSHING and RECEIVING

Oilers

Passing

Gifford Nielsen: 4-of-11, 41 yards, 1 TD, 2 INT
Dan Pastorini: 4-of-16, 16 yards, 0 TD, 3 INT

Rushing

Earl Campbell: 16 carries for 38 yards
Ronnie Coleman: 7 carries for 22 yards
Boobie Clark: 5 carries for 15 yards
Tim Wilson: 7 carries for 19 yards
Rob Carpenter: 4 carries for 8 yards

Receiving

Earl Campbell: 1 catch for 4 yards
Billy Johnson: 2 catches for 32 yards
Conrad Rucker: 1 catch for 13 yards
Mike Renfro: 1 catch for 12 yards
Guido Merkens: 1 catch for 9 yards, 1 TD
Tim Wilson: 1 catch for -10 yards
Rob Carpenter: 1 catch for -3 yards

Steelers

Passing

Terry Bradshaw: 12-of-29, 198 yards, 2 TD, 2 INT

Rushing

Terry Bradshaw: 3 carries for -3 yards
Franco Harris: 14 carries for 42 yards
Sidney Thornton: 7 carries for 20 yards, 1 TD
Rocky Bleier: 2 carries for 14 yards
Greg Hawthorne: 3 carries for 9 yards, 1 TD

Receiving

Lynn Swann: 5 catches for 95 yards
Franco Harris: 1 catch for 18 yards
Sidney Thornton: 1 catch for 16 yards, 1 TD
Rocky Bleier: 1 catch for 9 yards
John Stallworth: 1 catch for 20 yards
Jim Smith: 1 catch for 18 yards, 1 TD
Greg Hawthorne: 1 catch for 8 yards
Randy Grossman: 1 catch for 14 yards

DEFENSE

Oilers

Interceptions

Mike Reinfeldt: 1 for 23 yards
Art Stringer: 1 for 0 yards

Steelers

Interceptions

John Banaszak: 1 for 3 yards
Jack Lambert: 1 for 2 yards
Mike Wagner: 2 for 19 yards
Dirt Winston: 1 for 41 yards, 1 TD

KICK RETURNS

Oilers

Kickoffs

Ronnie Coleman: 4 for 88 yards, 22.0 avg.
Guido Merkens: 1 for 13 yards, 13.0 avg.
Tim Wilson: 2 for 30 yards, 15.0 avg.

Punts

Billy Johnson: 3 for 1 yard, 0.3 avg.

Steelers

Kickoffs

Larry Anderson: 1 for 27 yards, 27.0 avg.
Robin Cole: 1 for 3 yards, 3.0 avg.

Punts

Jim Smith: 8 for 65 yards, 8.1 avg.

KICKING and PUNTING

Oilers

Kicking

Toni Fritsch: 1-for-1 PAT

Punting

Cliff Parsley: 9 for 415 yards, 46.1 avg.

Steelers

Kicking

Matt Bahr: 5-for-5 PAT, 1-for-2 FG

Punting

Craig Colquitt: 7 for 281 yards, 40.1 avg.

Week 3

Sept. 16
Busch Memorial Stadium
St. Louis, MO

Pittsburgh Steelers vs **St. Louis Cardinals**

	1Q	2Q	3Q	4Q	Total
Steelers	7	0	0	17	24
Cardinals	9	6	6	0	21

Associated Press

ST. LOUIS — Rookie Matt Bahr's field goal produced a last-minute victory Sunday for the Pittsburgh Steelers, but the lion's share of the credit went to the National Football League kingpins' rock-ribbed defense.

"They were able to turn it around," said Steelers coach Chuck Noll of the performance by Pittsburgh's vaunted "Steel Curtain" in the closing 30 minutes.

"Our whole football team, I think, came back from adverse circumstances. I think that's the mark of a champion," Noll said following a 24-21 triumph over the St. Louis Cardinals.

The defensive effort, which was rewarded when Bahr booted a 20-yard field goal with 13 seconds left, was especially gratifying to tackle John Banaszak.

"We're happy," said Banaszak, who helped Pittsburgh restrict St. Louis to 37 net yards in the final two periods.

"Team defense is what it's all about. We just played 11-man defensive football," he said.

"There are people who are going to try to knock you off when you're on top of the totem pole. It's going to make their season. If we play somebody who's 1-9 a few weeks from now, that's a big thing for them."

En route to their victory, the Steelers (3-0) rallied from a 21-7 deficit and overcame the Cardinals (1-2) with a 17-point explosion in the final 15 minutes.

Bahr's field goal capped a Pittsburgh march from its own 29 in the closing minutes to extend the Steelers' string of victories to 11 games, including last January's 35-31 triumph over the Dallas Cowboys in Super Bowl XIII.

In winning, the Steelers overcame two interceptions and two losses of fumbles, which helped the Cardinals grab a 21-7 advantage late in the third quarter.

Rocky Bleier's four-yard run narrowed the St. Louis lead to 21-14 with eight seconds gone in the closing period. Terry Bradshaw clicked on a five-yard scoring pass to Benny Cunningham with 8:07 remaining, and Bahr's kick split the uprights for the winning points.

Although stymied by the tough Steeler defense, St. Louis grabbed a

9-0 lead in the opening 12 minutes and led 15-7 at halftime.

Rookies Ottis Anderson, the University of Miami burner, and Theotis Brown, the former UCLA star, ran for Cardinals touchdowns, and Steve Little and Mike Wood combined for three field goals. Until the final quarter, Pittsburgh's only score came on an 18-yard pass from Bradshaw to John Stallworth.

Jim Hart and Mel Gray hooked up on a 48-yard pass play to set up the 12-yard touchdown gallop by Anderson early in the opening quarter for St. Louis.

One of two Pittsburgh fumbles led to a 22-yard field goal by Little, making it 9-0 soon afterward. Bradshaw then whipped four straight pass completions, the final one to Stallworth, as the Steelers drew to 9-7, but Ken Stone's interception of a Bradshaw aerial led to Brown's one-yard touchdown smash in the second quarter.

Bradshaw was carried from the field on a stretcher with a badly bruised left ankle late in the second quarter, but returned to action at the start of the final half.

His first pass of the third quarter was picked off by St. Louis' Carl Allen, with a 24-yard field goal by Wood following. Willard Harrell then returned a punt 68 yards to the Pittsburgh 13 to set up a 27-yard field goal by Wood, which closed the Cards' scoring.

Bleier, who rushed for 73 yards on 13 carries, scored only seconds into the closing quarter at the end of an 80-yard Steelers advance.

Jim Smith's 38-yard punt return preceded Bradshaw's pass to Cunningham for the tying touchdown.

On the winning drive, a 28-yard pass from Bradshaw to Bleier preceded Bahr's field goal.

		SCORING	PIT	STL
1st	Cardinals	Ottis Anderson 12 yard rush (kick failed)	0	6
	Cardinals	Steve Little 22 yard field goal	0	9
	Steelers	John Stallworth 18 yard pass from Terry Bradshaw (Matt Bahr kick)	7	9
2nd	Cardinals	Theotis Brown 1 yard rush (kick failed)	7	15
3rd	Cardinals	Mike Wood 24 yard field goal	7	18
	Cardinals	Mike Wood 27 yard field goal	7	21
4th	Steelers	Rocky Bleier 4 yard rush (Matt Bahr kick)	14	21
	Steelers	Bennie Cunningham 5 yard pass from Terry Bradshaw (Matt Bahr kick)	21	21
	Steelers	Matt Bahr 20 yard field goal	24	21

	TEAM STATS	
	PIT	STL
First downs	25	12
Rush-Yards-TD	42-164-1	31-106-2

Comp-Att-Yards-TD-INT	17-35-242-2-2	12-25-132-0-0
Sacked-Yards	1-8	3-26
Net pass yards	234	106
Total yards	398	212
Fumbles-Lost	7-2	1-1
Turnovers	4	1
Penalties-Yards	6-55	5-45

PASSING, RUSHING and RECEIVING

Steelers

Passing

Terry Bradshaw: 14-of-31, 206 yards, 2 TD, 2 INT
Mike Kruczek: 3-of-4, 36 yards

Rushing

Terry Bradshaw: 3 carries for -3 yards
Rocky Bleier: 13 carries for 73 yards, 1 TD
Greg Hawthorne: 9 carries for 34 yards
Franco Harris: 13 carries for 29 yards
Sidney Thornton: 7 carries for 28 yards

Receiving

Rocky Bleier: 2 catches for 44 yards
John Stallworth: 6 catches for 80 yards, 1 TD
Bennie Cunningham: 5 catches for 72 yards, 1 TD
Greg Hawthorne: 2 catches for 9 yards
Lynn Swann: 2 catches for 37 yards

Cardinals

Passing

Jim Hart: 12-of-24, 132 yards
Ottis Anderson: 0-of-1, 0 yards

Rushing

Theotis Brown: 14 carries for 69 yards, 1 TD
Jim Hart: 1 carry for 0 yards
Ottis Anderson: 16 carries for 37 yards, 1 TD

Receiving

Theotis Brown: 2 catches for 17 yards
Ottis Anderson: 5 catches for 11 yards
Mel Gray: 1 catch for 48 yards
Pat Tilley: 2 catches for 39 yards
Gary Parris: 1 catch for 13 yards
Dave Stief: 1 catch for 4 yards

DEFENSE

Cardinals

Interceptions

Carl Allen: 1 for 7 yards
Ken Stone: 1 for 30 yards

KICK RETURNS

Steelers

Kickoffs

Larry Anderson: 3 for 90 yards, 30.0 avg.

Punts

Jim Smith: 6 for 75 yards, 12.5 avg.

Cardinals

Kickoffs

John Barefield: 1 for 22 yards, 22.0 avg.
Roy Green: 3 for 74 yards, 24.7 avg.
Willard Harrell: 1 for 28 yards, 28.0 avg.

Punts

Willard Harrell: 2 for 75 yards, 37.5 avg.

KICKING and PUNTING

Steelers

Kicking

Matt Bahr: 3-for-3 PAT, 1-for-2 FG

Punting

Craig Colquitt: 6 for 250 yards, 41.7 avg.

Cardinals

Kicking

Steve Little: 0-for-2 PAT, 1-for-2 FG
Mike Wood: 2-for-3 FG

Punting

Steve Little: 7 for 304 yards, 43.4 avg.

Week 4

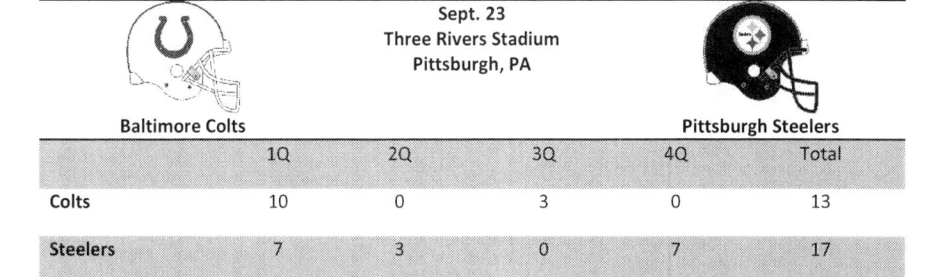

	Sept. 23 Three Rivers Stadium Pittsburgh, PA				
Baltimore Colts				**Pittsburgh Steelers**	
	1Q	2Q	3Q	4Q	Total
Colts	10	0	3	0	13
Steelers	7	3	0	7	17

It was just another routine afternoon for the Band-Aid Brigade. Ho-Hum. It is getting to be a familiar plot. Terry Bradshaw goes off with an injury and then comes charging back to rally the team. They've got this business of fourth-quarter comebacks down to a science.

The reality, of course, is that it isn't quite as easy as it looks. The Steelers are stuck together with enough tape and Band-Aids to stretch from here to Pasadena. But they refused to crack. Their defense again hung tough, and they came from behind in the fourth quarter for the third time in four games.

That was the scenario again yesterday at Three Rivers Stadium before 49,483 fans as a fourth-quarter, Bradshaw-to-Bennie-Cunningham screen pass — a play they hadn't used in two years — rallied them to a 17-13 victory over the Baltimore Colts.

They're now 4-0 and have won a team-record 12 straight games and 21 of their last 23, but nobody is talking about a juggernaut. They're only talking about surviving.

Steelers-Col

Baltimore — FG Mike-Mayer 27
Steelers — Stallworth 47 pass from Bradshaw (Bahr kick)
Baltimore — Carr 36 pass from Landry (Mike-Mayer kick)
Steelers — FG Bahr 25
Baltimore — FG Mike-Mayer 24
Steelers — Cunningham 28 pass from Bradshaw (Bahr kick)

A — 49,483

	Colts	Steelers
First downs	17	17
Rushes-yards	36-97	36-157

Coach Chuck Noll, who paced the sidelines and was continually lashing out at his players in frustration during the game, reacted by giving his troops today and tomorrow off to mend their wounds.

Noll had barely two-thirds of his team in action. Six players, Franco Harris, L.C. Greenwood, Ron Johnson, Steve Furness, Dwight White and Theo Bell, sat out the game. Two others, Lynn Swann and Moon Mullins, limped off with muscle pulls. Jack Lambert, who injured his shoulder in practice Friday, played mainly on passing downs.

Three ailing linemen who had hoped

s Summary

```
188          Passing yards         235
149          Return yards           33
17-34-2      Passes              19-30-3
6-38         Punts                 4-45
2-0          Fumbles-lost          1-1
3-31         Penalties-yards       6-58
```

INDIVIDUAL LEADERS

RUSHING — Baltimore, Washington 21-65, Leaks 10-22, Landry 4-8. Steelers, Thornton 13-129, Hawthorne 7-16, Bleier 10-14.

PASSING — Baltimore, Landry 17-34-2-195. Steelers, Bradshaw 19-29-2-249.

RECEIVING — Receiving, Baltimore, Carr 4-68, McCauley 4-52, McCall 2-25, Doughty 2-22. Steelers, Stallworth 4-82, Cunningham 3-68, Bleier 6-41, Thornton 3-33.

---

to sit out — Jon Kolb, Steve Courson and Sam Davis, were all rushed into the fray during emergencies.

Loren Toews, who had been declared out of the game on Friday, was declared in on the Colts' final series when the Steelers were playing the pass.

"We were rotating our injured," said Courson with a wry comment that had a lot of truth to it.

Courson came in when Mullins limped off. When Courson's knee started acting up, Sam Davis was rushed in. When Davis' hamstring got sore, Courson returned.

After Baltimore's Ron Fernandes, who is playing because John Dutton is home in Nebraska, rushed past Ted Petersen to crunch Bradshaw in the third period, Kolb was rushed in at tackle for Petersen to help keep Bradshaw in one piece.

Fernandes, who said he got Bradshaw with a "blind-side rib shot," said, "I knew he'd come back. Heck, he came back last week after he left on a stretcher."

This time, Bradshaw was only shaken up and missed just two plays. But Mike Kruczek threw an interception on the second one.

With all this going on, it wasn't that surprising that Greg Landry guided the Colts to a 13-10 lead after three quarters.

Landry was playing a nifty cat-and-mouse guessing game with the Steeler defense. His best guess came in the first quarter when he called an audible as the Steelers lined up everybody at the line of scrimmage to blitz on a third-and-three play at the Steeler 36.

Landry's audible was for a takeoff

(Continued on Page 15.)

(Continued from Page 11.)

pass to Roger Carr, who hauled it in for a 36-yard touchdown pass over J.T. Thomas. The coverage left Thomas in a one-on-one situation.

Landry noted with a grin that the Steelers didn't try that blitz again the rest of the day.

Joe Greene said, "When you get burned, you don't need to stick your hand in the fire again."

But the Steelers felt they fooled Landry by faking it a few times, and they guessed right on occasion. One time was when things looked bleak for the Steelers. Right after Kruczek's interception, Landry faced a second-and-15 at the Steeler 17.

He was looking for the Steelers to be in man-to-man coverage, but they were in a zone. Landry threw an interception right into Jack Ham's arms.

"He guessed right at times, but we outguessed him that time," Ham noted.

Two plays later, Sid Thornton skirted right end, was sprung by a Mike Webster block on the safetyman and went 75 yards down the sidelines before being hauled down at the 11.

Unfortunately, on the next play (the first of the final quarter), Rocky Bleier was hit as he took the handoff and fumbled it back.

The Steelers didn't get it back until there was just 8:53 left.

They were on their own 16. It was time for a long drive. They got it. They moved 84 yards in seven plays.

Thornton ran for 17, and Hawthorne caught a five-yard pass, then ran for 19. Bleier then caught a four-yard pass, ran for three and pulled in an eight-yard pass.

Cunningham then went 28 yards with a screen pass — a play last used against Dallas in 1977 — for the touchdown that won it. The Colts got it into Steeler territory twice after that, but the defense held.

It was a victory, but the Steelers knew it was a close call.

"Injuries are an easy way out, but we didn't play that well on defense," Ham said. "Give Landry credit, though. He did a good job."

The injuries are definitely affecting the offense. As Greene noted, "You can cover up things on defense, but you can't cover them up on offense. Timing is so essential."

Bradshaw said, "We're having a tough time, but, we'll charge up before it is over."

How long can the Steelers keep surviving these close calls with a patched-up lineup?

"Until hell freezes over," Greene promised. But, even though Greene said he never doubted they'd win, he admitted he wasn't quite as confident of a comeback as he was against St. Louis last week.

There were times out there yesterday when it definitely seemed a bit chilly for the Steelers.

		SCORING	BAL	PIT
1st	Colts	Steve Mike-Mayer 27 yard field goal	3	0
	Steelers	John Stallworth 47 yard pass from Terry Bradshaw (Matt Bahr kick)	3	7
	Colts	Roger Carr 36 yard pass from Greg Landry (Steve Mike-Mayer kick)	10	7
2nd	Steelers	Matt Bahr 25 yard field goal	10	10
3rd	Colts	Steve Mike-Mayer 24 yard field goal	13	10
4th	Steelers	Bennie Cunningham 28 yard pass from Terry Bradshaw (Matt Bahr kick)	13	17

	TEAM STATS	
	BAL	PIT
First downs	17	17
Rush-Yards-TD	36-97-0	26-157-0

Comp-Att-Yards-TD-INT	17-34-195-1-2	19-30-249-2-3
Sacked-Yards	1-7	2-14
Net pass yards	188	235
Total yards	285	392
Fumbles-Lost	2-0	1-1
Turnovers	2	4
Penalties-Yards	5-51	6-58

PASSING, RUSHING and RECEIVING

Colts

Passing

Greg Landry: 17-of-34, 195 yards, 1 TD, 2 INT

Rushing

Greg Landry: 4 carries for 8 yards
Joe Washington: 21 carries for 65 yards
Don McCauley: 1 carry for 2 yards
Roosevelt Leaks: 10 carries for 22 yards

Receiving

Joe Washington: 3 catches for 19 yards
Roger Carr: 4 catches for 68 yards, 1 TD
Don McCauley: 4 catches for 52 yards
Roosevelt Leaks: 2 catches for 8 yards
Reese McCall: 2 catches for 25 yards
Glenn Doughty: 2 catches for 23 yards

Steelers

Passing

Terry Bradshaw: 19-of-29, 249 yards, 2 TD, 2 INT
Mike Kruczek: 0-of-1, 0 yards

Rushing

Sidney Thornton: 13 carries for 129 yards
Terry Bradshaw: 1 carry for -2 yards
Rocky Bleier: 10 carries for 14 yards
Greg Hawthorne: 2 carries for 16 yards

Receiving

Sidney Thornton: 3 catches for 33 yards
John Stallworth: 4 catches for 83 yards, 1 TD
Bennie Cunningham: 3 catches for 68 yards, 1 TD
Rocky Bleier: 6 catches for 41 yards
Greg Hawthorne: 1 catch for 5 yards
Lynn Swann: 1 catch for 12 yards
Randy Grossman: 1 catch for 7 yards

DEFENSE

Colts

Interceptions

Lyle Blackwood: 1 for 3 yards
Nesby Glasgow: 1 for -1 yard
Doug Nettles: 1 for 30 yards

Steelers

Interceptions

Jack Ham: 1 for 2 yards
Jack Lambert: 1 for 0 yards

KICK RETURNS

Colts

Kickoffs

Nesby Glasgow: 4 for 91 yards, 22.8 avg.

Punts

Nesby Glasgow: 3 for 26 yards, 8.7 avg.

Steelers

Kickoffs

Anthony Anderson: 1 for 12 yards, 12.0 avg.
Larry Anderson: 3 for 35 yards, 11.7 avg.

Punts

Jim Smith: 2 for 6 yards, 3.0 avg.

KICKING and PUNTING

Colts

Kicking

Steve Mike-Mayer: 1-for-1 PAT, 2-for-2 FG

Punting

Bucky Dilts: 6 for 232 yards, 38.7 avg.

Steelers

Kicking

Matt Bahr: 2-for-2 PAT, 1-for-2 FG

Punting

Craig Colquitt: 4 for 182 yards, 45.5 avg.

Week 5

	1Q	2Q	3Q	4Q	Total
Pittsburgh Steelers					
Steelers	0	7	0	7	14
Eagles	0	7	10	0	17

Sept. 30
Veterans Stadium
Philadelphia, PA

Philadelphia Eagles

PHILADELPHIA (AP) — How do you make your team feel that it is better than the world champions? Coach Dick Vermeil tried it by reading a slogan to his Philadelphia Eagles: "No one can make you feel inferior unless you allow it to happen."

Vermeil also played a hunch as he pulled out all the stops in his team's 17-14 triumph over the previously unbeaten Pittsburgh Steelers Sunday.

Both teams now are 4-1 in the National Football League divisional races.

"I named John Bunting captain for today (Sunday) because I had a feeling about how much he wanted this game. He's the 'Mother Hen' of our club, the grandmother of our whole football team. He's the biggest worrier on the team next to me."

Maybe it was just coincidence, but it was Bunting who intercepted a Terry Bradshaw pass in the third period and returned it 15 yards to the Steelers' 2-yard line to set up the winning touchdown.

The Eagles were leading 10-7 at the time of Bunting's interception. Wilbert Montgomery scored from the one on second down and Tony Franklin kicked his second conversion. The score offset a late fourth period 37-yard TD pass from Bradshaw to John Stallworth.

All week, Vermeil refused to categorize the game as the potential turning point in his slightly more than three-year rebuilding program. He told everyone who broached the subject that the Eagles already had turned the corner and were ready to line up against any team in the NFL.

But his post-game comments belied his pre-game bravado.

"This game was more important to us because we beat the world champs," Vermeil said. "We raised a level of confidence within our coaching staff, our organization and myself."

Vermeil then equated the triumph with a previous thrill. "It's as good as the Rose Bowl," said the coach, referring to the Jan. 1, 1976, startling upset of Ohio State by his UCLA Bruins.

As for the Steelers, a team racked with injuries to key performers, coach Chuck Noll insisted that he and his staff did not overlook the Eagles.

"They forced us to make mistakes and then took advantage of them," said Noll.

Noll also said he wasn't bothered by the end of Pittsburgh's two-year, 12-game winning streak.

"I don't care about streaks ... What I'm interested in is winning our division," Noll said.

The Steelers scored first for a 7-0 second quarter lead. Linebacker Jack Ham made his 28th career interception, the most among active linebackers in the NFL. Pittsburgh moved 47 yards on seven plays, with Sidney Thornton scoring from the seven. Matt Bahr converted.

The Eagles came right back, taking the kickoff to their 20, and driving 80-yards on eight plays to tie the score. Quarterback Ron Jaworski completed passes of 13 to Scott Fitzkee, and 30 and 27 to tight end Keith Krepfle. Leroy Harris scored from the one, and rookie Tony Franklin converted.

The Eagles took the opening kickoff of the second half and moved to the Steelers' 33, a 19 yard pass from Jaworski to Fitzkee highlighting the drive. When the attack stalled, Franklin trotted out and booted a 48 yard field goal to make it 10-7.

Bunting's interception setup Montgomery's TD, and it was all over but for two key defensive plays. The first came with 12:25 left in the final period on an interception by Herman Edwards in the end zone.

The second came with 8:52 remaining. Pittsburgh had moved from its 43 to the Eagles' two, a pair of 18-yard Bradshaw pass completions keying the drive. On third and two from the two, Franco Harris smashed into the line.

Harris was met by linebacker Frank LeMaster.

"I wasn't going to get a solid hit, so I thought I might as well go for the ball," said LeMaster. He did just that and middle guard Ken Clarke recovered at the goal line for Philadelphia.

Harris said of the fumble: "I held the ball too low."

Noll said the Steelers could make a thousand excuses. "If Harris hadn't fumbled ... If Bradshaw hadn't been intercepted (in the end zone) ... but it's no use ... We simply didn't get it going ... It's as simple as that."

Noll spoke of a fumbled snap by Eagles' punter Max Runager that the kicker picked up and booted away. He said that might have made a difference. He also referred to a call on an onsides kick at the end with the score 17-14.

"It was wrong. The play happened in front of me. The ball traveled more than 10 yards and (Matt) Bahr (the kicker) fell on it. The official ruled it illegal touching," Noll said.

But the Steelers' coach chose to give the Eagles credit. He said Vermeil's team won on a great effort all down the line from kicking through offense and defense, and he had nothing but great admiration for the Eagles.

Bradshaw said the Steelers may have played too conservative. "Maybe we should have been more aggressive. We wanted to use our running game. But maybe we should have thrown more," Bradshaw said.

		SCORING	PIT	PHI

2nd	Steelers	Sidney Thornton 7 yard rush (Matt Bahr kick)	7	0
	Eagles	Leroy Harris 1 yard rush (Tony Franklin kick)	7	7
3rd	Eagles	Tony Franklin 48 yard field goal	7	10
	Eagles	Wilbert Montgomery 1 yard rush (Tony Franklin kick)	7	17
4th	Steelers	John Stallworth 37 yard pass from Terry Bradshaw (Matt Bahr kick)	14	17

	TEAM STATS	
	PIT	PHI
First downs	19	18
Rush-Yards-TD	29-139-1	44-135-2
Comp-Att-Yards-TD-INT	12-26-176-1-2	11-20-158-0-2
Sacked-Yards	1-7	1-10
Net pass yards	169	148
Total yards	308	283
Fumbles-Lost	2-2	3-0
Turnovers	4	2
Penalties-Yards	6-37	10-70

PASSING, RUSHING and RECEIVING

Steelers

Passing

Terry Bradshaw: 12-of-26, 176 yards, 1 TD, 2 INT

Rushing

Sidney Thornton: 16 carries for 88 yards, 1 TD
Franco Harris: 11 carries for 44 yards

Rocky Bleier: 1 carry for 1 yard
Greg Hawthorne: 1 carry for 6 yards

Receiving

John Stallworth: 5 catches for 102 yards, 1 TD
Theo Bell: 2 catches for 30 yards
Bennie Cunningham: 1 catch for 19 yards
Rocky Bleier: 2 catches for 16 yards
Randy Grossman: 2 catches for 9 yards

Eagles

Passing

Ron Jaworski: 11-of-20, 158 yards, 0 TD, 2 INT

Rushing

Wilbert Montgomery: 28 carries for 98 yards, 1 TD
Ron Jaworski: 3 carries for 9 yards
Leroy Harris: 12 carries for 30 yards, 1 TD
Billy Campfield: 1 carry for -2 yards

Receiving

Wilbert Montgomery: 1 catch for 15 yards
Keith Krepfle: 4 catches for 95 yards
Scott Fitzkee: 2 catches for 32 yards
Leroy Harris: 3 catches for -2 yards
Harold Carmichael: 1 catch for 18 yards

DEFENSE

Steelers

Interceptions

Jack Ham: 1 for 6 yards
Jack Lambert: 1 for 0 yards

Eagles

Interceptions

John Bunting: 1 for 13 yards
Herman Edwards: 1 for 0 yards

KICK RETURNS

Steelers

Kickoffs

Anthony Anderson: 1 for 18 yards, 18.0 avg.
Larry Anderson: 3 for 65 yards, 21.7 avg.

Punts

Theo Bell: 2 for 13 yards, 6.5 avg.

Eagles

Kickoffs

Wally Henry: 1 for 29 yards, 29.0 avg.

Punts

Wally Henry: 2 for 9 yards, 4.5 avg.

KICKING and PUNTING

Steelers

Kicking

Matt Bahr: 2-for-2 PAT

Punting

Craig Colquitt: 4 for 164 yards, 41.0 avg.

Eagles

Kicking

Tony Franklin: 2-for-2 PAT, 1-for-1 FG

Punting

Max Runager: 5 for 225 yards, 45.0 avg.

Week 6

Oct. 7
Municipal Stadium
Cleveland, OH

Pittsburgh Steelers	1Q	2Q	3Q	4Q	Cleveland Browns Total
Steelers	21	9	7	14	51
Browns	0	14	7	14	35

It should have been easy ... a laugher. It turned out to be a track meet, and one of the most remarkable football games the Pittsburgh Steelers and Cleveland Browns have ever played.

"I remember looking up at the scoreboard and thinking, 'Thirty-seven points should be enough to win this game,'" said Steelers offensive tackle Jon Kolb with a grin. "Then I remember thinking, 'Forty-four points is surely enough.' Then I remember thinking, 'Man, 51 points has got to be enough.' I'm glad I was finally right."

"We nipped 'em 51-35," Pittsburgh quarterback Terry Bradshaw laughed. "Excitin' wasn't it?"

That it was. In a contest that resembled something out of the old American Football League, the Steelers defeated the Browns before 81,260 stunned fans at Municipal Stadium. Even the Pittsburgh faithful who traveled the Turnpike to get to Cleveland couldn't believe what they saw.

Pittsburgh set a new team record with 361 yards rushing and rolled up 522 yards total offense, the most under head coach Chuck Noll. For a while the Steelers even flirted with making NFL history by having three backs rush for 100 yards apiece. Only Franco Harris managed that, but Sidney Thornton and Rocky Bleier weren't too far behind.

Harris had the fourth best game of his illustrious career and gained 153 yards on 19 carries, including a 71-yard TD romp over right tackle. Meanwhile, Thornton picked up 98 yards on 18 tries and Bleier collected 81 on four carries.

"Everything was just working perfectly on offense," said Bleier, who had the longest run of his career in the fourth quarter when he went 70 yards for a touchdown on a third-and-one play. "I mean, how many times do you see two guys score on runs of 70 yards against a goal-line defense?"

What made the offensive explosion even sweeter for Pittsburgh was that St. Louis knocked off Houston 24-17. That means the Steelers are alone atop the AFC Central Division with a 5-1 record, while Houston and Cleveland have 4-2 marks.

Cleveland defensive end Mike St. Clair tried to get the Browns and their fans charged up when he came out during the introductions waving a "Browns' Bag," which is Cleveland's equivalent to the Terrible

Towel. But Bradshaw and company rolled the Browns' defense up and stuffed it in that bag with 21 first quarter points.

"We were making the big plays and making things happen," said Bradshaw, who hit on his first nine passes and completed 12 of 21 for 161 yards and three scores. "I haven't played emotionally all year, but I was fired up this week. I was really excited.

"And you saw Franco and Rocky running. I don't know where they got that stuff about either of them losing a step. They both ran away from defenders on those big plays, especially Franco. You can tell he's starting to get juiced up."

It was Harris' first 100-yard game since last Dec. 3, and even he had to admit the 71-yard run and 100-yard game felt pretty darn good.

"Yeah, and this was the kind of game I needed," Harris said quietly. "I really wasn't thinking about anything on that run. I go by the philosophy that if you ever think too much out there you're in trouble. Once you get a step on somebody, don't look back ... if they catch you, they catch you."

While the Pittsburgh offense was going crazy, the defense was having problems stopping the Browns. Or more specifically, quarterback Brian Sipe.

Sipe tried to rally Cleveland and connected on 22 of 41 passes for 351 yards and five touchdowns, all personal highs. But he still came up short.

"I don't care about respectability. I'd rather win," Sipe said in the empty Cleveland locker room. "I don't care about statistics, I just want to get to the playoffs."

Even though it looked like the Steelers relaxed a bit and started playing a prevent defense after gaining the big lead, Noll said that wasn't the case.

"What happens is they (Cleveland) quit doing when you expect them to because they have to play catch up," Noll explained. "So they start doing things differently and you try to adjust, and pretty soon everything goes to hell.

"Sipe's statistics speak for his performance, but we have a lot of people hurt on defense and that didn't help either. A prevent defense? No, we were just playing a loose defense."

Still, you have to give the Browns credit. They didn't pack it in, and had Pittsburgh not come up with a 15-play, 94-yard scoring drive that ate up all but 36 seconds of the last nine minutes it might have been a different story.

"It was a page out of the past," Noll said with a smile. "For us it was a rebirth of our offense. This is the first game we've really been healthy on offense, and we went out and got the job done. Next week we hope to have Lynn (Swann) back, then we'll be 100 percent on offense."

Get out the calculators.

		SCORING	PIT	CLE
1st	Steelers	Bennie Cunningham 7 yard pass from Terry Bradshaw (Matt Bahr kick)	7	0
	Steelers	Sidney Thornton 10 yard pass from Terry Bradshaw (Matt Bahr kick)	14	0
	Steelers	Franco Harris 71 yard rush (Matt Bahr kick)	21	0
2nd	Steelers	Jim Smith 14 yard pass from Terry Bradshaw (kick failed)	27	0
	Browns	Reggie Rucker 32 yard pass from Brian Sipe (Don Cockroft kick)	27	7
	Browns	Ozzie Newsome 18 yard pass from Brian Sipe (Don Cockroft kick)	27	14
	Steelers	Matt Bahr 42 yard field goal	30	14
3rd	Steelers	Franco Harris 25 yard rush (Matt Bahr kick)	37	14
	Browns	Calvin Hill 14 yard pass from Brian Sipe (Don Cockroft kick)	37	21
4th	Steelers	Rocky Bleier 70 yard rush (Matt Bahr kick)	44	21
	Browns	Dave Logan 30 yard pass from Brian Sipe (Don Cockroft kick)	44	28
	Browns	Dave Logan 13 yard pass from Brian Sipe (Don Cockroft kick)	44	35
	Steelers	Sidney Thornton 1 yard rush (Matt Bahr kick)	51	35

	TEAM STATS	
	PIT	CLE
First downs	21	24
Rush-Yards-TD	45-361-4	24-93-0
Comp-Att-Yards-TD-INT	12-21-161-3-0	23-42-365-5-3
Sacked-Yards	0-0	0-0
Net pass yards	161	365
Total yards	522	458
Fumbles-Lost	2-1	4-2

Turnovers	1	5
Penalties-Yards	9-84	1-3

PASSING, RUSHING and RECEIVING

Steelers

Passing

Terry Bradshaw: 12-of-21, 161 yards, 3 TD, 0 INT

Rushing

Franco Harris: 19 carries for 153 yards, 2 TD
Sidney Thornton: 18 carries for 98 yards, 1 TD
Rocky Bleier: 4 carries for 81 yards, 1 TD
Greg Hawthorne: 4 carries for 29 yards

Receiving

Sidney Thornton: 1 catch for 10 yards, 1 TD
John Stallworth: 4 catches for 96 yards
Rocky Bleier: 1 catch for 9 yards
Bennie Cunningham: 4 catches for 29 yards, 1 TD
Jim Smith: 2 catches for 17 yards, 1 TD

Browns

Passing

Brian Sipe: 22-of-41, 351 yards, 5 TD, 3 INT
Johnny Evans: 1-of-1, 14 yards

Rushing

Brian Sipe: 2 carries for 4 yards
Mike Pruitt: 15 carries for 73 yards
Calvin Hill: 5 carries for 8 yards
Dino Hall: 1 carry for 7 yards
Cleo Miller: 1 carry for 1 yard

Receiving

Mike Pruitt: 4 catches for 33 yards
Ozzie Newsome: 6 catches for 97 yards, 1 TD
Dave Logan: 5 catches for 91 yards, 2 TD
Calvin Hill: 4 catches for 68 yards, 1 TD
Reggie Rucker: 2 catches for 56 yards, 1 TD
Ricky Feacher: 1 catch for 14 yards
Willis Adams: 1 catch for 6 yards

DEFENSE

Steelers

Interceptions

Donnie Shell: 1 for 0 yards
Mike Wagner: 2 for 12 yards

KICK RETURNS

Steelers

Kickoffs

Larry Anderson: 3 for 65 yards, 21.7 avg.
Greg Hawthorne: 1 for 23 yards, 23.0 avg.

Punts

Theo Bell: 1 for 0 yards, 0.0 avg.

Browns

Kickoffs

Dino Hall: 9 for 172 yards, 19.1 avg.

Punts

Dino Hall: 2 for 58 yards, 29.0 avg.

KICKING and PUNTING

Steelers

Kicking

Matt Bahr: 6-for-7 PAT, 1-for-1 FG

Punting

Craig Colquitt: 5 for 180 yards, 36.0 avg.

Browns

Kicking

Don Cockroft: 5-for-5 PAT, 0-for-1 FG

Punting

Johnny Evans: 2 for 65 yards, 32.5 avg.

Week 7

	Oct. 14 Riverfront Stadium Cincinnati, OH				
Pittsburgh Steelers				Cincinnati Bengals	
	1Q	2Q	3Q	4Q	Total
Steelers	3	0	0	7	10
Bengals	7	20	0	7	34

It resembled an Easter egg hunt more than a football game.

The Cincinnati Bengals kept finding official NFL balls bouncing on the green artificial turf at Riverfront Stadium and they grabbed them with the glee of frolicking youngsters.

The result was that the Steelers were left with egg on their faces.

The Steelers managed to do the impossible. They managed to outbungle the Bungling Bengals.

They fumbled the ball nine times and lost seven of them – both records for futility in the Chuck Noll era – and Terry Bradshaw threw in a pair of interceptions as the Steelers were routed by the Cincinnati Bengals 34-10 before 52,381 fans.

The game was decided in a two-minute span in the second period when the Bengals converted three fumbles into 20 points, including a 14-point splurge in 15 seconds. Fielding Yost had the point-a-minute team at Michigan. The Bengals were a point-a-second team.

"It was just a complete lack of concentration," Joe Greene said after the game, and nobody argued.

Bradshaw fumbled three snaps from center early in the third period.

"It's like dancing to two different numbers and neither is our song," he said. "If my dog don't bite me when I get home I'll be OK. You just laugh and make jokes because you don't want to cry."

It may have been the most embarrassing moment since the Steelers became a playoff team in 1972. It was the first time in the last eight years that they have lost to a team destined to finish at .500 or below.

"Sure, it's embarrassing," Bradshaw said. "You're a pro athlete and you look like that. It's embarrassing."

The loss left the Steelers, who won their first seven last year, at 5-2, while the Bengals are 1-6. The Steelers dropped into a first-place tie with Houston while Denver and Dallas are coming up on the schedule.

Steelers coach Chuck Noll said, "I guess we answered all your questions. The Bengals aren't that bad. They deserved the victory. They forced errors."

There had been much debate about whether the Bengals were better than their 0-6 record coming in. The ironic thing is that they did not even look that good while handling the Steelers their most lopsided setback since they lost to Houston by 26 points back in 1971.

On the first scrimmage play of the game, Ken Anderson threw an interception. On the fifth play, he fell down. The Bengals managed four turnovers, but the Steelers trumped that with their nine turnovers. It was meaningless that the Steelers even had a 327-284 edge in yardage.

Dick Jauron, the Bengals defensive back, said of the Steeler turnovers, "You won't see the Pittsburgh Steelers do that again in a long time. I'll be surprised if you ever see it again."

Gary Burley, the outspoken former Pitt defensive lineman, said he even predicted the upset. "Yesterday, a reporter asked me if we could win. I said Pittsburgh would come in here all overconfident and relaxed. I predicted we'd win 35-14. I was wrong a little bit, but hey, I'm not Jimmy the Greek."

It was figured the Steelers would be flat and have a letdown after their exciting 51-35 win over Cleveland last week. It seems both teams left their games in Cleveland last week because the Browns lost on Sunday, too.

It all started with 10:23 left in the second quarter when the Steelers took over on their own 20 after a Bengals punt with the Bengals leading 7-3.

On first down, John Stallworth caught a 25-yard pass from Bradshaw, then fumbled when he was hit. Ken Riley, who recovered two fumbles and intercepted a pass, pounced on it and ran to the Steelers' 31.

Five plays later, Pete Johnson banged into the end zone from the 1-yard line and the score was 13-3 even though Chris Bahr missed the extra point.

Fifteen seconds later, the Bengals were in the end zone again.

Chris Bahr boomed the kickoff in the end zone and Larry Anderson hesitated as he seemed ready to down the ball. But he then decided to run it out. He was flipped and, as he was tackled, he fumbled.

Somebody named Howie Kurnick, a rookie from the University of Cincinnati, picked it up and ran it 12 yards into the end zone. That made it 20-3 and things were getting serious.

"I was just flying through and all of a sudden, it was on the ground," Kurnick said.

The next time, it took the Bengals three plays to get into the end zone. On a third-and-one play, Franco Harris went to his left but was stacked up short of the first down. He was stripped of the ball. Jim LeClair picked it up and ran it 27 yards into the end zone.

"I just happened to look down and it was at my feet. I thought that I'd better do something about it, so I picked it up and ran," LeClair said.

After the play, Harris just knelt on the turf and looked toward the end zone. Last week, he and Rocky Bleier went for touchdowns on third-and-one plays. This time, he gave up a touchdown and it was 27-3.

In the second half, on another third-and-one play, Harris burst for a first down, then fumbled the ball away.

"You don't get much lower than this," Harris said. "I don't know what happened."

The Bengals had blown a 24-point lead to Houston earlier this year, but the Steelers never gave them a chance to collapse. Mike Webster and Bradshaw – they each took the blame – fumbled the snap on the fourth play of the second half and lost the ball. Eddie Edwards recovered it. They next time they got the ball, they fumbled it twice and lost it the second time.

The Bengals fumbled it right back – twice in the third quarter the Bengals gave the ball right back to the Steelers on the first play after a turnover – but it did not make a difference.

The Steelers were a beaten team.

"It's a season of highs and lows, just like in life," Greene said. "This was one of the low points. I don't feel as bad today as I did in Philadelphia two weeks ago, but I don't know what you can read into that."

		SCORING	PIT	CIN
1st	Steelers	Matt Bahr 46 yard field goal	3	0
	Bengals	Dan Ross 7 yard pass from Ken Anderson (Chris Bahr kick)	3	7
2nd	Bengals	Pete Johnson 1 yard rush (kick failed)	3	13
	Bengals	Howard Kurnick 12 yard fumble return (Chris Bahr kick)	3	20
	Bengals	Jim LeClair 27 yard fumble return (Chris Bahr kick)	3	27
4th	Bengals	Rick Walker 14 yard pass from Ken Anderson (Chris Bahr kick)	3	34

Steelers	John Stallworth 33 yard pass from Terry Bradshaw (Matt Bahr kick)	10	34

	TEAM STATS	
	PIT	CIN
First downs	16	19
Rush-Yards-TD	18-64-0	45-170-1
Comp-Att-Yards-TD-INT	21-40-275-1-2	9-20-120-2-2
Sacked-Yards	1-12	2-6
Net pass yards	263	114
Total yards	327	284
Fumbles-Lost	9-7	2-2
Turnovers	9	4
Penalties-Yards	7-58	5-43

PASSING, RUSHING and RECEIVING

Steelers

Passing

Terry Bradshaw: 21-of-40, 275 yards, 1 TD, 2 INT

Rushing

Terry Bradshaw: 3 carries for 0 yards
Franco Harris: 9 carries for 45 yards
Sidney Thornton: 6 carries for 19 yards

Receiving

John Stallworth: 6 catches for 126 yards, 1 TD
Jim Smith: 5 catches for 75 yards
Franco Harris: 4 catches for 29 yards
Bennie Cunningham: 4 catches for 38 yards

Sidney Thornton: 1 catch for 10 yards
Greg Hawthorne: 1 catch for -3 yards

Bengals

Passing

Ken Anderson: 9-of-20, 120 yards, 2 TD, 2 INT

Rushing

Charles Alexander: 19 carries for 91 yards
Ken Anderson: 3 carries for 28 yards
Archie Griffin: 12 carries for 21 yards
Deacon Turner: 7 carries for 25 yards
Pete Johnson: 3 carries for 8 yards, 1 TD
Nathan Poole: 1 carry for -3 yards

Receiving

Charles Alexander: 1 catch for 5 yards
Archie Griffin: 4 catches for 65 yards
Dan Ross: 2 catches for 21 yards, 1 TD
Don Bass: 1 catch for 15 yards
Rick Walker: 1 catch for 14 yards, 1 TD

DEFENSE

Steelers

Interceptions

Mel Blount: 1 for 0 yards
Dirt Winston: 1 for 7 yards

Bengals

Interceptions

Reggie Williams: 2 for 5 yards

KICK RETURNS

Steelers

Kickoffs

Anthony Anderson: 1 for 25 yards, 25.0 avg.
Larry Anderson: 4 for 84 yards, 21.0 avg.

Punts

Theo Bell: 4 for 34 yards, 8.5 avg.

Bengals

Kickoffs

Jim Browner: 2 for 39 yards, 19.5 avg.
Howard Kurnick: 1 for 13 yards, 13.0 avg.

Punts

Dick Jauron: 1 for 10 yards, 10.0 avg.
Vaughn Lusby: 2 for 17 yards, 8.5 avg.

KICKING and PUNTING

Steelers

Kicking

Matt Bahr: 1-for-1 PAT, 1-for-2 FG

Punting

Craig Colquitt: 4 for 174 yards, 43.5 avg.

Bengals

Kicking

Chris Bahr: 4-for-5 PAT, 0-for-1 FG

Punting

Pat McInally: 7 for 282 yards, 40.3 avg.

Week 8

	Oct. 22 Three Rivers Stadium Pittsburgh, PA	
Denver Broncos		Pittsburgh Steelers

	1Q	2Q	3Q	4Q	Total
Broncos	7	0	0	0	7
Steelers	7	21	0	14	42

By VITO STELLINO
Post-Gazette Sports Writer

The real Steelers came back home last night.

The fumbling, stumbling imposters of recent weeks disappeared before a sea of 49,699 towel-waving fans at Three Rivers Stadium.

For the first time since last January in Miami, the Steelers looked like a real Super Bowl champion.

They put it all together to crush the shell-shocked Denver Broncos, 42-7.

The Steelers finally stopped admiring their Super Bowl rings and started playing football again.

They did it just in time, too, because "America's Team" — the Dallas Cowboys — will be in town next Sunday for a rematch of Super Bowl XIII.

This will be the regular-season game of the year and will be the Steelers' chance to show they can do it week in and week out.

They know they cannot spend much time celebrating last night's win. They have to get ready for Dallas after a short week. They know the challenge.

Even before the game, Joe Greene said, "Even if we blow out Denver, which is a good possibility, we've got to show we can do it against the Cowboys."

As the Steeler fans whooped it up at the end of the game, one of them held up a sign reading: "Bring On the Cowboys."

For the Cowboy fans watching in "America," things had to look a bit ominous. They saw the same Terry Bradshaw they saw in Miami last January.

This game had Steeler football stamped all over it as they rolled up 530 net yards. And when the Steelers are the Steelers, it is Bradshaw who is leading the way.

He completed 18 of 24 passes for 287 yards and two touchdowns.

The Cowboys had to notice another nemesis — Lynn Swann. He did not start and be played only parttime and he caught only two passes. But they went for 76 yards and a touchdown.

Swann caught seven against the Cowboys in the Super Bowl — in addition to getting the big call on the Benny Barnes play. Swann tripped and the official, Fred Swearingen, called pass interference. Pete Rozelle later apologized for the call. This time it will be the Steelers' chance to show they can beat the Cowboys even without Swearingen's flag.

The Cowboys will bring the best record in football (7-1) into this game while the Steelers lead the AFC Central Division with a 6-2 record.

The Broncos, who were wiped out by the Steelers, 33-10 in the playoffs last year on a wet, cold day, must have felt as if they were looking at instant replay on a beautiful, Indian summer evening.

Bradshaw has now put 21, 33 and 35 points on the board against the Broncos in less than 10 quarters in the last three games. He played only a half in the regular-season finale last year and Coach Chuck Noll pulled him with 9:24 to go in the fourth period last night with the Steelers leading, 35-7.

That is the equivalent of Red Auerbach lighting up his cigar because Noll does not like to take Bradshaw out. The subs pushed across another touchdown with Anthony Anderson scoring on a 10-yard run.

Sharing honors with Terry Bradshaw was Franco Harris, who carried the ball 17 times for 121 yards. It was the 32nd time — the second in the last three weeks — that Harris has gained more than 100 yards in a regular-season game. It was the first time he had done it against the Broncos' swarming 3-4 defense in a regular-season contest.

The Steelers made it look so easy that it was difficult to believe the team had lost two of its last three games and fumbled the ball nine times, while losing it seven times, in the loss to Cincinnati.

This time, the Steelers did not have a turnover in the entire first half while they took a 28-7 lead. They wound up having just one fumble — by Sid Thornton — and Bradshaw threw one interception.

The Steelers played intense, crisp football and that is how they avoided the turnovers.

The Steelers also came up with the big plays and big plays turn games around.

The Steelers had three of them in the first half and they all resulted in touchdowns. There was a 56-yard run by

(Continued on Page 16.)

(Continued from Page 13.)

Franco Harris on a third-and-three play on the Steelers' first possession, a 65-yard pass from Bradshaw to Swann in the second quarter on a second-and-four play and a 54-yard Bradshaw pass to Randy Grossman on a first down in the second period.

Those three plays broke the Broncos' back.

It was Franco who first got the big crowd excited. Denver took the opening kickoff and burned the Steeler defense a bit. Craig Morton, starting because Norris Weese had a bad knee, threw a 22-yard pass to Haven Moses on the third play and Jon Keyworth ran 13 yards before the Broncos were forced to punt.

The Steelers took over and Harris ran five yards and Thornton two. That made it a third-and-three play and the fans were quiet. They seemed to be waiting for something to happen. It happened.

Bradshaw pitched to Harris, who swept around left end and then cut across the field, going 56 yards before Bernard Jackson pulled him down from behind on the Bronco 17-yard line.

Three plays later, Swann caught an 11-yard touchdown pass.

Morton managed to trump that touchdown. Three plays later, Moses caught a 64-yard touchdown strike from Morton. J.T. Thomas, playing safety at the time, banged into Moses, but bounced off and Ron Johnson could not catch him.

With the score tied, 7-7, the teams traded punts, but the Steelers got good field position and drove 38 yards for a second score. Jim Smith, alternating with Swann, caught a 20 yarder on the Bronco two and Harris dove in for the score.

The next two times the Steelers got the ball, it was big-play time.

Swann beat Louis Wright, the all-pro cornerback, on the 65 yarder before Bernard Jackson caught him from behind on the Bronco 16. Three plays later, Harris swept four yards around left end for the score. That made it 21-7 with 8:55 elapsed.

The next time the Steelers got the ball, Randy Grossman, starting because Bennie Cunningham was bothered with recurring headaches, caught a 54 yarder down the sidelines. Three plays later, Jim Smith caght a 19 yarder, then Thornton banged in from the one for the 28-7 halftime lead.

The Steelers put the game away with a 12-play, 80-yard drive which was climaxed early in the fourth period by Thornton's 17-yard touchdown catch of a Bradshaw pass.

Bradshaw then retired to the sidelines to savor the victory.

		SCORING	DEN	PIT
1st	Steelers	Lynn Swann 11 yard pass from Terry Bradshaw (Matt Bahr kick)	0	7
	Broncos	Haven Moses 64 yard pass from Craig Morton (Jim Turner kick)	7	7
2nd	Steelers	Franco Harris 2 yard rush (Matt Bahr kick)	7	14
	Steelers	Franco Harris 4 yard rush (Matt Bahr kick)	7	21
	Steelers	Sidney Thornton 1 yard rush (Matt Bahr kick)	7	28
4th	Steelers	Sidney Thornton 17 yard pass from Terry Bradshaw (Matt Bahr kick)	7	35
	Steelers	Anthony Anderson 10 yard rush (Matt Bahr kick)	7	42

	TEAM STATS	
	DEN	PIT
First downs	16	27
Rush-Yards-TD	17-53-0	42-236-4
Comp-Att-Yards-TD-INT	18-36-305-1-2	21-27-294-2-1
Sacked-Yards	4-29	0-0
Net pass yards	276	294
Total yards	329	530
Fumbles-Lost	2-1	2-2
Turnovers	3	3
Penalties-Yards	7-68	5-26

PASSING, RUSHING and RECEIVING

Broncos

Passing

Craig Morton: 16-of-31, 261 yards, 1 TD, 1 INT
Craig Penrose: 2-of-5, 44 yards, 0 TD, 1 INT

Rushing

Craig Morton: 2 carries for 1 yard
Jon Keyworth: 4 carries for 29 yards
Rob Lytle: 4 carries for 6 yards
Otis Armstrong: 4 carries for 10 yards
Larry Canada: 1 carry for 2 yards
Jim D. Jensen: 1 carry for 4 yards
Zachary Dixon: 1 carry for 1 yard

Receiving

Haven Moses: 5 catches for 133 yards, 1 TD
Riley Odoms: 6 catches for 94 yards
Rob Lytle: 4 catches for 23 yards

Otis Armstrong: 1 catch for 16 yards
Rick Upchurch: 1 catch for 24 yards
Larry Canada: 1 catch for 15 yards

Steelers

Passing

Terry Bradshaw: 18-of-24, 267 yards, 2 TD, 1 INT
Mike Kruczek: 3-of-3, 27 yards

Rushing

Franco Harris: 17 carries for 121 yards, 2 TD
Terry Bradshaw: 2 carries for 5 yards
Sidney Thornton: 9 carries for 27 yards, 1 TD
Jim Smith: 1 carry for 12 yards
Greg Hawthorne: 3 carries for 17 yards
Anthony Anderson: 5 carries for 34 yards, 1 TD
Rocky Bleier: 4 carries for 18 yards
Rick Moser: 1 carry for 2 yards

Receiving

Franco Harris: 4 catches for 23 yards
Lynn Swann: 2 catches for 76 yards, 1 TD
Sidney Thornton: 4 catches for 45 yards, 1 TD
Jim Smith: 5 catches for 55 yards
Randy Grossman: 1 catch for 54 yards
Greg Hawthorne: 2 catches for 23 yards
John Stallworth: 3 catches for 18 yards

DEFENSE

Broncos

Interceptions

Bob Swenson: 1 for 0 yards

Steelers

Interceptions

Jack Lambert: 1 for 23 yards
Donnie Shell: 1 for 0 yards

KICK RETURNS

Broncos

Kickoffs

Larry Canada: 1 for 8 yards, 8.0 avg.
Chris Pane: 5 for 111 yards, 22.2 avg.

Steelers

Kickoffs

Larry Anderson: 2 for 31 yards, 15.5 avg.

Punts

Theo Bell: 3 for 8 yards, 2.7 avg.

KICKING and PUNTING

Broncos

Kicking

Jim Turner: 1-for-1 PAT

Punting

Luke Prestridge: 5 for 178 yards, 35.6 avg.

Steelers

Kicking

Matt Bahr: 6-for-6 PAT

Punting

Craig Colquitt: 1 for 56 yards, 56.0 avg.

Week 9

Dallas Cowboys	Oct. 28 Three Rivers Stadium Pittsburgh, PA	Pittsburgh Steelers

	1Q	2Q	3Q	4Q	Total
Cowboys	0	3	0	0	3
Steelers	0	7	7	0	14

the pros

Associated Press

PITTSBURGH — Terry Bradshaw stood on the sidelines Sunday and marveled at what his Pittsburgh teammates were doing to Roger Staubach and the rest of the Dallas Cowboys.

"This is the best the defense has played all year," the Pittsburgh quarterback said after the Steelers wrecked Dallas' running game, flattened Staubach and rode Franco Harris' touchdown runs of one and 48 yards to a 14-3 victory over the Cowboys.

"If we play against everybody the way we played against Dallas, we'll be back in the Super Bowl," Bradshaw said after the Steelers had registered their fourth straight victory over the Cowboys including the triumphs in Super Bowls X and XIII.

The victory boosts the Steelers to 7-2 on the season, still good for first place in the AFC Central. The loss actually did not harm the Cowboys in the NFC East standings. Dallas (7-2) still leads Washington and Philadelphia by one game. Both the Redskins and Eagles were upset Sunday.

Tony Dorsett, who had run for more than 100 yards in each of Dallas' previous four games, carried 19 times for 73 yards, all but six of the yards the Cowboys punched out on the ground against the Steelers.

"Execution, that's the key," said Dorsett, who went to school at the University of Pittsburgh. "If you can't execute, you're not going to run on Hopewell High, much less the 'Steel Curtain.'

"On first downs, we got either one yard or no yards. You have to get something on first down," he added. And Staubach confirmed: "We had no success running on first down. We ended up with a lot of second-and-10s, so we had to begin passing on first downs, passing more than we would have wanted to."

"They shut us down," said Dallas coach Tom Landry. "We probably played as poorly offensively as we have all year. We had two or three chances to get in for a touchdown and didn't do it. If we get in even once, the game's entirely different."

"Their rush, the blitz, gave us some problems," said Staubach. "Their defensive line did a good job."

With 13½ minutes to play, Staubach, under pressure on almost every passing down, eluded tackles by Gary Dunn and John Banaszak, only to be decked by left end L. C. Greenwood. Staubach suffered a concussion and after several anxious moments was led off the field.

However, Staubach was lucid when the game was over, and was able to talk with reporters. Through glazed eyes, he said, "I'm tingling. Tingling all over."

With five minutes to go, Dallas running back Preston Pearson also was injured and was removed from the field on a stretcher. He suffered bruised ribs and a sprained knee.

Harris, who gained 102 yards on 18 carries for the day, scored the only touchdown Pittsburgh needed with his fourth-down, one-yard dive 47 seconds into the second period. It capped a nine-play, 63-yard march highlighted by Terry Bradshaw's passes of 17 and 11 yards to John Stallworth. Bradshaw finished the day by completing 11 of 25 passes for 126 yards.

Staubach, who wound up completing 11 of 25 passes for 113 yards, brought the Cowboys back into position for Rafael Septien's 32-yard field goal with 5:12 gone in the second quarter.

But on the first play from scrimmage following a Dallas punt midway in the third period, Harris burst through a hole off left guard, shook off Cowboys right tackle Randy White, then ducked past safety Cliff Harris and raced unchallenged into the end zone.

After Harris' one-yard plunge behind a block by tight end Randy Grossman, Staubach completed passes of 17 and 13 yards to Drew Pearson and 13 yards to Billy Joe DuPree. That put the ball on the Pittsburgh 15.

But Dorsett lost three yards on first down and gained only one after failing to find a receiver on a planned option pass. On third down, Staubach hit Butch Johnson in the middle of the end zone, but the ball bounced straight up, and before it came back down to Johnson, linebacker Dennis Winston knocked him out from under it, forcing the Cowboys to settle for Septien's field goal.

The three points scored by the Cowboys were their fewest since a 23-3 loss to the New York Giants in the final game of the 1972 season.

Septien missed another 32-yard field-goal attempt late in the third period, kicking the ball wide to the left after Staubach had completed passes of 17 yards to Drew Pearson and 22 yards to DuPree in a drive from the Dallas 32 to the Pittsburgh 11. Dorsett ran for 21 yards in that march, the longest single run against the Steelers this season.

With less than four minutes remaining in the second period, the Cowboys facing a fourth-and-five from their 31, punter and reserve quarterback Danny White took the snap and rolled right, throwing an incompletion that gave the Steelers the ball. But after driving to the Dallas 14, three incompletions by Bradshaw brought Matt Bahr out for a 32-yard field-goal attempt. He also missed, wide to the left.

	Cowboys	Steelers
First downs	14	14
Rushes-yards	23-77	35-172
Passing yards	109	115
Return yards	39	
Passes	16-27-1	11-25-0
Punts	7-40	6-39
Fumbles-lost	0-0	0-0
Penalties-yards	4-30	4-45
Dallas	0 3 0 0 — 3
Pittsburgh	0 7 7 0 — 14

Pit—Harris 1 run (Bahr kick)
Dal—FG Septien 32
Pit—Harris 48 run (Bahr kick)
A—50,199

INDIVIDUAL LEADERS
RUSHING—Dallas, Dorsett 19-73. Pittsburgh, Harris 18-102, Thornton 14-46.
PASSING—Dallas, Staubach 11-25-0-113. White 2-17-1-45. Pittsburgh, Bradshaw 11-25-0-126.
RECEIVING—Dallas, D.Pearson 5-69, DuPree 3-53. Pittsburgh, Stallworth 7-98, Swann 3-21.

		SCORING	DAL	PIT
2nd	Steelers	Franco Harris 1 yard rush (Matt Bahr kick)	0	7
	Cowboys	Rafael Septien 32 yard field goal	3	7
3rd	Steelers	Franco Harris 48 yard rush (Matt Bahr kick)	3	14

	TEAM STATS	
	DAL	PIT
First downs	16	16
Rush-Yards-TD	23-79-0	35-173-2
Comp-Att-Yards-TD-INT	18-42-208-0-1	11-25-126-0-0
Sacked-Yards	3-9	1-11
Net pass yards	199	115
Total yards	278	288
Fumbles-Lost	1-0	0-0
Turnovers	1	0
Penalties-Yards	6-40	4-45

PASSING, RUSHING and RECEIVING

Cowboys

Passing

Roger Staubach: 11-of-25, 113 yards
Danny White: 7-of-17, 95 yards, 0 TD, 1 INT

Rushing

Tony Dorsett: 19 carries for 73 yards
Roger Staubach: 1 carry for 4 yards
Scott Laidlaw: 1 carry for 0 yards
Robert Newhouse: 2 carries for 2 yards

Receiving

Drew Pearson: 5 catches for 89 yards
Tony Dorsett: 3 catches for 8 yards
Billy Joe DuPree: 5 catches for 53 yards
Ron Springs: 3 catches for 44 yards
Preston Pearson: 1 catch for 9 yards
Scott Laidlaw: 1 catch for 5 yards

Steelers

Passing

Terry Bradshaw: 11-of-25, 126 yards

Rushing

Franco Harris: 18 carries for 102 yards, 2 TD
Sidney Thornton: 14 carries for 68 yards
Terry Bradshaw: 2 carries for -5 yards
Rocky Bleier: 1 carry for 8 yards

Receiving

Franco Harris: 1 catch for -1 yard
John Stallworth: 7 catches for 98 yards
Lynn Swann: 3 catches for 29 yards

DEFENSE

Steelers

Interceptions

Donnie Shell: 1 for 0 yards

KICK RETURNS

Cowboys

Kickoffs

Steve Wilson: 2 for 27 yards, 13.5 avg.

Punts

Steve Wilson: 2 for 9 yards, 4.5 avg.

Steelers

Kickoffs

Larry Anderson: 2 for 44 yards, 22.0 avg.

Punts

Theo Bell: 6 for 39 yards, 6.5 avg.

KICKING and PUNTING

Cowboys

Kicking

Rafael Septien: 1-for-2 FG

Punting

Danny White: 7 for 278 yards, 39.7 avg.

Steelers

Kicking

Matt Bahr: 2-for-2 PAT, 0-for-1 FG

Punting

Craig Colquitt: 9 for 347 yards, 38.6 avg.

Week 10

		Nov. 4 Three Rivers Stadium Pittsburgh, PA			
Washington Redskins				Pittsburgh Steelers	
	1Q	2Q	3Q	4Q	Total
Redskins	0	7	0	0	7
Steelers	7	17	7	7	38

The Press
SPORTS
Mon., Nov. 5, 1979   C-1

Terry Bradshaw had his best statistics in a regular-season game in the National Football League, passing for 311 yards and four touchdowns yesterday as the Steelers whipped the Washington Redskins, 38-7.

His top two receivers, John Stallworth and Lynn Swann, both caught passes good for more than 100 yards, only the second time in their careers they have done that on the same day.

The Steelers totaled 545 yards offensively, their finest effort under Coach Chuck Noll, and had their third 500-plus yard effort in the last five weeks.

For the third week in a row, the Steelers dominated a playoff rival at Three Rivers Stadium, adding the Redskins to a list of victims that includes the Denver Broncos and Dallas Cowboys.

The Steelers remained in first place in the Central Division of the American Football Conference, and maintained a one-game edge over the Cleveland Browns, who beat the Philadelphia Eagles yesterday, 24-19.

The Houston Oilers have a chance to tie the Browns in the standings if they can defeat the Dolphins tonight in Miami.

Offensively, the Steelers scored 38 points against the Redskins, who had been the stingiest team in the NFL when it came to giving up points.

Defensively, they held the Redskins to a single touchdown, and no one has scored any more than that against the Steelers on their home turf this season.

And it all began on the front line. Noll knows that better than anybody.

"Whoever controls the line of scrimmage controls the game," Noll noted afterward.

The rushing and the passing begin with the blocking up front, and the defensive coverage begins with the rush.

"The line play was exceptional," said Noll. "We played super offensively and defensively, in every area, except possibly our kick-off coverage, which we'll have to work on."

No detail is too small to escape the coach's attention. The Steelers may be 8-2, and looking simply smashing, but Noll will not dwell on that. Trips to Kansas City and San Diego are next on the schedule, and he will address himself to new challenges — one at a time, of course.

"Our pass protection was outstanding," the coach continued. "We had great respect for the Redskins' pass rush, but our line gave Terry all the time he needed. It seemed like he had all day to throw."

Stallworth caught six passes for 126 yards and two touchdowns, an 11-yarder on the Steelers' second offensive series to get things going, and a 65-yard dazzler in the third quarter.

On the latter, Stallworth picked a ball out of the air with one hand after it bounced upward when he first attempted to catch it, and ran more than 40 yards for the touchdown. Noll classified it as "a circus catch comparable to one Stallworth made in the Super Bowl."

Stallworth knew where it all began yesterday.

"Terry had time to look for the second and sometimes the third receiver," he said. "We have, without a doubt, the best offensive line in the league. They did it today, and were equally good against Dallas, and just as good against Denver.

"They're all healthy now, and they're getting the rapport they had last year. They're playing super. It all starts with them. It's impossible for Terry to get the ball to us if they don't do their blocking."

Stallworth's 65-yard reception-and-run equaled an earlier one by Swann in the Denver game for the longest gainer by passing this season.

Swann, who caught five passes for 106 yards, said, "When the line is giving Terry time they are also giving me time to run my routes and put my moves on my man. It means so much."

In addition to Stallworth's two touchdowns, Bennie Cunningham scored on a 16-yard screen pass, Randy Grossman caught a 4-yard pass in the end zone and Rick Moser scored his first pro touchdown on a two-yard smash.

The interior linemen drawing the praise, left to right, are Jon Kolb, Sam Davis, Mike Webster, Moon Mullins and Larry Brown, for starters, and there is no slack when Ted Petersen and Steve Courson come in for spot duty.

"That's the thing that made the difference in our passing game last year," said Noll of the work of the offensive line. "I saw where a team in New York (the Giants) wanted to go with a big passing game this season. That's fine, but you better get the pass protection before you think about passing.

"The Redskins have some fine defensive linemen in Dave Butz, Diron Talbert, Coy Bacon, Karl Lorch and Joe Jones, but our guys got the job done against them today."

"Giving Terry time, that's the whole key," said Mullins, who came out of the game with a pinched nerve in his neck, but returned to action later. "Keeping Terry clean, that's our job. They put a lot of pressure on us; they were blitzing a lot, but we provided excellent pass protection as a unit."

Bradshaw said he has had many days when he was playing as well as he did against the Redskins, though he recognized that he never did better statistically, and he accomplished what he did in a little more than two quarters of play.

He left the game early in the third quarter — "my mind was scrambled" — after sustaining a head blow when he was tackled and fumbled on the final play of the first half.

"I don't worry about the yardage, but I do love those touchdowns," Bradshaw said. "I love to put points on the board."

He gave way to Mike Kruczek, who's from the Washington, D.C., area and was only too happy to continue the romp over the Redskins.

The Steelers were so much in command, Noll admitted that he considered inserting third-string quarterback Cliff Stoudt into the game for his first regular season outing in his three years on the team.

"Our pass protection is so good now," Bradshaw said. "That's why I don't run with the ball myself anymore. If I move now, it's to look and see other receivers. It's made me a better quarterback. A lot of big plays happen when I find that second or third receiver out there.

"Our offensive line works hard at giving me that extra second I have so much confidence in them now. I'm terrible about it sometimes. I just expect it. I don't even think about it anymore. I know I'll get it.

"I had all the time in the world. The main reason for that is because they tried to stop our running game. They brought up both safeties to support against the run on first down, so I just came out and started throwing on first down."

He completed 15 of 27, and had one interception.

"They were safety blitzing and everything," Bradshaw said, "and when they did that I hit John Stallworth on a flag pass and I hit Lynn Swann on a flag. I don't care who you are, there's no way you can cover our guys man-to-man, especially when the quarterback has a lot of time."

The offensive line saw to it that Terry had time, that's for sure.

"When you have everything going," said Bradshaw "it's a lot of fun."

		SCORING	WAS	PIT
1st	Steelers	John Stallworth 11 yard pass from Terry Bradshaw (Matt Bahr kick)	0	7
2nd	Redskins	John Riggins 4 yard rush (Mark Moseley kick)	7	7
	Steelers	Matt Bahr 21 yard field goal	7	10
	Steelers	Bennie Cunningham 16 yard pass from Terry Bradshaw (Matt Bahr kick)	7	17
	Steelers	Randy Grossman 4 yard pass from Terry Bradshaw (Matt Bahr kick)	7	24
3rd	Steelers	John Stallworth 65 yard pass from Terry Bradshaw (Matt Bahr kick)	7	31
4th	Steelers	Rick Moser 2 yard rush (Matt Bahr kick)	7	38

	TEAM STATS	
	WAS	PIT
First downs	17	26
Rush-Yards-TD	24-88-1	40-173-1
Comp-Att-Yards-TD-INT	15-34-159-0-2	20-34-390-4-1
Sacked-Yards	1-10	2-18

Net pass yards	149	372
Total yards	237	545
Fumbles-Lost	3-2	2-2
Turnovers	4	3
Penalties-Yards	2-10	8-45

PASSING, RUSHING and RECEIVING

Redskins

Passing

Joe Theismann: 14-of-31, 147 yards, 0 TD, 1 INT
Kim McQuilken: 1-of-3, 12 yards, 0 TD, 1 INT

Rushing

Joe Theismann: 4 carries for 20 yards
John Riggins: 13 carries for 56 yards, 1 TD
Bennie Malone: 5 carries for 12 yards
Clarence Harmon: 1 carry for 0 yards
Ike Forte: 1 carry for 0 yards

Receiving

John Riggins: 4 catches for 33 yards
Danny Buggs: 3 catches for 37 yards
Ricky Thompson: 1 catch for 35 yards
Benny Malone: 1 catch for 3 yards
Don Warren: 1 catch for 13 yards
Clarence Harmon: 1 catch for 12 yards
John McDaniel: 1 catch for 9 yards
Buddy Hardeman: 2 catches for 9 yards
Ike Forte: 1 catch for 8 yards

Steelers

Passing

Terry Bradshaw: 15-of-27, 311 yards, 4 TD, 1 INT
Mike Kruczek: 5-of-7, 79 yards

Rushing

Franco Harris: 15 carries for 62 yards
Anthony Anderson: 6 carries for 56 yards
Mike Kruczek: 2 carries for 0 yards
Rocky Bleier: 6 carries for 26 yards
Sidney Thornton: 6 carries for 13 yards
Rick Moser: 5 carries for 16 yards, 1 TD

Receiving

John Stallworth: 6 catches for 126 yards, 2 TD
Lynn Swann: 5 catches for 106 yards
Randy Grossman: 3 catches for 49 yards, 1 TD
Rocky Bleier: 1 catch for 10 yards
Sidney Thornton: 1 catch for 21 yards
Theo Bell: 1 catch for 31 yards
Bennie Cunningham: 2 catches for 29 yards, 1 TD
Jim Smith: 1 catch for 18 yards

DEFENSE

Redskins

Interceptions

Joe Lavender: 1 for -2 yards

Steelers

Interceptions

Mel Blount: 1 for 1 yard
Donnie Shell: 1 for 2 yards

KICK RETURNS

Redskins

Kickoffs

Ike Forte: 3 for 93 yards, 31.0 avg.
Buddy Hardeman: 3 for 55 yards, 18.3 avg.
Clarence Harmon: 1 for 19 yards, 19.0 avg.

Punts

Buddy Hardeman: 1 for 3 yards, 3.0 avg.

Steelers

Kickoffs

Larry Anderson: 1 for 20 yards, 20.0 avg.

Punts

Theo Bell: 2 for 5 yards, 2.5 avg.

KICKING and PUNTING

Redskins

Kicking

Mark Moseley: 1-for-1 PAT, 0-for-1 FG

Punting

Mike Bragg: 6 for 229 yards, 38.2 avg.

Steelers

Kicking

Matt Bahr: 5-for-5 PAT, 1-for-3 FG

Punting

Craig Colquitt: 1 for 31 yards, 31.0 avg.

Week 11

		1Q	2Q	3Q	4Q	Total
Pittsburgh Steelers	Nov. 11 Arrowhead Stadium Kansas City, MO					**Kansas City Chiefs**
Steelers		10	10	0	10	30
Chiefs		0	0	3	0	3

KANSAS CITY, Mo. — This is the kind of day it was for the Steelers:

Terry Bradshaw completed 17 of 29 passes for 232 yards and three touchdowns, but shook his head, grimaced and said yesterday, "It was the worst game I've played all year."

The dazed Kansas City Chiefs, who suffered a 30-3 licking at the hands of the Steelers for their worst beating of the year, had to wonder what Bradshaw might have done on a good day.

The funny thing is that Bradshaw, who is noted for poking fun at himself, was not kidding this time.

The spectre that haunts the Steelers — an ailment or an injury that could sideline their quarterback — almost happened this weekend.

There was a lot of doubt he would even play, much less throw for three touchdowns after he came down with a sudden attack of back spasms Saturday morning.

He was in obvious pain and had problems just walking from the Steelers' charter plane to the bus here Saturday. He spent the day in his hotel room, resting and gulping "10 or 12 pills" for the back ailment while Mike Kruczek studied the game plan in case he had to go in.

"I wasn't sure I'd be able to play," Bradshaw said. "I told Mike to make sure he knew the game plan. I slept sitting up, propped up with pillows."

If the attack had come 24 hours later, Bradshaw could not have played. But the medication worked, and Bradshaw felt well enough to play even if he was not vintage Bradshaw.

"I had no strength," he said. "I couldn't throw. I got winded. I didn't feel worth a darn. I was hoping I wouldn't get into a throwing match. I just didn't have a good day. I wasn't sitting in the pocket the way I normally do, I didn't throw the way I normally throw."

Bradshaw's shaky condition lent a note of drama to the game, but it went unnoticed by the 70,132 spectators at Arrowhead Stadium. In fact, there were 8,243 no-shows on a cold but clear day with temperatures in the 40s.

Both the fans in the stands and the ones who stayed at home and watched on TV had to wonder why Bradshaw was not throwing more because the Chiefs' defense was playing the run well, particularly on first downs. Bradshaw, however, often burned them on third-down plays. The Steelers zipped to a 20-0 halftime lead as he converted on nine of 12 third-down situations.

It is a measure of the Steeler team that they can win big even when the quarterback is not feeling well and the running game is bogged down.

The receivers took over as John Stallworth (four catches for 88 yards) and Lynn Swann (five for 55) made spectacular catches to back the defense and the special teams.

"The story was our defense, field position and kicking game," Coach Chuck Noll noted. Only one of the three Steeler touchdown drives was longer than 46 yards.

Bradshaw also used a bit of guile. He threw a 26-yard touchdown pass to Stallworth off a flea-flicker and threw a one-yard pass to tackle Larry Brown, who was a tight end on the short-yardage play. It was Brown's first regular-season touchdown catch since he was the starting tight end in 1975. Wait until the Dallas Cowboys see this. They will be calling the Steelers a finesse team.

Bradshaw also threw a 16-yard touchdown pass to Swann, who leaped up to snare the high pass and then came down with his feet in bounds. Matt Bahr, who had been having his problems while hitting on only seven of 15 field-goal attempts, popped in three from 31, 20 and 37 yards when drives bogged down.

The incredible thing is that this was basically a defensive game, yet the Steelers won, 30-3.

The Steelers are going through the schedule like a thresher in a Kansas wheatfield these days. Nothing stops them. They have won their last four games by a 124-20 margin since the debacle in Cincinnati. They are 9-2 for the season. A year ago at this point, they were 9-2 and they went on to finish 17-2.

Yet, the Steelers appear to be playing better now than they were a year ago when they lost two of four after winning the first seven. "We had our slump earlier this year," said Rocky Bleier.

The Steeler defense limited the Chiefs to 127 net yards and 65 yards rushing and just eight first downs. In their last four wins, the opposing offense has not rushed for 100 yards. The Steelers also knocked out runners Tony Reed (knee) and Arnold Morgado (broken right leg) for the season. That virtually caved in the Chiefs' season like an accordion. Kansas City is now 4-7, has lost five straight and are a running team with virtually no runners left.

(Continued on Page 11.)

(Continued from Page 9.)

Despite all that, the Chiefs were still in the game late in the third quarter. With the score still 20-3, they had a second-and-10 on the Steeler 35 after the Chiefs' second theft of a Bradshaw pass. Steve Fuller, the rookie quarterback who hit on only nine of 20 passes and was sacked four times, tried to burn the Steelers with a flea-flicker to Henry Marshall.

But safety Donnie Shell was not fooled, stayed with Marshall all the way and made the defensive play.

"The game could have changed on that one play," Joe Greene said. "If they had scored, they would have had the crowd behind them and some enthusiasm with the score 20-10 and a quarter to play. It was a big play on Donnie's part."

The Chiefs punted two plays later after a delay-of-game penalty ruined a field-goal attempt. They never made another move.

"I had fun out there," said Greene, who had pointed out that last week's game against Washington was a "dead" one. The Chiefs made a livelier effort, but the Steelers still swatted them away with ease.

It was an ideal time for a Steeler letdown, but it did not come.

"The letdown ain't going to happen," Greene said. "It's the wrong time of the-year for a letdown."

There is never any chance of a letdown when the defense is worried about the quarterback's health. The defense was ready to win this one, 7-3, if it had been necessary.

It was another cold and calculating day for the Steelers.

		SCORING	PIT	KAN

1st	Steelers	John Stallworth 26 yard pass from Terry Bradshaw (Matt Bahr kick)	7	0
	Steelers	Matt Bahr 31 yard field goal	10	0
2nd	Steelers	Lynn Swann 16 yard pass from Terry Bradshaw (Matt Bahr kick)	17	0
	Steelers	Matt Bahr 20 yard field goal	20	0
3rd	Chiefs	Jan Stenerud 42 yard field goal	20	3
4th	Steelers	Matt Bahr 37 yard field goal	23	3
	Steelers	Larry Brown 1 yard pass from Terry Bradshaw (Matt Bahr kick)	30	3

	TEAM STATS	
	PIT	KAN
First downs	20	8
Rush-Yards-TD	44-127-0	26-65-0
Comp-Att-Yards-TD-INT	17-29-232-3-2	9-20-89-0-1
Sacked-Yards	1-4	5-27
Net pass yards	228	62
Total yards	355	127
Fumbles-Lost	3-0	2-2
Turnovers	2	3
Penalties-Yards	4-30	4-42

PASSING, RUSHING and RECEIVING

Steelers

Passing

Terry Bradshaw: 17-of-29, 232 yards, 3 TD, 2 INT

Rushing

Terry Bradshaw: 2 carries for 10 yards
Franco Harris: 20 carries for 68 yards
Rocky Bleier: 12 carries for 24 yards
Anthony Anderson: 5 carries for 20 yards
Rick Moser: 2 carries for 4 yards
Greg Hawthorne: 2 carries for 3 yards
Mike Kruczek: 1 carry for -2 yards

Receiving

John Stallworth: 4 catches for 88 yards, 1 TD
Rocky Bleier: 3 catches for 40 yards
Lynn Swann: 5 catches for 55 yards, 1 TD
Bennie Cunningham: 2 catches for 29 yards
Jim Smith: 1 catch for 12 yards
Randy Grossman: 1 catch for 7 yards
Larry Brown: 1 catch for 1 yard, 1 TD

Chiefs

Passing

Steve Fuller: 9-of-20, 89 yards, 0 TD, 1 INT

Rushing

Tony Reed: 6 carries ror 14 yards
Mike A. Williams: 6 carries for 19 yards
Henry Marshall: 1 carry for 11 yards
Arnold Morgado: 10 carries for 12 yards
Horace Belton: 3 carries for 9 yards

Receiving

J.T. Smith: 3 catches for 47 yards
Tony Reed: 1 catch for 13 yards
Mike A. Williams: 2 catches for 4 yards
Tony Samuels: 1 catch for 18 yards
Henry Marshall: 1 catch for 5 yards
Arnold Morgado: 1 catch for 2 yards

DEFENSE

Steelers

Interceptions

Dirt Winston: 1 for 0 yards

Chiefs

Interceptions

M.L. Carter: 1 for 20 yards
Tom Howard: 1 for 19 yards

KICK RETURNS

Steelers

Kickoffs

Larry Anderson: 1 for 19 yards, 19.0 avg.

Punts

Theo Bell: 4 for 45 yards, 11.3 avg.

Chiefs

Kickoffs

Horace Belton: 6 for 115 yards, 19.2 avg.
Steve Gaunty: 1 for 30 yards, 30.0 avg.

Punts

J.T. Smith: 3 for 36 yards, 12.0 avg.

KICKING and PUNTING

Steelers

Kicking

Matt Bahr: 3-for-3 PAT, 3-for-3 FG

Punting

Craig Colquitt: 4 for 156 yards, 39.0 avg.

Chiefs

Kicking

Jan Stenerud: 1-for-2 FG

Punting

Bob Grupp: 7 for 266 yards, 38.0 avg.

Week 12

Nov. 18
San Diego Stadium
San Diego, CA

Pittsburgh Steelers vs **San Diego Chargers**

	1Q	2Q	3Q	4Q	Total
Steelers	0	0	7	0	7
Chargers	7	14	7	7	35

SAN DIEGO — The Steelers ought to check trainer Ralph Berlin's black bag to see if there is any snake oil in it.

Chargers Coach Don Coryell might have sold the Steelers some of that.

With all the cunning and convincing tones of the old-time traveling medicine man, or the come-on ability of a carnival pitchman, last week Coryell proclaimed the Pittsburgh Steelers to be "the finest team I've ever seen, the finest team in the history of pro football."

Everybody bought Coryell's proclamation, perhaps the Pittsburgh tourists more than anyone.

Yesterday Coryell and his Chargers went out and whipped the Steelers soundly, 35-7, more soundly than anybody else had beaten them this season.

"This game settled something once and for all," said Coach Chuck Noll, with more than a suggestion of sarcasm in his voice. "The greatest team of all time ... the Chargers are."

Did Coryell set up the Steelers for their fall? Did he roll out the red carpet when they came to town, and then yank it out from under them while they were admiring the blue sky and bright sun overhead?

"Words didn't do it," said Noll. "Deeds did it. They outhit us. They played very aggressively. They beat our butt. They did a good job and they just ran over us."

Noll studied a statistical report of the game, reading it the way a man in the military service might re-read a "Dear John" letter. He looked at the numbers, and he didn't like them any more than he liked the game. What did he see in the stats that he hadn't seen from the sideline?

"I see that we stunk," said Noll succinctly. "That's what I see."

Noll didn't point it out, but one statistic that tells a lot about the game is the Chargers gained more ground on the passing of Terry Bradshaw than the Steelers did.

Bradshaw, who simply had a bad day, completed 20 of 38 passes, mostly of the short variety to his running backs, for 125 yards. Meanwhile, five of his passes were intercepted and returned 171 yards. Bradshaw also was sacked four times for 39 yards in losses. And, the Steeler woes were compounded by three lost fumbles for a total of eight turnovers.

The Chargers' outside linebackers, Woody Lowe and Ray Preston, each picked off a pair of passes, and cornerback Mike Williams came up with the other interception.

Lowe returned his second interception 77 yards for a touchdown in the third quarter. Glen Edwards tipped the pass into Lowe's arms. It was a play that particularly galled Noll.

"We had guys walking off the field when they were returning the ball," noted Noll. "That happens when you believe your press clippings."

The Chargers' first score was set up when Preston intercepted a Bradshaw pass in the first period and returned it 35 yards to the Steelers' 37-yard line. Dan Fouts, San Diego's fine quarterback, passed 18 yards to wide receiver John Jefferson, then 16 yards to him for a touchdown.

In the second quarter, Fouts completed a nine-play, 72-yard drive with a 6-yard TD pass to tight end Bob Klein in the end zone. Klein caught the ball above Donnie Shell's outstretched hands.

Later in the quarter, Preston picked off a second Bradshaw pass and returned it 35 yards to the 5. Gerry Mullins made the tackle for the Steelers, as he did on three occasions in the contest, and was called for a personal foul for his overzealousness, putting the ball on the 2-yard line.

Fullback Bo Matthews bulled his way up the middle for his first touchdown this season.

So the Chargers had a 21-0 lead at halftime, and it could have been 35-0 if the Steelers' defense had not been so stout.

The Steelers seemed capable of making a comeback in the second half. Bradshaw had his best passing series of the game on the Steelers' second possession in the third period, and Rocky Bleier capped the drive with a 2-yard touchdown bolt.

But later in the period, Edwards deflected a pass intended for Lynn Swann into the hands of Lowe, who raced down the left sideline and just made it to the goal line.

"Thank God for Woodrow Lowe," offered Fouts after the game. "Their defense was awesome and they didn't give us anything. But their offense put the defense in bad positions. Their defense played a lot better than the score indicated. It should have been a 14-7 game in our favor, not a 35-7 game."

Another interception led to the Chargers' final touchdown. Big Wilbur Young, the Chargers' standout defensive end, got his hand on a ball thrown by Bradshaw, and this one was returned 18 yards to the 5-yard line by Mike Williams. Three plays later, Hank Bauer went up the middle for a 2-yard touchdown.

"I'm totally surprised by the final score," commented Klein. "They are such a super team. I didn't think we could score that many points against Pittsburgh."

"Everybody knew what to do today," said Bob Horn,

(Continued from Page B-5) middle linebacker for the Chargers. "We studied our game plans real hard this week. We stopped them on first and second down running, so they had to pass. We forced them away from their game plan."

Said defensive end Leroy Jones: "Our defense was just great. We knew if we could put pressure on Bradshaw our defensive backs would cover and we would have a great day."

Preston put it this way: "We noticed on film that Bradshaw was throwing the ball to spots where there'd be three or four defenders, and they were coming up with great catches. We felt if we could pressure him, we'd come up with some of those throws."

The Chargers were successful in covering the Steelers' deep receivers, Swann and John Stallworth, for the most part, and tight end Bennie Cunningham. They let backs Franco Harris and Rocky Bleier open, and Bradshaw threw often to both of them, but never for big gains. "That's what they gave us," Bradshaw said.

"We didn't play well, it's that simple," the Steeler quarterback continued. "When you lose and lose like that, it's always disillusioning. It's embarrassing, not to even make a game of it. I put too much pressure on our defense. They were playing with their backs to the wall all day."

Bradshaw doesn't believe that Coryell's comments about how great the Steelers are led to an overconfident approach to playing this game.

"Everybody's been saying that," Bradshaw said. "I'd like to think that we don't believe that stuff. But we're human and maybe we do. This will be good for us. Maybe people will quit saying 'the mighty Steelers,' and so forth.

"Now we're just another football team struggling to make the playoffs. Maybe we'll play better with a knife in our back."

Houston beat Cincinnati, 42-21, yesterday so the Oilers and Steelers are now tied for first place in the American Football Conference's Central Division with 9-3 records. Cleveland is one game behind after beating Miami, 30-24, in overtime.

The Browns will pay a visit to Three Rivers Stadium next Sunday.

"We better get our act together for these last few games against teams in our division," said Jack Lambert. "These games will determine our season. Don't ask me about how good our team is until the season's over."

Steeler Summary

How They Scored

		SCORING	PIT	SDG
1st	Chargers	John Jefferson 16 yard pass from Dan Fouts (Mike Wood kick)	0	7
2nd	Chargers	Bob Klein 6 yard pass from Dan Fouts (Mike Wood kick)	0	14

	Chargers	Bo Matthews 2 yard rush (Mike Wood kick)	0	21
3rd	Steelers	Rocky Bleier 2 yard rush (Matt Bahr kick)	7	21
	Chargers	Woodrow Lowe 77 yard interception return (Mike Wood kick)	7	28
4th	Chargers	Hank Bauer 2 yard rush (Mike Wood kick)	7	35

	TEAM STATS	
	PIT	SDG
First downs	14	14
Rush-Yards-TD	29-66-1	30-98-2
Comp-Att-Yards-TD-INT	20-38-164-0-5	11-25-137-2-2
Sacked-Yards	4-39	3-17
Net pass yards	125	120
Total yards	191	218
Fumbles-Lost	4-3	3-2
Turnovers	8	4
Penalties-Yards	7-38	9-60

PASSING, RUSHING and RECEIVING

Steelers

Passing

Terry Bradshaw: 18-of-36, 153 yards, 0 TD, 5 INT
Mike Kruczek: 2-of-2, 11 yards

Rushing

Franco Harris: 20 carries for 44 yards
Terry Bradshaw: 1 carry for 3 yards
Rocky Bleier: 8 carries for 19 yards, 1 TD

Receiving

Franco Harris: 7 catches for 50 yards
John Stallworth: 4 catches for 55 yards
Rocky Bleier: 4 catches for 28 yards
Lynn Swann: 2 catches for 28 yards
Rick Moser: 1 catch for 6 yards
Greg Hawthorne: 1 catch for 5 yards
Bennie Cunningham: 1 catch for -8 yards

Chargers

Passing

Dan Fouts: 11-of-24, 137 yards, 2 TD, 2 INT
Mike Fuller: 0-of-1, 0 yards

Rushing

Dan Fouts: 1 carry for 1 yard
Mike Thomas: 13 carries for 53 yards
Clarence Williams: 7 carries for 16 yards
Lydell Mitchell: 4 carries for 13 yards
Artie Owens: 2 carries for 10 yards
Hank Bauer: 2 carries for 3 yards, 1 TD
Bo Matthews: 1 carry for 2 yards, 1 TD

Receiving

John Jefferson: 5 catches for 106 yards, 1 TD
Mike Thomas: 1 catch for 4 yards
Clarence Williams: 3 catches for 16 yards
Bob Klein: 1 catch for 6 yards, 1 TD
Charlie Joiner: 1 catch for 5 yards

DEFENSE

Steelers

Interceptions

Ron Johnson: 1 for 0 yards
Jack Lambert: 1 for 0 yards

Chargers

Interceptions

Woodrow Lowe: 2 for 106 yards, 1 TD
Ray Preston: 2 for 60 yards
Mike H. Williams: 1 for 5 yards

KICK RETURNS

Steelers

Kickoffs

Larry Anderson: 3 for 55 yards, 18.3 avg.
Rick Moser: 1 for 6 yards, 6.0 avg.

Punts

Theo Bell: 3 for 42 yards, 14.0 avg.
Thom Dornbrook: 1 for 0 yards, 0.0 avg.

Chargers

Kickoffs

Artie Owens: 2 for 48 yards, 24.0 avg.

Punts

Mike Fuller: 3 for 5 yards, 1.7 avg.
Mike H. Williams: 1 for 9 yards, 9.0 avg.

KICKING and PUNTING

Steelers

Kicking

Matt Bahr: 1-for-1 PAT

Punting

Craig Colquitt: 5 for 173 yards, 34.6 avg.

Chargers

Kicking

Mike Wood: 5-for-5 PAT

Punting

Jeff West: 7 for 241 yards, 34.4 avg.

Week 13

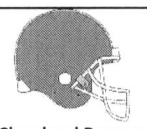

	Nov. 25 Three Rivers Stadium Pittsburgh, PA					
Cleveland Browns						Pittsburgh Steelers
	1Q	2Q	3Q	4Q	OT	Total
Browns	10	10	7	3	0	30
Steelers	3	10	0	17	3	33

This one could have been given an Oscar, an Emmy and a Clio.

The Steelers settled for passing out eight game balls. They had more heroes than they could count.

So you wanted exciting football? The Steelers and the Cleveland Browns believe the customer is always right. They gave 48,773 fans at Three Rivers Stadium the most exciting game of the year.

For the last six weeks, watching the Steelers had been about as exciting as watching paint dry. The games were always decided before the fourth quarter started. They won four games by a combined score of 124-20 and lost two by a total of 69-17.

This time, the drama was just starting to build when the fourth quarter opened. The Steelers didn't tie it 30-30 until Matt Bahr kicked a 21-yard field goal with 24 seconds left in regulation time, and they finally won it 33-30 on Bahr's 37-yarder with nine seconds left in overtime. It was the second straight time that the Browns lost here in overtime.

It probably would have been more fitting for the game to end in a tie. "It's a shame that either team had to lose," was a line heard in both locker rooms.

The players were weary warriors who had earned each other's respect in the long fray. "I gained a lot of respect for them," Joe Greene said.

John Banaszak chimed in, "There's no reason for them to hand their heads, because they came after us."

A tie probably wouldn't have hurt the Steelers because they still could have won the division by winning their last three games. They still have to win at Houston, but the win means they can afford to split their other two games against Cincinnati and Buffalo and still win the crown. The Steelers and Houston are tied at 10-3, while Cleveland, which plays Houston next week, is 8-5.

But the Steelers savored the hard-earned victory, and it was significant that they kept coming from behind. The Steelers handed out eight game balls to Bahr, Terry Bradshaw, Theo Bell, Steve Courson, Ted Peterson, Bennie Cunningham, L.C. Greenwood and Franco Harris. Courson and Peterson started in the line because Gerry Mullins and Jon Kolb were ailing.

This was an offensive show, and it would take a calculator to compute all the records set. The Steelers rang up 606 yards for the second highest total in the team's history and the most under Chuck Noll. Bradshaw's figured of 30 completions on 44 attempts and 364 yards were all career highs. They also set a team record with 36 first downs.

It was noteworthy, too, that Bradshaw completed nine passes to Harris and seven to Rocky Bleier. The Browns tried the San Diego strategy of dropping back to stop the bomb, but Bradshaw burned it by making the short game work.

"This was more satisfying than blowing them out," Bradshaw said. "It has to be the most gratifying win of the year. Let that stuff about the mighty Steelers and all of that garbage die. We're in a tough division. We could have given up several times and said the defense wasn't playing well, but we kept coming back."

The Steelers were resourceful and found a way to win, but they saluted Brian Sipe. "I was a fan of his back when they were trying to run him out of town," Bradshaw said.

Sipe completed 23 of 38 passes for 333 yards and three touchdowns, and he did it without a running game to back it up.

Bradshaw was working against a beat-up Cleveland defense as Franco Harris complemented his passing with a 151-yard game. The Browns tried a 3-4 defense at times, but the Steelers just shredded it.

In fact, the Steelers could have made it a blowout if it had not been for Sipe's performance and their own mistakes. The Steelers were far from perfect, but their mistakes made it more interesting. The Steelers came back from deficits of 10-0, 20-6 and 27-13 during the seesaw game.

As late as the fourth quarter, the Steelers kept trying to give it away. Trailing 27-20, they all but gave the Browns a field goal when Harris fumbled and Jack Lambert kept the drive alive by roughing Sipe on third down.

Trying to come back from a 10-point margin, Bradshaw managed to get sacked after getting a first down on the 1, but the Steelers came back to score anyway to cut the deficit to 30-27.

Bradshaw got sacked because his intended receiver, Randy Grossman, got jammed. Bradshaw could laugh when it was over as he said, "I didn't want to look at the sidelines. Chuck Noll wanted a piece of me. Oh, Lord, if we hadn't scored, I would have gone to the Browns' side. Grossman told me, 'He'd like to get a hold of you.'"

Bradshaw and Noll had their moments on their sidelines during the long game, but Bradshaw said that's just part of the game. "I know when I make a mistake and I'm upset and he wants to make a point, but I already know I messed up and here he comes and we start. It's better that we avoid each other. We're just too much alike in some respects. But it's just the heat of the game."

There was more heat to come. With the score 30-27, Robin Cole grabbed a face mask to give the Browns a first down at midfield. But Greenwood got 1 ½ of his 4 ½ sacks, the half with Steve Furness' help, and the Browns had to punt. Theo Bell returned the ball 27 yards to the 50 and the Steelers drove for the tying field goal.

In the overtime, Mel Blount and Ron Bolton traded interceptions, but it was a Browns' mistake that finally turned the game. The Steelers were guilty of illegal motion on a second-and-10 at their own 34. The Browns could have taken the play to make it third-and-nine. They accepted the penalty to make it second-and-15.

That extra down was critical because on third down Bradshaw scrambled 28 yards for a first down on the Browns' 38 and Bahr kicked the game-winner five plays later.

Sam Rutigliano, the Cleveland coach, first said, "I made a mistake." Later, he admitted he wanted to decline the penalty but said there was a "mixup" on the field and the Browns accepted it. Jack Gregory, the Cleveland lineman, said Rutigliano changed his mind after the penalty was accepted.

Whatever happened, it was the final turning point on a game that deserved to be mounted on a wall.

Greene, who said earlier the win over Washington was a "dead" game, smiled, "I would have enjoyed watching the whole 75 minutes."

There was enough excitement for an entire season.

		SCORING	CLE	PIT
1st	Browns	Ozzie Newsome 21 yard pass from Brian Sipe (Don Cockroft kick)	7	0
	Browns	Don Cockroft 20 yard field goal	10	0
	Steelers	Matt Bahr 45 yard field goal	10	3
2nd	Browns	Don Cockroft 32 yard field goal	13	3
	Steelers	Matt Bahr 34 yard field goal	13	6
	Browns	Dave Logan 16 yard pass from Brian Sipe (Don Cockroft kick)	20	6
	Steelers	Franco Harris 2 yard pass from Terry Bradshaw (Matt Bahr kick)	20	13
3rd	Browns	Calvin Hill 3 yard pass from Brian Sipe (Don Cockroft kick)	27	13

4th	Steelers	Franco Harris 1 yard rush (Matt Bahr kick)	27	20
	Browns	Don Cockroft 40 yard field goal	30	20
	Steelers	Franco Harris 3 yard rush (Matt Bahr kick)	30	27
	Steelers	Matt Bahr 21 yard field goal	30	30
OT	Steelers	Matt Bahr 37 yard field goal	30	33

	TEAM STATS	
	CLE	PIT
First downs	22	36
Rush-Yards-TD	24-62-0	45-255-2
Comp-Att-Yards-TD-INT	23-38-333-3-1	30-44-364-1-1
Sacked-Yards	7-50	1-13
Net pass yards	283	351
Total yards	345	606
Fumbles-Lost	1-0	3-2
Turnovers	1	3
Penalties-Yards	8-65	10-95

PASSING, RUSHING and RECEIVING

Browns

Passing

Brian Sipe: 23-of-38, 333 yards, 3 TD, 1 INT

Rushing

Brian Sipe: 3 carries for 30 yards
Calvin Hill: 5 carries for 10 yards
Mike Pruitt: 14 carries for 27 yards

Dino Hall: 1 carry for -3 yards
Cleo Miller: 1 carry for -2 yards

Receiving

Dave Logan: 7 catches for 135 yards, 1 TD
Ozzie Newsome: 5 catches for 77 yards, 1 TD
Calvin Hill: 4 catches for 51 yards, 1 TD
Mike Pruitt: 3 catches for 21 yards
Reggie Rucker: 2 catches for 36 yards
Dino Hall: 1 catch for 8 yards
Cleo Miller: 1 catch for 5 yards

Steelers

Passing

Terry Bradshaw: 30-of-44, 364 yards, 1 TD, 1 INT

Rushing

Franco Harris: 32 carries for 151 yards, 2 TD
Terry Bradshaw: 3 carries for 43 yards
Rocky Bleier: 10 carries for 61 yards

Receiving

Franco Harris: 9 catches for 81 yards, 1 TD
Rocky Bleier: 7 catches for 45 yards
John Stallworth: 6 catches for 75 yards
Bennie Cunningham: 4 catches for 68 yards
Lynn Swann: 3 catches for 48 yards
Randy Grossman: 1 catch for 47 yards

DEFENSE

Browns

Interceptions

Ron Bolton: 1 for 1 yard

Steelers

Interceptions

Mel Blount: 1 for 0 yards

KICK RETURNS

Browns

Kickoffs

Dino Hall: 8 for 162 yards, 20.3 avg.

Steelers

Kickoffs

Anthony Anderson: 6 for 80 yards, 13.3 avg.
Larry Anderson: 1 for 10 yards, 10.0 avg.

Punts

Theo Bell: 4 for 39 yards, 9.8 avg.

KICKING and PUNTING

Browns

Kicking

Don Cockroft: 3-for-3 PAT, 3-for-3 FG

Punting

Johnny Evans: 4 for 185 yards, 46.3 avg.

Steelers

Kicking

Matt Bahr: 3-for-3 PAT, 4-for-5 FG

Punting

Craig Colquitt: 1 for 35 yards, 35.0 avg.

Week 14

Cincinnati Bengals	Dec. 2 Three Rivers Stadium Pittsburgh, PA	Pittsburgh Steelers

	1Q	2Q	3Q	4Q	Total
Bengals	0	10	7	0	17
Steelers	10	14	10	3	37

Dr. Terry Bradshaw is ready to hang out his shingle.

The Steelers quarterback, who received an honorary doctorate degree from Alderson-Broaddus College in West Virginia last June, showed that he knows a few things about psychology.

Bradshaw knew he could do just about anything he wanted against the hapless Cincinnati Bengals, so he went in with an unusual game plan: He staged Lynn Swann Appreciation Day.

He made it a personal project to build up Swann's confidence in the twilight of a frustrating year. Bradshaw's five passes to Swann resulted in 192 yards and two touchdowns in a 37-17 rout of the Bengals.

"I've never done that before, but I was throwing to Lynn on purpose because he was getting down," Bradshaw said. "He had been having all kinds of problems this year and he wasn't himself. He's a proud individual and I'm sure he's disappointed in the season he's had.

"He came in from USC and walked into two Super Bowls, and this is the first year he's had problems. The Good Lord teaches a thing called humility. He's had to look at himself, but he proved he's back and that'll help our team. I'm anxious to see what Houston will do to stop him."

Swann, who was late to camp because of a court suit and then was injured with a dislocated toe and a pulled hamstring, did not play in the first Cincinnati game. He came into this game with just 29 catches while John Stallworth had 61.

It was a perfect game to try this strategy and add another dimension to the offense. The bungling "Bungles" were not as bad as advertised. They were worse. The Steelers all but stuffed them into a trash can and probably wished they could have done the same thing to a modern ruin called Three Rivers Stadium.

They had more problems with the stadium than the Bengals as the elevator and scoreboard broke down. Their only concern until Bradshaw suffered a wrist injury was whether the stadium was going to fall down before the game ended.

The remaining chilled fans in the crowd of 46,521 were stunned when Bradshaw came off the field holding his wrist after he fell and Eddie Edwards plopped on top of him. There were fears it was broken, but X-rays showed it was only a sprain.

Bradshaw, whose main concern seemed to be whether he would still be able to make a planned trip to his Louisiana farm this week, said he would be fine, but he will have to wait to see how it is Monday.

Bradshaw, who likes a good gag, climbed on his stool and yelled across the locker room, "Sidney, Sidney, bring me your pail. I'll stick my good wrist in it."

Sidney Thornton, the running back, came up with a delightful tale this week about how he cured a sprained ankle by sticking his good ankle in a mixture dreamed up by a voodoo lady called Miss Rudolph.

When he got serious, Bradshaw said of Edwards' hit, "I'm not going to call it a cheap shot, but all he had to do was this," as he slapped a reporter's arm. Since Bradshaw was on the ground, he only had to be touched.

It also brought up the usual questions about why Bradshaw was still in the game with a 17-point lead and five minutes left.

"Chuck Noll doesn't pull me until he feels very comfortable, and I understand that," Bradshaw said.

One of these days, Bradshaw could suffer a serious injury in the late minutes of a rout, and Noll would not be very comfortable if he had to watch the Super Bowl on television.

The victory gives the Steelers an 11-3 record and a one-game lead over the Oilers going into next Monday night's game at Houston, thanks to Cleveland's upset of the Oilers.

The surprising thing is that Cleveland's win means the Steelers have not yet officially clinched a playoff spot, despite some misinformation to the contrary. There is still a slight chance that the Steelers could finish in a three-way wild-car tie with San Diego and Cleveland at 11-5.

But that is quite remote, and the reality is that the Houston loss probably means the Steelers will win the AFC's Central Division title. Houston would have to beat them by more than 20 points to knock them out of it as long as the Steelers beat Buffalo in the finale.

But the Houston loss takes some of the drama out of next Monday night's game, and that disappointed Joe Greene, who likes the excitement of a big game. "As a football player, you get a charge and a thrill from playing in those kinds of games," he said. "It's still big, but it's different now."

After Greene made those comments, the Houston game took on added importance because of San Diego's loss to Atlanta. The Steelers now have the best record in pro football and can clinch home-field advantage for both AFC playoff games by winning their final two games.

Bradshaw made the Cincinnati game a rout with passes of 58, 45, 34 and 42 yards, which led to 28 points. Two went for touchdowns, and the other two set up touchdowns. Franco Harris handled the running game, gaining 92 yards to post his seventh 1,000-yard season.

Swann, talking about this year, said, "I wasn't really down, but I wasn't joking around as much as I usually do. I was a good deal more serious. But this presents more problems now for the opposing teams."

Stallworth was held to two catches because Bradshaw went to Swann. "I hope John understands," Bradshaw said.

Stallworth, who was the "other" receiver in the past, said, "That's one of the reasons he's a successful quarterback. He relates to people and has a rapport with us."

When Bradshaw was asked if he did this on his own, he smiled, "I'd never tell Chuck that. I hope you don't write this. I'll have to leave town."

As Stallworth came out of the shower, Bradshaw gave him a big hug. He thinks about the egos of all his receivers.

Just call him Dr. Bradshaw.

		SCORING	CIN	PIT
1st	Steelers	Matt Bahr 43 yard field goal	0	3
	Steelers	Lynn Swann 58 yard pass from Terry Bradshaw (Matt Bahr kick)	0	10
2nd	Steelers	Franco Harris 1 yard rush (Matt Bahr kick)	0	17
	Bengals	Chris Bahr 46 yard field goal	3	17
	Steelers	Rocky Bleier 1 yard rush (Matt Bahr kick)	3	24
	Bengals	Isaac Curtis 29 yard pass from Ken Anderson (Chris Bahr kick)	10	24
3rd	Bengals	Isaac Curtis 32 yard pass from Ken Anderson (Chris Bahr kick)	17	24
	Steelers	Lynn Swann 42 yard pass from Terry Bradshaw (Matt Bahr kick)	17	31
	Steelers	Matt Bahr 23 yard field goal	17	34
4th	Steelers	Matt Bahr 32 yard field goal	17	37

	TEAM STATS	
	CIN	PIT
First downs	21	24

Rush-Yards-TD	28-131-0	32-154-2
Comp-Att-Yards-TD-INT	20-36-258-2-0	17-29-339-2-1
Sacked-Yards	6-49	2-15
Net pass yards	209	324
Total yards	340	478
Fumbles-Lost	1-1	1-0
Turnovers	1	1
Penalties-Yards	4-29	6-45

PASSING, RUSHING and RECEIVING

Bengals

Passing

Ken Anderson: 20-of-36, 258 yards, 2 TD, 0 INT

Rushing

Ken Anderson: 5 carries for 46 yards
Pete Johnson: 18 carries for 51 yards
Charles Alexander: 2 carries for 13 yards
Archie Griffin: 2 carries for 12 yards
Deacon Turner: 1 carry for 9 yards

Receiving

Isaac Curtis: 5 catches for 119 yards, 2 TD
Pete Johnson: 4 catches for 22 yards
Dan Ross: 5 catches for 46 yards
Charles Alexander: 2 catches for 22 yards
Archie Griffin: 2 catches for 20 yards
Don Bass: 1 catch for 20 yards
Jim Corbett: 1 catch for 9 yards

Steelers

Passing

Terry Bradshaw: 17-of-29, 339 yards, 2 TD, 1 INT

Rushing

Terry Bradshaw: 1 carry for 2 yards
Franco Harris: 20 carries for 92 yards, 1 TD
Rocky Bleier: 11 carries for 60 yards, 1 TD

Receiving

Lynn Swann: 5 catches for 192 yards, 2 TD
Franco Harris: 2 catches for 27 yards
Rocky Bleier: 3 catches for 29 yards
Jim Smith: 2 catches for 48 yards
Bennie Cunningham: 3 catches for 25 yards
John Stallworth: 2 catches for 18 yards

DEFENSE

Bengals

Interceptions

Dick Jauron: 1 for 12 yards

KICK RETURNS

Bengals

Kickoffs

Howard Kurnick: 1 for 9 yards, 9.0 avg.
Deacon Turner: 7 for 129 yards, 18.4 avg.

Punts

Mike Levenseller: 1 for 4 yards, 4.0 avg.

Steelers

Kickoffs

Anthony Anderson: 3 for 52 yards, 17.3 avg.

Punts

Theo Bell: 3 for 29 yards, 9.7 avg.

KICKING and PUNTING

Bengals

Kicking

Chris Bahr: 2-for-2 PAT, 1-for-2 FG

Punting

Pat McInally: 4 for 162 yards, 40.5 avg.

Steelers

Kicking

Matt Bahr: 4-for-4 PAT, 3-for-3 FG

Punting

Craig Colquitt: 2 for 63 yards, 31.5 avg.

Week 15

Dec. 10
Astrodome
Houston, TX

Pittsburgh Steelers — Houston Oilers

	1Q	2Q	3Q	4Q	Total
Steelers	0	0	3	14	17
Oilers	0	7	3	10	20

The Houston Oilers, following sage advice, declined to spit into the wind or step on Superman's cape.

Having come within one second of defeating the world champion Pittsburgh Steelers, Oilers quarterback Dan Pastorini politely fell on the ball for the final play of the game at the Steelers' 1-yard line and the Oilers trotted into the dressing room with a 20-17 victory on "Monday Night Football."

The Oilers had better sense and sportsmanship than to rub the Steeler noses in the Astroturf.

"Pittsburgh is too good a team to rub their noses in a loss," Oilers coach Bum Phillips said.

"If the touchdown would have made a difference in the division championship, we could have scored," Pastorini said. "We weren't trying to rub their faces in it."

The Oilers had accomplished their goal. They kept the Steelers from clinching their sixth straight AFC Central Division championship and kept alive their own chances of claiming a title for the first time since 1967.

"After the way we lost to them the first time we played this year we had to be a little psyched up," Pastorini said. "So we just went out and got a little sweet revenge."

The Oilers, who lost to the Steelers 34-5 in last season's AFC Championship Game and 38-7 in their first meeting this season, clearly were ready for the challenge this time.

Houston held the Steelers to four first downs in the opening half and took a 7-0 halftime lead on a 25-yard pass from Pastorini to Ken Burrough. They went ahead 13-3 on field goals of 24 and 34 yards by Toni Fritsch in the third and fourth quarters.

The record crowd of 55,293 in the Astrodome and a national television audience kept waiting for the sleeping giant Steelers to wake up and they finally did.

Matt Bahr kicked a 37-yard field goal in the third quarter and Lynn Swann ran nine yards for a touchdown on an end around play that narrowed the Oilers' lead to 13-10.

But the Oilers didn't fold. Rob Carpenter ran four yards with 2:10 to play to boost the lead to 20-10.

Pittsburgh quarterback Terry Bradshaw whipped the Steelers to the game's final touchdown with a 34-yard bomb to John Stallworth with 1:18 left in the game. But the Steelers tried an onsides kick that found its way to Houston tight end Mike Barber.

"They took that damn football and ran it down our throats for five minutes and scored a touchdown," Steelers defensive tackle Joe Greene said of Carpenter's touchdown. "That was as disappointing as anything that happened and they did it the way they weren't supposed to."

The Oilers weren't supposed to be able to run on the Steelers but that's where Oilers running back Earl Campbell came into the picture with 109 yards on 33 carries, his first 100-yard performance ever against the Steelers.

The Oilers' performance brought words of praise from Steelers coach Chuck Noll.

"I thought the Houston Oilers played the best game I have ever seen them play," Noll said. "I'd like to play Houston every week of the season. That would be interesting, wouldn't it?"

Following Bradshaw's 34-yard touchdown to Stallworth, the quarterback said:

"We have them right where we wanted them. They couldn't play us tight. I had it all planned. We were going to go for the field goal."

Bradshaw took the blame for the loss. "I haven't been playing as well in the big games as I should," he said.

Bradshaw was intercepted twice by the Oilers. Art Stringer returned the first theft 21 yards in the second quarter and linebacker Robert Brazile's 26-yard return in the second quarter set up Houston's first touchdown.

It was suggested to Brazile that Bradshaw, recovering from a sprained wrist, was not throwing as well as usual.

"I don't know," Brazile quipped, "he threw me a perfect strike."

		SCORING	PIT	HOU
2nd	Oilers	Ken Burrough 25 yard pass from Dan Pastorini (Toni Fritsch kick)	0	7
3rd	Steelers	Matt Bahr 37 yard field goal	3	7
	Oilers	Toni Fritsch 24 yard field goal	3	10
4th	Oilers	Toni Fritsch 34 yard field goal	3	13
	Steelers	Lynn Swann 9 yard rush (Matt Bahr kick)	10	13
	Oilers	Rob Carpenter 4 yard rush (Toni Fritsch kick)	10	20
	Steelers	John Stallworth 34 yard pass from Terry Bradshaw (Matt Bahr kick)	17	20

	TEAM STATS	
	PIT	HOU
First downs	15	20
Rush-Yards-TD	22-120-1	54-190-1
Comp-Att-Yards-TD-INT	14-29-237-1-2	10-17-170-1-0
Sacked-Yards	3-19	1-10
Net pass yards	218	160
Total yards	338	350
Fumbles-Lost	1-0	1-0
Turnovers	2	0
Penalties-Yards	10-79	4-28

PASSING, RUSHING and RECEIVING

Steelers

Passing

Terry Bradshaw: 14-of-29, 237 yards, 1 TD, 2 INT

Rushing

Terry Bradshaw: 1 carry for 20 yards
Franco Harris: 12 carries for 59 yards
Lynn Swann: 1 carry for 9 yards, 1 TD
Rocky Bleier: 8 carries for 32 yards

Receiving

Franco Harris: 3 catches for 32 yards
Bennie Cunningham: 2 catches for 67 yards
John Stallworth: 3 catches for 64 yards, 1 TD
Lynn Swann: 4 catches for 50 yards
Rocky Bleier: 1 catch for 6 yards
Randy Grossman: 1 catch for 18 yards

Oilers

Passing

Dan Pastorini: 10-of-16, 170 yards, 1 TD, 0 INT
Gifford Nielsen: 0-of-1, 0 yards

Rushing

Earl Campbell: 33 carries for 109 yards
Dan Pastorini: 1 carry for -2 yards
Tim Wilson: 10 carries for 47 yards
Rob Carpenter: 7 carries for 25 yards, 1 TD
Rich Caster: 1 carry for 5 yards
Mike Barber: 1 carry for 6 yards
Boobie Clark: 1 carry for 0 yards

Receiving

Earl Campbell: 2 catches for 22 yards
Ken Burrough: 3 catches for 48 yards, 1 TD

Rob Carpenter: 1 catch for 12 yards
Rich Caster: 1 catch for 24 yards
Mike Barber: 1 catch for 22 yards
Mike Renfro: 1 catch for 25 yards
Ronnie Coleman: 1 catch for 17 yards

DEFENSE

Oilers

Interceptions

Robert Brazile: 1 for 26 yards
Art Stringer: 1 for 21 yards

KICK RETURNS

Steelers

Kickoffs

Larry Anderson: 3 for 72 yards, 24.0 avg.
Greg Hawthorne: 1 for 23 yards, 23.0 avg.

Punts

Theo Bell: 3 for 19 yards, 6.3 avg.

Oilers

Kickoffs

Ronnie Coleman: 2 for 37 yards, 18.5 avg.
Carter Hartwig: 1 for 23 yards, 23.0 avg.

Punts

Rich Ellender: 2 for 6 yards, 3.0 avg.

KICKING and PUNTING

Steelers

Kicking

Matt Bahr: 2-for-2 PAT, 1-for-2 FG

Punting

Craig Colquitt: 4 for 184 yards, 46.0 avg.

Oilers

Kicking

Toni Fritsch: 2-for-2 PAT, 2-for-3 FG

Punting

Cliff Parsley: 5 for 174 yards, 34.8 avg.

Week 16

Dec. 16
Three Rivers Stadium
Pittsburgh, PA

Buffalo Bills   Pittsburgh Steelers

	1Q	2Q	3Q	4Q	Total
Bills	0	0	0	0	0
Steelers	7	7	7	7	28

Let's start with the good news.
The Steelers took what Joe Greene called the "first step" yesterday, swatting the hapless Buffalo Bills, 28-0, before 48,002 chilled fans at Three Rivers Stadium. The triumph gave the Steelers the Central Division crown for the seventh time in the last eight years and qualified them for home-field advantage in a first-round playoff game Dec. 29 or 30.
But it was the bad news that may turn out to be the most significant development of the day. It was certainly the most chilling.
The Steelers announced that Jack Ham, who injured his ankle early in the Houston game last Monday night, will need possible "fusion type" surgery on the ankle and will be sidelined for the rest of the season.

Going into the playoffs without Ham is a prospect that has to worry the Steelers. Greene called it a "major problem," and no one argued the point.

The only consolation is that the Steelers have two weeks to prepare to survive without Ham and to get the rest of their walking wounded healthy before their playoff game.

The Steelers are, in effect, using two players to replace Ham, with Dennis Winston starting and giving way to Loren Toews on passing downs.

The Steelers also hope to get their offensive line healthy before the next game. Jon Kolb and Sam Davis were held out while Mike Webster, who suffered a bruised kidney in the Houston game, played yesterday with a flak jacket to protect his kidneys. Webster, who has the build of an oak tree, brushed it off, but finally conceded that the "doctors were very concerned."

The Steelers will not know their first playoff opponent until next Sunday and will not even have it narrowed to two choices until tonight's San Diego-Denver game is ended. In the wild-card game next week, Houston is going to play the loser of the San Diego-Denver game. If Houston wins, the Steelers will host Mi-

(Continued on Page 13, Column 1)

ami. If either Denver or San Diego wins the wild-card game, the Steelers will host that club.

It was a satisfying if not memorable victory for the Steelers, who finished their regular season at 12-4. The most notable thing about it was Sidney Thornton's return to form. Thornton, who had been hobbled for more than a month by an ankle injury, replaced Rocky Bleier late in the first period and rushed 51 yards in 10 carries for a 5.1-yard average. Thornton again seems to have wrestled the starting job away from Bleier for the playoffs.

Terry Bradshaw hit on 14 of 27 passes for 209 yards and a touchdown although he had two intercepted, and Franco Harris rushed for exactly 100 yards in 21 carries. The defense also got a shutout, its first since the 1977 opener against San Francisco.

The game got sloppy in the second half. In one stage of seven third-quarter plays, there were three fumbles, two interceptions.

Buffalo came out as if it were ready to play when Joe Ferguson hit Jerry Butler with a 27-yard pass on the game's opening play from scrimmage. The Bills marched to the Steeler 14 where they had a fourth-and-one play. Chuck Knox, the Buffalo coach, then made a strange call. With nothing to lose and everything to gain, he decided not to gamble for the first down.

This is typical Knox strategy. He is a conservative coach in a profession known for conservative men. When he coached Los Angeles, Knox ordered a fourth-down field goal from the one-foot line in a 1976 playoff game against Minnesota. The Vikings blocked the kick and ran it back for a touchdown.

Nick Mike-Mayer made the first field-goal attempt, but the Bills were penalized for not getting the play off in time. He then tried a 36 yarder, and Greene blocked it.

The rest of the game mostly featured mini-brawls. As one wit said, a football game seemed in danger of breaking out at any moment. The Bills seemed more interested in brawling. Knox told his players all week that they could not be intimidated by the Steelers and they seemed to be trying to get in the first blow.

Dwight White said the Steelers sometimes turn the other cheek because they never get the "benefit of the doubt" in these scuffles.

"We've heard a long time that we're dirty and we intimidate and we've caught a lot of hell," Dwight White said. "We like to be respected for more than being the bully on the block, but we reacted because we were provoked."

Jim Haslett, the Pittsburgh native

playing his first game at Three Rivers Stadium, seemed to set the tone when he was ejected for what appeared to be kicking Bradshaw in the head — Haslett said it was an accident. Whatever happened, Bradshaw got a bloody scalp which will prevent him from wearing his toupee, but he missed only one play until he was yanked with seven minutes left by Chuck Noll, who had his 100th regular-season victory sewn up.

There were many other scuffles and frequent offsetting penalties. John Banaszak, who said he had been a "nice guy" too long, Greene and Jack Lambert were among the players involved.

Greene's incident was almost funny. Greene said he slugged tackle Joe Devlin, who had been holding him, and Devlin yelled, "I'm not going to be intimidated by you."

Greene said he wanted to laugh. "I thought that was just rhetoric for the papers. But, damn, they believe it," he said. Greene just shook his head and said the players apologized and that was it.

Buffalo could not do much against the Steelers, legally or illegally and wound up with just 156 yards in total offense.

"I feel good about it," Banaszak said. "We had some things to prove on defense. We'd been criticized and we'd given up a lot of points, but we shut them down."

The game was one-sided and dull in the second half, but Greene was pleased with that kind of game. "It would have been a bummer if it'd been close in a must game against a team like Buffalo."

As White said, "When the stage is set and the curtain is pulled, it's the Steeler time of the year."

Now they are ready to go after their fourth championship in the last six years — a feat that has been accomplished just once since the modern era began after World War II. If they do it, they are going to have to do it without Jack Ham. That will not be easy.

		SCORING	BUF	PIT
1st	Steelers	Lynn Swann 20 yard pass from Terry Bradshaw (Matt Bahr kick)	0	7
2nd	Steelers	Franco Harris 1 yard rush (Matt Bahr kick)	0	14
3rd	Steelers	Sidney Thornton 8 yard rush (Matt Bahr kick)	0	21
4th	Steelers	Franco Harris 11 yard rush (Matt Bahr kick)	0	28

	TEAM STATS	
	BUF	PIT

First downs	8	24
Rush-Yards-TD	24-78-0	45-214-3
Comp-Att-Yards-TD-INT	11-31-103-0-2	14-27-209-1-2
Sacked-Yards	2-25	1-8
Net pass yards	78	201
Total yards	156	415
Fumbles-Lost	1-1	3-2
Turnovers	3	4
Penalties-Yards	7-56	6-47

PASSING, RUSHING and RECEIVING

Bills

Passing

Joe Ferguson: 11-of-31, 103 yards, 0 TD, 2 INT

Rushing

Mike Collier: 16 carries for 49 yards
Joe Ferguson: 1 carry for 0 yards
Roland Hooks: 2 carries for 16 yards
Terry Miller: 5 carries for 13 yards

Receiving

Mike Collier: 4 catches for 11 yards
Jerry Butler: 3 catches for 54 yards
Roland Hooks: 1 catch for 7 yards
Frank Lewis: 1 catch for 22 yards
Lou Piccone: 1 catch for 6 yards
Joe Shipp: 1 catch for 3 yards

Steelers

Passing

Terry Bradshaw: 14-of-27, 209 yards, 1 TD, 2 INT

Rushing

Franco Harris: 21 carries for 100 yards, 2 TD
Terry Bradshaw: 2 carries for 10 yards
Sidney Thornton: 10 carries for 51 yards, 1 TD
Mike Kruczek: 1 carry for 22 yards
Rick Moser: 3 carries for 11 yards
Greg Hawthorne: 4 carries for 9 yards
Anthony Anderson: 2 carries for 8 yards
Rocky Bleier: 2 carries for 3 yards

Receiving

Franco Harris: 2 catches for 18 yards
Sidney Thornton: 2 catches for 55 yards
Lynn Swann: 3 catches for 61 yards, 1 TD
John Stallworth: 4 catches for 39 yards
Bennie Cunningham: 3 catches for 36 yards

DEFENSE

Bills

Interceptions

Mario Clark: 1 for 13 yards
Jeff Nixon: 1 for 10 yards

Steelers

Interceptions

Larry Anderson: 1 for 19 yards
Donnie Shell: 1 for 8 yards

KICK RETURNS

Bills

Kickoffs

Keith Moody: 4 for 89 yards, 22.3 avg.
Leonard Willis: 1 for 33 yards, 33.0 avg.

Punts

Keith Moody: 1 for 1 yard, 1.0 avg.

Steelers

Kickoffs

Larry Anderson: 1 for 30 yards, 30.0 avg.

Punts

Theo Bell: 10 for 105 yards, 10.5 avg.

KICKING and PUNTING

Bills

Kicking

Nick Mike-Mayer: 0-for-2 FG

Punting

Rusty Jackson: 10 for 402 yards, 40.2 avg.

Steelers

Kicking

Matt Bahr: 4-for-4 PAT, 0-for-2 FG

Punting

Craig Colquitt: 4 for 176 yards, 44.0 avg.

Divisional Playoffs

Dec. 30
Three Rivers Stadium
Pittsburgh, PA

Miami Dolphins — Pittsburgh Steelers

	1Q	2Q	3Q	4Q	Total
Dolphins	0	0	7	7	14
Steelers	20	0	7	7	34

PITTSBURGH — As the Pittsburgh Steelers headed for their dressing room in a joyous tromp, Joe Greene headed the opposite way in the concrete tunnel that snakes through the guts of Three Rivers Stadium.

Just as his badly whipped rivals got there, this giant of a man so ill-identified as "Mean Joe" reached the door of the quarters lent Sunday to the Miami Dolphins.

As each of the defeateds came by, Greene clasped them with a taped paw. A sincere, poignant and respectful goodbye to the NFL team that used to be the greatest, from a beautiful monster who leads the team that is now the runaway king.

"If we had won this one, and gone on to take the Super Bowl," said Don Shula, the Miami coach, "there could have been a case for us as the best team of the Seventies. But how can there be any contest now, the Steelers have three Super Bowls won ... and it looks like four."

PITTSBURGH HIT Miami with a fist of steel Sunday, bolting to a 20-0 first-quarter lead and then winning with 34-14 ease to advance to next Sunday's AFC Championship Game against its divisional brothers, those gut guys called the Houston Oilers.

The Steeler running game humbled the Dolphins' heretofore-proud defense early on the 24-degree afternoon, and then Terry Bradshaw hit touchdown bullets to his wideout wonders — John Stallworth and Lynn Swann — to all but eliminate Miami in the first 15 minutes.

Houston (12-5) meets Pittsburgh (13-4) at 1 p.m. next Sunday for the AFC championship and, at 5 o'clock, the orange darlings from Tampa Bay play the Los Angeles Rams at Tampa Stadium.

Bradshaw mastered the Dolphins totally, completing 21 of 31 passes for 230 yards and those two scores. Franco Harris scored twice and it was running, by him and by Sidney Thornton, that softened the Dolphins' underbelly and made them ducks in a shooting gallery for Bradshaw.

NEXT WEEK WILL be the third Oiler-Steeler game of the season. Pittsburgh won in a 38-7 laugher early in the year, but at the shank of the season, Houston, with Earl Campbell and Dan Pastorini healthier than now, won a 20-17 fight.

With critical injuries drydocking runner Campbell, thrower Pastorini and catcher Ken Burrough, Houston was recognized by America as a shock winner in Saturday's 20-17 AFC semifinal.

Asked about the Oilers' so-called miracle, Steeler coach Chuck Noll said, "It would be difficult for us to respect the Oilers more than we already do."

And, it is difficult for most of the pro football nation to be more awed by a team than it is at this moment by three-time Super Bowl champion Pittsburgh.

The Steeler defense made running a crime for the Dolphins, holding Miami to a net 25 yards in 22 attempts. Bob Griese passed for 118 yards and relief quarterback Don Strock gained 125, but mostly in hopeless desperation.

"WE DIDN'T panic when it got to 20-0 in the first quarter," Griese said. "When we scored early in the second half to make it 20-7, we thought we had a real chance. Then, Pittsburgh drove it right down the field and put it out of reach."

Pittsburgh received the opening kickoff and thundered 62 yards in 13 plays to score on a one-yard blast by the 235-pound Thornton. Miami ran three offensive plays, punted to the Steelers and that triggered a 62-yard scoring drive that made it 13-0.

The trend was obvious.

On the touchdown play, Bradshaw evaded Miami rushers as he did so well all day and joined with Stallworth on 17 yards of pass-run artistry. The Dolphins did manage to block the second extra-point kick by Matt Bahr. But then Miami ran three more plays and once again had to punt. Pittsburgh danced 56 yards in six plays this time and it was 20-0. For the score, Bradshaw pulled a great escape from Miami's pass rush and found Swann sitting all alone for a 20-yard completion.

MIAMI'S ONLY points of the long, cold Sunday came off a break. The drive went just 11 yards after officials charged that a Dolphin punt bounded off the leg of Steeler return man Dwayne Woodruff. It was ruled a fumble, although TV replays didn't show the ball touching Woodruff, and Miami's Don Bessillieu recovered. Griese passed seven yards to Duriel Harris in the end zone. It was 20-7, the closest Miami ever got.

Pittsburgh was to have none of this competition stuff. The Steelers again marched it through the Miami defense as if the opponent were little more than a friendly punching bag. They covered 69 yards in 12 plays with Rocky Bleier running the last one.

MOST OF THE figures on the stat sheet showed how awesome Pittsburgh had been. For one thing, the third-down efficiency was astonishing. Fourteen times the Steelers faced third-down situations and 11 times they made it. During the time it was getting to be 20-0, Pittsburgh made its first seven third-down challenges in a row.

Miami leaves the playoffs with a 10-7 record for this season, which will be Don Shula's next to last there as head coach unless he and Joe Robbie reach a new contractual arrangement.

Shula isn't nodding to anything. There are rumors about him replacing Dan Devine at Notre Dame after his Dolphin deal runs out following 1980. The Baltimore Colts would love to have him back there. Shula is only saying he'll wait and see, make that decision when he must.

		SCORING	MIA	PIT
1st	Steelers	Sidney Thornton 1 yard rush (Matt Bahr kick)	0	7
	Steelers	John Stallworth 17 yard pass from Terry Bradshaw (kick failed)	0	13
	Steelers	Lynn Swann 20 yard pass from Terry Bradshaw (Matt Bahr kick)	0	20
3rd	Dolphins	Duriel Harris 7 yard pass from Bob Griese (Uwe von Schamann kick)	7	20
	Steelers	Rocky Bleier 1 yard rush (Matt Bahr kick)	7	27
4th	Steelers	Franco Harris 5 yard rush (Matt Bahr kick)	7	34
	Dolphins	Larry Csonka 1 yard rush (Uwe von Schamann kick)	14	34

	TEAM STATS	
	MIA	PIT
First downs	16	27
Rush-Yards-TD	22-25-1	40-159-3

Comp-Att-Yards-TD-INT	22-40-243-1-2	21-31-230-2-0
Sacked-Yards	3-19	1-10
Net pass yards	224	220
Total yards	249	379
Fumbles-Lost	0-0	3-3
Turnovers	2	3
Penalties-Yards	4-35	8-41

PASSING, RUSHING and RECEIVING

Dolphins

Passing

Don Strock: 8-of-14, 125 yards, 0 TD, 1 INT
Bob Griese: 14-of-26, 118 yards, 1 TD, 1 INT

Rushing

Bob Griese: 1 carry for 1 yard
Gary Davis: 2 carries for 12 yards
Delvin Williams: 8 carries for 1 yard
Larry Csonka: 10 carries for 20 yards, 1 TD
George Roberts: 1 carry for -9 yards

Receiving

Nat Moore: 5 catches for 93 yards
Duriel Harris: 3 catches for 61 yards, 1 TD
Gary Davis: 2 catches for 24 yards
Tony Nathan: 3 catches for 27 yards
Delvin Williams: 6 catches for 26 yards
Bruce Hardy: 2 catches for 12 yards
Bob Torrey: 1 catch for 0 yards

Steelers

Passing

Terry Bradshaw: 21-of-31, 230 yards, 2 TD, 0 INT

Rushing

Franco Harris: 21 carries for 83 yards, 1 TD
Sidney Thornton: 12 carries for 52 yards, 1 TD
Greg Hawthorne: 2 carries for 15 yards
Rocky Bleier: 4 carries for 13 yards, 1 TD
Anthony Anderson: 1 carry for -4 yards

Receiving

Franco Harris: 5 catches for 32 yards
John Stallworth: 6 catches for 86 yards, 1 TD
Sidney Thornton: 3 catches for 34 yards
Jim Smith: 4 catches for 41 yards
Lynn Swann: 3 catches for 37 yards, 1 TD

DEFENSE

Steelers

Interceptions

Dirt Winston: 1 for 3 yards
Dwayne Woodruff: 1 for 0 yards

KICK RETURNS

Dolphins

Kickoffs

Gary Davis: 2 for 14 yards, 7.0 avg.
Tony Nathan: 4 for 73 yards, 18.3 avg.

Steelers

Kickoffs

Larry Anderson: 1 for 26 yards, 26.0 avg.
Greg Hawthorne: 1 for 20 yards, 20.0 avg.

Punts

Theo Bell: 3 for 31 yards, 10.3 avg.
Dwayne Woodruff: 1 for 0 yards, 0.0 avg.

KICKING and PUNTING

Dolphins

Kicking

Uwe von Schamann: 2-for-2 PAT

Punting

George Roberts: 4 for 145 yards, 36.3 avg.

Steelers

Kicking

Matt Bahr: 4-for-5 PAT

Punting

Craig Colquitt: 2 for 59 yards, 29.5 avg.

AFC Championship Game

Jan. 6
Three Rivers Stadium
Pittsburgh, PA

Houston Oilers   Pittsburgh Steelers

	1Q	2Q	3Q	4Q	Total
Oilers	7	3	0	3	13
Steelers	3	14	0	10	27

When it was all said and done, the Steelers had survived. They had persevered. They had met all the tests and overcome all the obstacles during the long grind of a 16-game regular season and two playoff games.

With the maturity and experience of a three-time Super Bowl champion, the Steelers turned back the gritty Houston Oilers 27-13 before 50,475 chilled but cheering fans at Three Rivers Stadium in the AFC Championship Game.

The hard-earned victory in the game that was closer than the score sounded earned them the right to make their fourth Super Bowl trip. They will be in the Rose Bowl in Pasadena, Calif., on Jan. 20 to meet NFC champion Los Angeles in Super Bowl XIV. The Rams won the NFC title with a 9-0 triumph over the Tampa Bay Buccaneers in Tampa.

This was not one of the vintage Steelers performances. It was not one they will hang on the wall. If it had been just another game in November, it might have been called sluggish at times. The Steelers continued to be plagued by the turnover problem they had to overcome all year.

Terry Bradshaw threw an interception into Vernon Perry's arms for a touchdown and Theo Bell fumbled a punt trying to make a diving catch. The Steelers got a first down on the 4 and had to settle for a field goal. They committed costly penalties and dropped a couple of key passes.

But they had the poise and maturity to overcome all that and put 14 points on the board in the second period to take the lead for good.

They now have a shot at their fourth Super Bowl crown in the last six years. If they get it, they can go for Vince Lombardi's record of five championships in a seven-year span.

Rocky Bleier, who grew up in Wisconsin rooting for the Packers, said, "As a fan, you never realize how tough it is." Dwight White echoed, "It was no picnic all year long. It was tough."

It is always tougher to stay on top when every team is shooting at you, but they survived. That is the mark of a champion.

They survived because the defense held Earl Campbell to 15 net yards in 17 carries and shut the Oilers down to 24 net yards rushing after holding Miami to just 25 last week.

They survived because Bradshaw overcame his early interception to throw for 219 yards and two touchdowns.

They survived because an old pro like Bleier, who has started in 12 playoff games and has been on the winning side 11 times, rushed for 52 yards and caught three passes for 39 yards.

They survived because Franco Harris was the leading rusher for both sides for the 13th time in 16 playoff games.

They survived because Bennie Cunningham overcame a costly motion penalty and a couple of dropped passes to haul in a touchdown grab.

They survived because the patched-up offensive line did the job.

And they survived because ... well, because they were lucky at times. As Branch Rickey once said, "Luck is the residue of design."

John Stallworth said, "You need four things – a great offense, a great defense, great special teams and a lot of luck. We had it all today."

Stallworth caught a touchdown pass in the second period to snap a 10-10 tie after Lynn Swann just missed leaping up and tipping the pass.

"I thought it was for me," Swann said. "It's a good thing I didn't tip it." Stallworth chimed in, "I got a few gray hairs watching him go for it. I thought he might tip it."

And then they had the good fortune that a critical official's call went their way. For all the fans who were bitter about Willie Spencer's call last month in Houston, it has to be remembered that these things go both ways.

In fact, there was a sense of déjà vu about this game. It was reminiscent at times of last January's Super Bowl. The Steelers overcame a seven-point deficit to take a seven-point lead at halftime. They bogged down in the third quarter when they played it conservatively with poor field position. Then the official's call went their way.

This time is was not Bennie Barnes-Lynn Swann. It was Mike Renfro-Ron Johnson. On the third-to-last play of the third quarter, Houston had a first down on the Steelers' 6 after driving from its own 14.

Dan Pastorini fired a pass to Renfro in the right corner of the end zone. Renfro leaped over Johnson and came down with his feet in bounds. But the official, side judge Don Orr, ruled Renfro did not have possession when he came down.

It was obvious on the instant replay that his feet were in bounds, but the camera did not show conclusively whether he had possession. The definitive word will have to come from NFL Films.

It did not help that Orr made a tentative signal with his hands and officials then conferred a couple of minutes before ruling no touchdown.

"I hope the call was right," Joe Greene said. "If it was, we'll feel a lot better and Houston will feel a lot better. It's already taken some of the excitement out of the game."

Houston failed in its next two plays and had to settle for a field goal. Instead of tying the game 17-17, the Oilers trailed 17-13.

It is curious that, in two of the last three AFC title games, an official's call has been critical. In the 1977 Denver-Oakland game, Rob Lytle fumbled the ball but Ed Marion ruled no fumble. Denver then scored a touchdown en route to a 20-17 victory.

After Houston settled for the field goal, the Steelers drove 55 yards to set up a 35-yard Matt Bahr field goal for a 20-13 lead with almost 10 minutes left.

Houston punched out a pair of first downs, but Guido Merkens fumbled while catching a 12-yard pass for the second one. Donnie Shell grabbed it on the Oilers' 45 and the Steelers then marched in the clinching touchdown.

The Steelers are now 13-4 in playoff games the last eight years and have won five consecutive playoff games while ringing up 33, 34, 35, 34 and 27 points. But this was the most difficult one of the last two years.

"I wanted to win so badly that I got myself all worked up and I didn't relax," Bradshaw said. "I've played better, but I'll take the results."

"I was mad at myself about that interception, but Chuck Noll said not to worry. I had been thinking about this game for three days and I couldn't sleep or eat."

		SCORING	HOU	PIT
1st	Oilers	Vernon Perry 75 yard interception return (Toni Fritsch kick)	7	0
	Steelers	Matt Bahr 21 yard field goal	7	3
2nd	Oilers	Toni Fritsch 21 yard field goal	10	3
	Steelers	Bennie Cunningham 16 yard pass from Terry Bradshaw (Matt Bahr kick)	10	10
	Steelers	John Stallworth 20 yard pass from Terry Bradshaw (Matt Bahr kick)	10	17
4th	Oilers	Toni Fritsch 23 yard field goal	13	17
	Steelers	Matt Bahr 39 yard field goal	13	20
	Steelers	Rocky Bleier 4 yard rush (Matt Bahr kick)	13	27

	TEAM STATS	
	HOU	PIT
First downs	11	22
Rush-Yards-TD	22-24-0	36-161-1
Comp-Att-Yards-TD-INT	20-29-212-0-1	18-30-219-2-1
Sacked-Yards	1-9	3-22
Net pass yards	203	197
Total yards	227	358
Fumbles-Lost	4-2	1-1
Turnovers	3	2
Penalties-Yards	2-10	5-34

PASSING, RUSHING and RECEIVING

Oilers

Passing

Dan Pastorini: 19-of-28, 203 yards, 0 TD, 1 INT
Gifford Nielsen: 1-of-1, 9 yards

Rushing

Tim Wilson: 4 carries for 9 yards
Earl Campbell: 17 carries for 15 yards
Rich Caster: 1 carry for 0 yards

Receiving

Tim Wilson: 7 catches for 60 yards
Mike Renfro: 3 catches for 52 yards
Ronnie Coleman: 2 catches for 46 yards
Earl Campbell: 1 catch for 11 yards
Rob Carpenter: 5 catches for 23 yards
Guido Merkens: 1 catch for 12 yards
Mike Barber: 1 catch for 8 yards

Steelers

Passing

Terry Bradshaw: 18-of-30, 219 yards, 2 TD, 1 INT

Rushing

Franco Harris: 21 carries for 85 yards
Terry Bradshaw: 1 carry for 25 yards
Rocky Bleier: 13 carries for 52 yards, 1 TD
Sidney Thornton: 1 carry for -1 yard

Receiving

Franco Harris: 6 catches for 50 yards
Rocky Bleier: 3 catches for 39 yards
Lynn Swann: 4 catches for 64 yards
John Stallworth: 3 catches for 52 yards, 1 TD
Bennie Cunningham: 2 catches for 14 yards, 1 TD

DEFENSE

Oilers

Interceptions

Vernon Perry: 1 for 75 yards, 1 TD

Steelers

Interceptions

Dwayne Woodruff: 1 for 0 yards

KICK RETURNS

Oilers

Kickoffs

Rob Carpenter: 1 for 4 yards, 4.0 avg.
Rich Ellender: 4 for 47 yards, 11.8 avg.
Carter Hartwig: 1 for 13 yards, 13.0 avg.

Punts

Rich Ellender: 2 for 8 yards, 4.0 avg.

Steelers

Kickoffs

Larry Anderson: 4 for 82 yards, 20.5 avg.

Punts

Theo Bell: 3 for 8 yards, 2.7 avg.

KICKING and PUNTING

Oilers

Kicking

Toni Fritsch: 1-for-1 PAT, 2-for-2 FG

Punting

Cliff Parsley: 4 for 120 yards, 30.0 avg.

Steelers

Kicking

Matt Bahr: 3-for-3 PAT, 2-for-3 FG

Punting

Craig Colquitt: 3 for 153 yards, 51.0 avg.

Super Bowl XIV

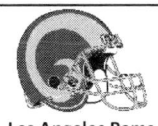

		Jan. 20 Rose Bowl Pasadena, CA			
Los Angeles Rams					Pittsburgh Steelers
	1Q	2Q	3Q	4Q	Total
Rams	7	6	6	0	19
Steelers	3	7	7	14	31

It wasn't overwhelming, but Pittsburgh's 31-19 triumph over the dogged Los Angeles Rams in Super Bowl XIV gave the Steelers a legitimate claim to the title of the greatest team in pro football history.

The Steelers, sparked by a 73-yard touchdown pass from Terry Bradshaw to John Stallworth and a key interception by Jack Lambert, surged to their fourth NFL title in the last six years when they rallied in the final period to defeat the underdog Rams.

The unprecedented fourth Super Bowl victory did not come easily as the lead changed hands six times before Bradshaw finally put the heavily favored Steelers ahead to stay with 12:04 left in the game on the touchdown bomb to Stallworth.

"Everybody's been shooting for us for the last eight years, and it (the victory) came against the Rams – whom we have never beaten," said Bradshaw, who was named the game's Most Valuable Player. "It's quite a remarkable collection of athletes."

Bradshaw, 31, a 10-year veteran, said, "I felt more pressure than at any other time," and added that the pass to Stallworth was a "60 percent slot hook and go," a play developed only a week ago.

"I ran the pass eight times in practice and I didn't like it, but it worked today," Bradshaw said. "This is my most satisfying Super Bowl."

Victorious coach Chuck Noll said, "This victory is probably the best we've ever had," as he accepted the Super Bowl trophy from NFL Commissioner Pete Rozelle. Noll said the Rams "ran the ball very well and played great defense," but he credited his team with coming up with the great plays and strong game-ending defense that enabled the Steelers to win.

Trailing 19-17, the Steelers looked lethargic as they were bogged down with a third-and-eight at their 27. But Bradshaw, having his difficulties with three interceptions, calmly stepped back and hit Stallworth in full stride at the Rams' 30. The All-Pro wide receiver easily outraced Rod Perry to the end zone.

The scoring pass was Bradshaw's second of the game and ninth in his Super Bowl career, breaking the record held by Dallas' Roger Staubach. Stallworth also set a record with the third Super Bowl scoring reception of his career.

Bradshaw, who hit 14 of 21 passes for 309 yards, won his second straight Super Bowl MVP award, tying the record of Bart Starr, the former Green Bay quarterback and now their head coach. Starr won the honor in each of the first two Super Bowls.

Los Angeles, an 11-point underdog, refused to give in and with young Vince Ferragamo guiding them moved to a first-and-10 at the Steelers' 32. But Ferragamo tested the Pittsburgh pass defense once too often and Lambert, the Steelers' All-Pro middle linebacker, ended the Rams' dream of winning a Super Bowl in their first appearance in the NFL title game by intercepting Ferragamo's pass over the middle and returning it 16 yards to the Steelers' 30.

Lambert, who led the Steelers with 10 tackles, said the Rams "played a ballgame. Every time we scored, they scored. It took a while before we could really shut them down."

Bradshaw applied the crushing blow when he threw a 45-yard pass to Stallworth to the Los Angeles 22, setting up Franco Harris' second touchdown of the game – a one-yard burst off left tackle. Harris' TD dive came with 1:49 remaining after a pass interference penalty against Rams cornerback Pat Thomas.

The Steelers extended the AFC's domination over NFC rivals in the Super Bowl with the 10th victory in 14 Super Bowls for the conference, formerly the American Football League before a 1970 merger with the NFL. The Steelers won all three of their previous Super Bowls, beating Dallas twice and Minnesota once. A Super Bowl record crowd of 103,985 watched Pittsburgh clinch its fourth title.

"They didn't outplay us at all," said Los Angeles coach Ray Malavasi. "They got a couple of lucky plays on us and that pretty much did it. They made a couple of big plays and we didn't.

"We didn't get it this time, but by God we'll get another shot at it. Pittsburgh doesn't try to surprise anyone. They executed and they won."

Pittsburgh, which trailed 13-10 at halftime, roared into the lead on its first possession of the second half when Larry Anderson, who turned in a record kickoff returning performance, took the kickoff back 37 yards to the Steelers' 39. Four plays later, Bradshaw hit Lynn Swann, who made a leaping 47-yard TD reception between Nolan Cromwell and Thomas.

Swann was injured later in the third quarter and saw no further action.

The gritty Ferragamo, second to former New York Jet Joe Namath as the youngest quarterback ever to start a Super Bowl, refused to rattle and needed just four plays to put Los Angeles back ahead. On third-and-seven from his 26, Ferragamo threw a 50-yard pass to Billy Waddy to the Steelers' 24 and on the next play running back Lawrence McCutcheon took a pitchout to the right and stunned the Steelers with a 24-yard touchdown pass to Ron Smith. The kick failed and L.A. led 19-17.

Bradshaw then hit Stallworth with a high, arching pass – just beyond the reach of Perry's frantic dive – to put the Steelers ahead for good.

"They were not fancy, but they came right at us," said Pittsburgh's veteran defensive tackle, Mean Joe Greene. "I expected the Rams to play better than they ever had and they did. We didn't play the way we think we can in the first half. The easiest thing to attribute that to was the great execution of the Rams.

"They played their hearts out. They believed."

The Rams made believers out of the Steelers in the first half and surged to a 13-10 lead when Frank Corral kicked a 45-yard field goal with just six seconds to go.

Pittsburgh went 55 yards in 11 plays on its first possession and went ahead 3-0 on rookie Matt Bahr's 41-yard field goal just 7:29 into the game.

Rocky Bleier had first-down runs of nine and eight yards and Bradshaw hit Harris for 32 yards to set up Bahr's kick – which came after Bradshaw barely overthrew a wide-open Swann in the end zone.

Pittsburgh then attempted an onside kick but the strategy backfired when rookie linebacker George Andrews recovered for Los Angeles at the Rams' 41. On the second play from scrimmage, Wendell Tyler weaved 39 yards down the left side to the Steelers' 14 and six plays later Cullen Bryant banged over left tackle from the Steelers' 1-yard line to put Los Angeles ahead 7-3. Tyler's run was the longest against the Steelers this season.

Pittsburgh struck right back as Anderson returned the kickoff 45 yards to the Rams' 47. Bradshaw hit Bennie Cunningham with passes of eight and 13 yards and threw to Swann for 12 more to set up a first-and-goal on the Rams' 5. Two plays later, Harris sprinted around right end untouched to push the Steelers ahead 10-7 just 2:08 into the second period.

Los Angeles again came back thanks to a key pass interference call against Pittsburgh safety Donnie Shell.

Ferragamo hit Tyler for 11 yards and McCutcheon for 16 to set up a second-and-12 on the Steelers' 38. Shell was called for elbowing Waddy along the right sideline and the Rams had a first down on the Steelers' 18. Four plays later, Corral tied the game 10-10 with a 31-yard field goal.

Pittsburgh, which committed a league-high 52 turnovers during the regular season, then coughed up a costly one when Bradshaw was intercepted by Dave Elmendorf, who returned it 10 yards to the Steelers' 39.

Ferragamo, taking over with 3:05 left in the half, hit three quick passes for 36 yards and, after a 14-yard sack, Corral connected from 45 yards out for the 13-10 lead. Ferragamo finished with 15 completions in 25 attempts for 212 yards. He was sacked four times for 42 yards in losses.

"The offense played well and the defense played well," said Ferragamo. "We played good enough football to win. We all played well. It's too bad we couldn't win.

"On the interception, Waddy went deep and Lambert made a deep drop into the zone. He made a good interception. I probably should have gone deep into the end zone with it."

The Rams' defense, which helped carry the team into the Super Bowl with a 9-0 shutout of Tampa Bay in the NFC title game, held Pittsburgh to 84 yards rushing but was unable to pressure Bradshaw, who was not sacked.

Harris, the leading rusher in NFL playoff history, managed only 46 yards on 20 carries. Tyler, who had to be helped from the field on five different occasions, was the game's leading rusher with 60 yards on 17 carries.

Stallworth, who set a club record with 70 receptions this year, caught three passes for 121 yards and Swann caught five for 79 yards before leaving the game with a head injury midway through the third period.

		SCORING	RAM	PIT
1st	Steelers	Matt Bahr 41 yard field goal	0	3
	Rams	Cullen Bryant 1 yard rush (Frank Corral kick)	7	3
2nd	Steelers	Franco Harris 1 yard rush (Matt Bahr kick)	7	10
	Rams	Frank Corral 31 yard field goal	10	10
	Rams	Frank Corral 45 yard field goal	13	10
3rd	Steelers	Lynn Swann 47 yard pass from Terry Bradshaw (Matt Bahr kick)	13	17
	Rams	Ron B. Smith 24 yard pass from Lawrence McCutcheon (kick failed)	19	17
4th	Steelers	John Stallworth 73 yard pass from Terry Bradshaw (Matt Bahr kick)	19	24
	Steelers	Franco Harris 1 yard rush (Matt Bahr kick)	19	31

	TEAM STATS	
	RAM	PIT

First downs	16	19
Rush-Yards-TD	29-107-1	37-84-2
Comp-Att-Yards-TD-INT	16-26-236-1-1	14-21-309-2-3
Sacked-Yards	4-42	0-0
Net pass yards	194	309
Total yards	301	393
Fumbles-Lost	0-0	0-0
Turnovers	1	3
Penalties-Yards	2-26	6-65

PASSING, RUSHING and RECEIVING

Rams

Passing

Vince Ferragamo: 15-of-25, 212 yards, 0 TD, 1 INT
Lawrence McCutcheon: 1-of-1, 24 yards, 1 TD, 0 INT

Rushing

Vince Ferragamo: 1 carry for 7 yards
Wendell Tyler: 17 carries for 60 yards
Cullen Bryant: 6 carries for 30 yards, 1 TD
Lawrence McCutcheon: 5 carries for 10 yards

Receiving

Wendell Tyler: 3 catches for 20 yards
Billy Waddy: 3 catches for 75 yards
Cullen Bryant: 3 catches for 21 yards
Lawrence McCutcheon: 1 catch for 16 yards
Preston Dennard: 2 catches for 32 yards
Drew Hill: 1 catch for 28 yards
Ron B. Smith: 1 catch for 24 yards, 1 TD
Terry Nelson: 2 catches for 20 yards

Steelers

Passing

Terry Bradshaw: 14-of-21, 309 yards, 2 TD, 3 INT

Rushing

Terry Bradshaw: 3 carries for 9 yards
Franco Harris: 20 carries for 46 yards, 2 TD
Sidney Thornton: 4 carries for 4 yards
Rocky Bleier: 10 carries for 25 yards

Receiving

John Stallworth: 3 catches for 121 yards, 1 TD
Franco Harris: 3 catches for 66 yards
Lynn Swann: 5 catches for 79 yards, 1 TD
Sidney Thornton: 1 catch for 22 yards
Bennie Cunningham: 2 catches for 21 yards

DEFENSE

Rams

Interceptions

Eddie Brown: 1 for 6 yards
Dave Elmendorf: 1 for 10 yards
Rod Perry: 1 for -1 yard

Steelers

Sacks

John Banaszak (1), Robin Cole (1), Steve Furness (1) and J.T. Thomas (1)

Interceptions

Jack Lambert: 1 for 16 yards

KICK RETURNS

Rams

Kickoffs

George Andrews: 1 for 0 yards, 0.0 avg.
Eddie Hill: 3 for 47 yards, 15.7 avg.
Jim Jodat: 2 for 32 yards, 16.0 avg.

Punts

Eddie Brown: 1 for 4 yards, 4.0 avg.

Steelers

Kickoffs

Larry Anderson: 5 for 162 yards, 32.4 avg.

Punts

Theo Bell: 2 for 17 yards, 8.5 avg.
Jim Smith: 2 for 14 yards, 7.0 avg.

KICKING and PUNTING

Rams

Kicking

Frank Corral: 1-for-2 PAT, 2-for-2 FG

Punting

Ken Clark: 5 for 220 yards, 44.0 avg.

Steelers

Kicking

Matt Bahr: 4-for-4 PAT, 1-for-1 FG

Punting

Craig Colquitt: 2 for 85 yards, 42.5 avg.

1979 NFL Standings

AFC

East	W	L	PF	PA
Miami Dolphins	10	6	341	257
New England Patriots	9	7	411	326
New York Jets	8	8	337	383

	W	L	PF	PA
Buffalo Bills	7	9	268	279
Baltimore Colts	5	11	271	351

Central	W	L	PF	PA
Pittsburgh Steelers	12	4	416	262
Houston Oilers	11	5	362	331
Cleveland Browns	9	7	359	352
Cincinnati Bengals	4	12	337	421

West	W	L	PF	PA
San Diego Chargers	12	4	411	246
Denver Broncos	10	6	289	262
Seattle Seahawks	9	7	378	372
Oakland Raiders	9	7	365	337
Kansas City Chiefs	7	9	238	262

NFC

East	W	L	PF	PA
Dallas Cowboys	11	5	371	313
Philadelphia Eagles	11	5	339	282
Washington Redskins	10	6	348	295
New York Giants	6	10	237	323
St. Louis Cardinals	5	11	307	358

Central	W	L	PF	PA
Tampa Bay Buccaneers	10	6	273	237
Chicago Bears	10	6	306	249
Minnesota Vikings	7	9	259	337